THE
WEST WING

The West Wing Book Production Team:

Randall Warner, Television Executive
John Wells Productions

Isabelle Richard, Category Manager
Skye Van Raalte-Herzog, Manager of Book Production
Warner Bros. Worldwide Publishing

A Tour of The West Wing photographs by Ron Jaffe

Pg ii–iii, xi–3 © John & Dallas Heaton/CORBIS, Pg iv © Richard T. Nowitz/CORBIS,
Pg vi © Charles O'Rear/CORBIS, Pg 39 © Bettman/CORBIS, Pg 74 © Mark Thiessen/CORBIS,
Pg 104 © Joseph Sohm;Visons of America/CORBIS, Pg 172–175 ©Richard T. Nowitz/CORBIS,
Pg 176 © Joseph Sohm;Visons of America/CORBIS, Pg 230 © Bettman/CORBIS, Pg 345 © Craig Aurness/
CORBIS, Pg 350 © Wally Mc Namee/CORBIS, Pg 8–345 © Joseph Sohm;Visons of America/CORBIS

All other photographs © Warner Bros.

First published 2002 by Pocket Books, a division of Simon & Schuster, Inc.

First published in Great Britain 2002 by Channel 4 Books
an imprint of Pan Macmillan Ltd
20 New Wharf Road, London N1 9RR
Basingstoke and Oxford

www.panmacmillan.com

Associated companies throughout the world

ISBN 07522 65091

3 5 7 9 8 6 4 2

A CIP Catalogue record for this book is available from the British Library.

Printed and bound in Great Britain by Butler & Tanner, Frome, Somerset.

Book design by Richard Oriolo
Cover design by Regina Starace

Front cover photo by C. Lee/PhotoLink/PictureQuest

THE
WEST WING

CREATED BY

AARON SORKIN

SEASON ONE

SEASON TWO

FOREWORD

There is an old theatrical adage, "If it ain't on the page it ain't on the stage," which clearly points to the fundamental necessity of good writing for success. In each episode of *The West Wing*, viewers are greeted with a familiar theme and the now recognizable names and faces of the nine regular cast members. At the end of each episode, however, three men appear in name only without whom there simply is no *West Wing*. They are Executive Producer John Wells, Executive Producer and Director Tommy Schlamme, and Writer/Creator Aaron Sorkin.

Although I was the last actor to join the cast for the pilot (in the summer of '99), I was the first to predict the show's success, based in large measure on my experience a few years earlier working with Aaron Sorkin on *The American President*. I'll return to Mr. Sorkin in a few paragraphs. For now, let me share some personal and professional experiences of working with arguably the finest group of actors ever assembled for an hour-long drama series in American Television History: Stockard Channing, Dulé Hill, Allison Janney, Rob Lowe, Janel Moloney, Richard Schiff, John Spencer, and Bradley Whitford.

When I agreed to do the pilot, the character of President Bartlet was a sometime thing, only appearing in about twenty percent of the episodes as a so-called recurring character. The focus of the series was the people who staff the West Wing rather than the Oval Office and the first family. About a month after the pilot was completed, to my surprise I was invited to become a regular for the whole series, and I could not have been more pleased, since I knew from the start that this project was something very special indeed.

The focus of the series is still the West Wing, and while Bartlet is a pivotal character, he is no more so than the others. If an audience doesn't care about these people they won't get the series. One must be drawn in by them, to their work, to their individual personalities, to their individual characters, to the struggles in their personal lives. They come from a place and they stand for something. As for the actors who play them, for me it was love at first sight, and we have bonded in a very real "family" sense. Sometimes as I watch the show at home, I'm overwhelmed by individual performances, almost forgetting that I am a part of this show as well. "Did you see what he did?" And, "Did you hear what she said?" I am so impressed with the level of talent. Each episode is read around a table at lunch with all the players, producers, writers, and director present. It is the only time in the episode where all of us come together. The rest of the time we gather in smaller groups for filming.

Then there's the scripts, and I return happily to Mr. Sorkin, who we do not take for granted. On the contrary. His attention to detail is fundamental to his writing, hence it must become so in our acting as well. We all know that that's how it lives. It's very disciplined, with very, very specific dialogue. Every inch of every page is filled with musical notes, composed to be played by different instruments.

In the beginning, I have to say frankly, my discipline was not in line with the program. I was a bit too cavalier, and I was not always attentive to the very letter of the word. But gradually I came to realize that I was in the wrong. And when I surrendered to the word and was ruled specifically by the text, I learned a wonderful freedom. Aaron Sorkin indeed is a masterful composer. You can do your own riff, and you can improvise—but it's not the same composition. And the end result is different. I think all of the cast came to that realization at different stages of the production. And now we're all in sync.

What kind of an administration is the Bartlet administration? We like to think that we project the ideal way to serve. Naturally, we can't always solve every problem, but we'll always identify them. There's a lot of politicking, of course, that's what we do for a living—the characters, that is. But there's no proselytizing. It may be that we have given bureaucracy, or at least bureaucrats, a good name! We've certainly given them a face, and a heart, and a breath. And we've given recognition to their humanity and their public service.

Before the show began to air, I hesitated to tell people what it was about, or to get too excited talking about it, because my feeling was that it was too good to succeed on network television. I'd explain, "There'll be no car chases, no fist fights, no gun battles, no special effects. There's no sex." It sounded like the kiss of death.

We kind of held our breath when we started. Then, with each episode, we began to gain more viewers and more confidence in where we were headed. By the end of the first year, we knew that not only did we have a good show, we had an audience. We even had fans! They call themselves "Wingnuts!" On many college campuses, the show has become a Wednesday night civics party. They have pizza and watch together in the dorms. We're required viewing for a lot of high school civics and American history classes, because people realize that this show offers a form of entertainment *and* throws in how a bill actually gets passed. How the Executive branch interacts with the Judicial, the Legislative, and, of course, the Military.

We are not the real deal, of course. We're only a fantasy. And yet, within this fantasy we have to be credible. We committed to a certain course in the very beginning, long before the show was popular. We had a goal. You can call it liberal. You can call it Democratic. You can call it Humanist. However it is perceived, we were pointing the direction where this ideal administration would lead the nation, and we stay the course, trusting that people will find some measure of their own ideals and, perhaps, experience some degree of expansion to their own imaginations.

What's next!
Martin Sheen

ACKNOWLEDGMENTS

Special thanks to: Aaron Sorkin, Thomas Schlamme, and John Wells.

Extra special thanks to: Dulé Hill, Allison Janney, Rob Lowe, Janel Moloney, Richard Schiff, Martin Sheen, John Spencer, and Bradley Whitford. Timothy Busfield, Stockard Channing, Marlee Matlin, and Emily Procter. Melissa Fitzgerald, Kathryn Joosten, Devika Parikh and NiCole Robinson. Patrick H. Caddell, Thomas Del Ruth, Kevin Falls, Kenneth Hardy, Kristin Harms, Dee Dee Myers, Lawrence O'Donnell, Jr., Lyn Elizabeth Paolo, Blanche Sindelar, and Ellen Totleben.

Many many thanks to: Aeden Babish, Kinney K. Booker, Lauren Carpenter, Lisa Croisette, John Eakin, Nia Figueroa, Steve Fogelson, Phil Gonzales, Carolyn Hadfield, Hilda Hagopian, Ron Jaffe, Mindy Kanaskie, Cheryl Kaye, Kathy Kelly-Brown, Curt King, Erin Lowery, Rebecca Marks, Sharan Magnuson, Toni Moston, Claudia Ortopan, Tim Raniere, Lauren Schmidt, Andrew Shipps, Brett Shuemaker, Steve Sonn, Alan Sowles, Maria Stasi, Andrew Stearn, and Kathleen Tucci.

A very heart-felt thank you to Llewellyn Wells.

SEASON ONE

". . . do ordain and establish . . ."

PILOT

In the bar of the Georgetown Four Seasons Hotel, Sam Seaborn (Rob Lowe) is having a drink with his friend Billy (Marc Grapey), a reporter. It's late and as his friend chatters and his glass empties, Sam turns his attention to the beautiful woman eyeing him from across the bar.

First thing next morning, Leo McGarry (John Spencer) is at home in Chevy Chase relaxing and doing the crossword puzzle. The peace of the morning is broken when the phone rings—it's Potus. As the sun rises over Washington, D.C., the rest of the White House senior staff gets the same call. C. J. Cregg (Allison Janney) gets a page and immediately falls off the treadmill at the gym; Josh Lyman (Bradley

Whitford) is woken up by the pager at his desk, and Toby Ziegler (Richard Schiff) gets word from the cockpit as his plane approaches Washington National.

As for Sam, he obviously consummated his evening eye contact because he wakes up in the bedroom of the dark-haired beauty from the night before. The woman, Laurie (Lisa Edelstein), reads him his page. Sam, still dripping from the shower, immediately says he's sorry, he has to go.

LAURIE: Tell your friend Potus that he's got a funny name and he should learn how to ride a bicycle.

SAM: I would, but he's not my friend, he's my boss, and it's not his name, it's his title.

LAURIE: "Potus?"

SAM: President of the United States.

And with that, we enter the West Wing of the White House. Leo McGarry, the chief of staff, walks briskly through the West Wing corridors, efficiently taking care of business. Staffers and aides bark information at him as he plunges through offices and hallways. The news of the morning is that 1,200 Cuban refugees are at sea trying to reach Miami. If they survive the trip, they'll arrive around sunset. On home turf, Josh Lyman is in hot water, having insulted the entire Christian right with a thoughtless remark on a TV show the night before. Leo makes it clear the President's furious and Josh's job is in real jeopardy.

When he reaches the Oval Office, Leo tells the President's secretary, Mrs. Landingham (Kathryn Joosten), that her boss broke Leo's expensive bike, he's a klutz. A grandmother and bodyguard all in one, Mrs. Landingham says she doesn't like that kind of language in the Oval Office. Leo gathers his staff, gauges reactions about the Cuban crisis, Josh's faux pas on televison, and the fallout from the President's accident. All in all, it's a typical morning's work.

Behind closed doors in his office, Josh watches and rewatches a tape of his gaffe on *Capital Beat*. Unable to change the moment, he sits and stares at the television, watching himself tell his fellow guest Mary Marsh (Annie Corley), an important religious conservative, that her God got caught cheating on his taxes. Josh's assistant, Donna Moss (Janel Moloney), comes to the door with a cup of coffee. Josh turns, but barely acknowledges the steaming cup in her hand. He asks Donna how long she's worked for him. "A year and a half," she says.

JOSH: And when was the last time you brought me a cup of coffee?

DONNA thinks . . .

JOSH: (cont.) It was never. You've never brought me a cup of coffee.

DONNA: (picking up the mug) If you're going to make a big deal out of—

JOSH: Donna, if I get fired I get fired.

DONNA: Do you think he's gonna do it?

JOSH: (beat) No.

Toby, in a rare moment of sympathy and peacekeeping, tells Josh that he's arranged a meeting over coffee that afternoon with Marsh and the Reverend Al Caldwell. Josh isn't wild about begging for apologies, but Toby abruptly insists that this meeting take place. When he says he wants to help Josh save his job, he adds that Josh shouldn't take his concern as a gesture of friendship.

As he's leaving, Toby waves a newspaper in front of Josh—he read that Mandy Hampton (Moira Kelly) just came to town. Josh snatches the article, leans back, and says to himself that it's a good picture of her. He wonders who she's working for and what brought her back to the political arena.

She has not come back as a friend, though. Mandy's consulting for Senator Lloyd Russell, a man popular with white suburban women, upper-middle-class black men, and the teacher's union, and who's no friend of the President. In other words, someone who might be a serious political rival to the President down the road.

Before the coffee meeting brings too much chaos to the table, Leo has a conversation with the Reverend Al Caldwell (F. William Parker). The President told Leo to fire Josh—the administration is taking this very seriously. However, the President thinks Caldwell's gotten too close to religious extremists like Mary Marsh and John Van Dyke; Caldwell claims he needs them for political muscle.

Sam returns a page and is surprised to hear a woman answer "Cashmere Escorts." In rushing from Laurie's shower, out the door, and to the White House, Sam realizes he must have switched pagers with her by mistake. Losing his pager is suddenly the least of his problems; he calls Laurie, he needs to see her.

Josh needs the scoop on Mandy and her presence in D.C., so they arrange to meet for lunch. They're only a few bites into their sandwiches when a couple of students recognize them: "Didn't you guys used to be a thing?" one of them asks. They did. Listening to her discuss her job and her new boss, Josh figures out that not only is Mandy working for Lloyd Russell, she's dating him, too. Mandy exacts some revenge by telling Josh something he doesn't know: *The New York Times* is going to run a poll with a 48 percent unfavorable rating for the administration.

Knowing how this situation could explode in his face, Sam goes to Laurie's apartment to retrieve his pager. Before Sam can say what's on his mind, Laurie preempts him: "Am I a hooker?" "No, no," Sam says. He asks if it's *possible* she's a "*very* high-priced *call* girl." That's how he'd put

it. No holds barred, she is. Laurie admits she should have told him, but she wanted Sam to like her. Here's his biggest problem: he does.

Al Caldwell's group is shown to the Mural Room as a crowd of nine-year-olds waits in the Roosevelt Room. Sam has been given the ultimate responsibility of teaching Leo's daughter's class about the history of the White House, something he admits he knows nothing about. What's worse, he doesn't even know which one is Leo's daughter.

The kids are transfixed by Sam, without understanding a word he's saying. He fumbles through some stuff about his former career as a lawyer before Mallory O'Brian (Allison Smith), the teacher, asks him about the building. Now Sam's really in trouble. He says the White House was built several years ago; the Roosevelt Room is named for the eighteenth President, FDR; and the chairs were made from lumber from a captured pirate ship. Miss O'Brian yanks Sam into the corridor: "Are you a moron?" She tells Sam the eighteenth President was Ulysses S. Grant and that the Roosevelt Room is named for Theodore Roosevelt, of whom there is a large painting on the wall. Is it possible that the Deputy Communications Director, in charge of crafting the message of the White House, knows *nothing* about the White House?

Sam knows he's whipped, but before Mallory goes back in, Sam asks which of the kids is Leo McGarry's daughter. He thinks if he can make her laugh, his life would be much easier. Mallory is at her wits' end, and wants to know why should she make his life easier.

SAM: Ms. O'Brian, I understand your feelings, but please believe me when I tell you that I'm a nice guy having a bad day. I just found out that the *Times* is publishing a poll that says a considerable number of Americans feel the White House has lost energy and focus. A perception that's not likely to be altered by video footage of the President riding his bicycle into a tree. As we speak, the Coast Guard is fishing Cubans out of the Atlantic Ocean while the governor of Florida wants to blockade the port of Miami. A good friend of mine's about to be fired for going on television and making sense, and it turns out I accidentally slept with a prostitute last night. Now would you please, in the name of compassion, tell me which one of these kids is my boss's daughter.

MALLORY: That would be me.

SAM: You.

MALLORY: Yes.

SAM: Leo's daughter's fourth grade class.

MALLORY: Yes.

SAM: (pause) This is bad on so many levels.

Rob Lowe (Sam Seaborn)
I came in and read that for Aaron for the audition. We did eight pages, by memory. Did it once. Everybody laughed a lot. But when it was done, it was dead silent and Aaron turned to John Wells and said, "I told you the scene was funny." It was a magical moment. When I walked out, the people in the outer office were like, "What are you doing in there? Nobody's ever laughed like that." I knew where the funny was.

The inevitable moment has come: Josh, Toby, and C.J. meet the representatives of the religious right. Remembering Toby's advice, Josh is polite, even humble. In his best rehearsed voice, he says he wasn't speaking for the President, he was glib and insulting, and he apologizes. But Mary Marsh pushes all apologies aside—she just wants to deal. Josh insulted them; what do they get? "Public morals, school prayer, or pornography, take your pick," she says. And she insists they deal only with Toby since she's sure Josh'll be gone by the end of the day. She tells Josh it was only a matter of time: "That New York sense of humor." Josh shrugs it off, but Toby quietly interrupts, "She meant Jewish." Josh doesn't want to go there and Caldwell tries to move the meeting along.

John Van Dyke tries to make a point about the First Commandment, but Toby and Mary Marsh are squaring off on Biblical trivia. "The First Commandment says 'honor thy father.'" Toby is enraged: If they are going to argue, they should at least get the Commandments right. "'Honor thy father' is the Third Commandment." "Then what's the First Commandment?" asks Van Dyke.

Out of nowhere, a booming voice silences the room. There's a man standing in the doorway supporting himself with a cane. And

Martin Sheen
(President Bartlet)

One of my favorite scenes in the whole series was in the pilot. There's an eight- or nine-page scene they shot with John Spencer where he goes through the whole West Wing and takes us into the Oval Office for the first time. We see it, and it's stunning. It's like walking into a church and seeing the main altar. Mrs. Landingham is trailing behind him as if he might leave some vulgarity in his path. And she's not having it. "Watch your language in here, sir." That was a special moment. It says we respect this institution. No matter who's in there, the presidency itself is very special to all of us.

he says, in answer to Van Dyke's question, "I am the Lord your God. Thou shalt worship no other God before me." With tremendous presence, President Jed Bartlet (Martin Sheen) enters the room. Spiritedly, Van Dyke asks if our children can buy pornography at a street corner for five dollars, isn't that too high a price for free speech? No, says the President, it's too high a price for pornography. Bartlet's clearly in no mood to debate with extremists. He pointedly asks Reverend Al Caldwell how many times he's asked him to denounce the fringe group, the Lambs of God?

It seems Church and State have met once again. His wife, Abbey, told him not to do anything when he's angry but he was as angry as he's ever been when he got on that bike the other day. It seems his twelve-year-old grand-

daughter, Annie, gave an interview in a teen magazine, and in the midst of conversations on boys and fashion, she mentioned her feelings on a woman's right to choose. The President has read his Bible from cover to cover and he asks which part of it inspired the Lambs of God to send his granddaughter a Raggedy Ann doll with a knife stuck through its throat. Without allowing another moment of discussion, he tells

DEE DEE MYERS (CONSULTANT)
Aaron Sorkin called me and said he'd written a pilot for a series about the White House and asked me if I'd like to be a consultant on it. I said I would, since I thought the pilot was really good. But I didn't think anyone would ever make it, and I thought, Gosh, the last thing that people are going to want at the end of a day of news dominated by White House intrigue is a TV show about White House intrigue.

JOHN SPENCER (LEO MCGARRY)
When we'd done the pilot there was a fifty-fifty chance. People are so bored with all of this, the last thing they're gonna want to look at is Washington, D.C., politics. Other people would say "absolutely." People were jonesing for this at this point because they watched the real-life drama every night and that's going to be over and what are we going to do? We didn't know which way it would go. It obviously went the second way.

Caldwell to denounce these people. And until he does, "you can all get your fat asses out of my White House."

Once the group has gone, Bartlet addresses his staff with the simultaneous love and strictness of a father. He reprimands them for taking a little break, thinking about their personal lives or about keeping their jobs. He wants to get to work: 1,200 Cubans left Havana this morning, 700 turned back, 350 are missing, presumed drowned, and 137 have been taken into custody in Miami. "With the clothes on their backs they came through a storm," Bartlet says. "And those that didn't die want a better life. They want it here. Talk about impressive. My point is this: Break's over."

Rob Lowe
The thing that first drew me to playing Sam was his big soliloquy in the pilot. It was the humor—I knew it was hilarious when I read it. I also thought it was really well suited to what I naturally bring as an actor. Some parts you have to use more out of your tool kit than others. This part, I just felt like everything I had done in my life, every experience I had ever had, everything I've ever read, enjoyed, loved—every failure I've ever had, every success, led me to this point to be able to play Sam.

POST HOC,
ERGO PROPTER HOC

I t's a typical morning in the West Wing as C.J. runs down the checklist of things to do, things to discuss, things to begin, and things to finish off. Her most difficult task is breaking it to the President that the Ryder Cup team won't come to the White House for a photo op because Bartlet made a joke about golf. C.J. says the President's sense of humor has cost them before, like the time he quipped about big hats during the campaign and lost the state of Texas. That's not true, Bartlet says. As he is fond of doing, he quotes Latin: "*Post hoc, ergo propter hoc*," he tells C.J. "After it, therefore because of it."

Unfortunately, it's not always sound reasoning: They all know they didn't lose Texas because of the President's hat joke.

Martin Sheen
I don't speak Latin. I speak some phrases because I was an altar boy when I was a kid. I loved it. My pastor, Monsignor John Sheridan at Our Lady of Malibu, is my coach for the Latin. I get some Latin, I call him up.

For Toby Ziegler, the Ryder Cup snub is further evidence that the administration needs help avoiding these huge public potholes. And Toby knows at least one consultant who's looking for work: Mandy Hampton. Mandy lost her only client once Lloyd Russell (John Bedford Lloyd) sold out to the White House, his price a high-profile spot at the Democratic convention. Mandy is furious at Russell. She practically runs him down on the sidewalk to confront him, and tell him he's denying himself a shot at the prize. If Russell's accepted the chance to nominate the President in the future, it means the White House is making sure he won't be getting nominated himself.

Mandy is certain the White House will be partying after Russell's climb down but Russell tells her the President's staff are serious men and women. They certainly won't be gloating.

JOSH: Victory is mine, victory is mine, great day in the mornin', people, victory is mine! . . . I drink from the keg of glory, Donna; Donna, now bring me the finest muffins and bagels in all the land!

At a press briefing, a reporter quotes Vice President Hoynes, commenting on the White House position on the A3-C3 as saying, "This is a time when the President needs our support." The reporter senses that the language is strained but C.J. deflects attention away from this potential minefield by making a joke about the Ryder Cup team or, as she puts it, "Twelve guys named Flippy."

After his disastrous flub with Mallory O'Brian, Sam knows he needs to confide in someone he trusts, explain that he really likes Laurie and he wants to see her again despite her job as a call girl. Josh is stunned by Sam's earnest confession, but knows the White House doesn't need this complication or bad press. He suggests Sam take the news to his boss, Toby.

SAM: About a week ago, I accidentally slept with a prostitute.

TOBY: Really?

SAM: Yes.

TOBY: You *accidentally* slept with a prostitute?

SAM: A call girl.

TOBY: Accidentally.

SAM: Yes.

TOBY: (pause) I don't understand. Did you trip over something?

SAM: I didn't know she was a call girl.

TOBY: There wasn't a red flag when she charged you money in exchange for sex?

The news gets worse. Sam tells Toby he was with Bill Kenworthy, *The Wall Street Journal* reporter, when he met Laurie at a bar. So the only people who know, says Toby with a sigh, are the two of them, the hooker, the President's deputy chief of staff, and *The Wall Street Journal*. He

throws his hands in the air. The administration doesn't need an opposition party, they do well enough on their own.

C.J. approaches Vice President John Hoynes (Tim Matheson), who looks like a man with an agenda, flanked by an eager staff as he gives sound bites to journalists. She begs for a second of Hoynes's time to discuss how his quote might be misinterpreted. Trying to remain polite and respectful, C.J. explains it's not the first time this kind of thing has happened, this makes three in five weeks. Hoynes is quick to blow C.J. off, assuring her he's got his own press secretary.

Navy physician Captain Morris Tolliver (Reuben Santiago-Hudson) has been showing off photographs of his wife, Angela, and their ten-day-old baby, Corey. Tolliver has been filling in for the President's regular physician, but before Tolliver administers Bartlet a quick physical, Leo McGarry interrupts to ask him if he'd like the job permanently. The President likes talking to him, he lightens the load of the day-to-day strain and chaos. Tolliver is honored and delighted, he can take over after he comes back from a trip to a teaching hospital in Jordan. From their interactions, even in the face of medical exams, it's obvious Tolliver and the President have a relationship reminiscent of a father and his grown son.

Dee Dee Myers

People had a lot of questions. "What does it look like when the President goes through a door? Does he go in first? Do his agents go in? Are there people around him?" Almost always, agents will walk into a room first, particularly if it's a room where there are non-White House staff types. And then the President will walk through the door by himself and then staff will follow. It's not obvious. You realize that you haven't given it a lot of thought to exactly how it's different than when anybody else walks through a door.

BARTLET: Morris, I made a joke about golfers and it consumes the whole damn building.

MORRIS: When you open your mouth you're speaking into a pretty loud microphone.

BARTLET: Jokes like that are part of my folksy charm, Morris. It's at the very heart of my popularity.

MORRIS: Don't you have an approval rate of like three percent or something?

BARTLET: We're having some trouble getting the word out.

As they banter on as friends, Bartlet admits he's not at ease with the Joint Chiefs. He's concerned they'd think him weak if they knew he truly doesn't feel violent toward his country's enemies. Morris wisely tells the President to give it time. "You've got a once-in-a-generation mind," he says, "and ultimately they'll respect that."

After rehashing the ups and downs of the West Wing and the public face of the White House, Josh and Toby agree a media consultant would be helpful. Josh deadpans he's "put on talent shows with more polish" than some of the events around the White House, and he's all for the idea, as long as they don't hire Mandy Hampton. Leo is the next rung of approval, and he's immediately on board, suggesting they hire . . . Mandy Hampton. Leo asks Josh if he can think of any reason not to hire her that isn't personal. "Yes," says Josh. "She used to be my girlfriend." After a little coaxing and a deadly look from Leo, Josh relents, as long as she understands she reports to him and to Toby. He'll draw up an organizational chart with lines and arrows so it'll be clear.

Josh is given hiring privileges and finds Mandy and her assistant, Daisy, in their bare office, drinking. They're trying to think of people to hit up for work. Sucking in all his pride, Josh asks if they would like to come and work for the President of the United States. Mandy retorts, it took him long enough. And as for Josh's rules of established hierarchy—he can dream on.

Josh has other problems mounting on the homefront. Donna lost him a hundred dollars by selecting Central Indiana State over Notre Dame in a football pool. She wants him to help her make another pick.

> **DONNA**: Who do you like, Rocky Mountain College or Purdue?
> **JOSH**: I'll tell you what. Can you give me Yeshiva University over the Dallas Cowboys?

Leo asks C.J. if she spoke with Hoynes about the quote. She's vague about their conversation, explaining that there was just a miscommunication with Hoynes and that he's back on board. Leo's not convinced and he goes straight to the source. He calls Hoynes to his office and confronts him, asking if he blew C.J. Cregg off that morning. "When she tells you something," Leo says, "I want you to consider it a directive from this office." Hoynes has too many thoughts colliding in his head to let it go.

> **HOYNES**: Leo, I've had it up to here with you and your pal. I get shoved in a broom closet—
> **LEO**: Excuse me. Me and my "pal."
> **HOYNES**: Yes.
> **LEO**: You're referring to President Bartlet?

HOYNES: Yes.

LEO: Refer to him that way.

HOYNES: G'night, Leo.

LEO: Don't do what you're doing, John.

HOYNES: You're a world-class political operative, Leo, why the hell *shouldn't* I keep doing what I've been doing?

LEO: 'Cause I'll win and you'll end up playing celebrity golf the rest of your life.

HOYNES: How long do you expect me to stick around here and be his whipping boy?

LEO: Give this President anything less than your full-throated support and you're gonna find out exactly how long.

Against all the advice of his co-workers and friends, Sam returns to the Four Seasons looking for Laurie. It can be ugly when anger and affection collide, and Sam knows he has to keep his cool. He finds Laurie at a table with a woman and two businessmen, and it's clear she's working but it's too late for a getaway. Sam skips the small talk and says he's going to go to the bar to call his friend, the assistant U.S. attorney general, maybe he'd like to join them. That breaks up the party pretty quickly, and Laurie glares at Sam before walking out. Sam follows her, undaunted. He won't give up.

Laurie is enraged at the scene she just witnessed. She says she was never going to cause trouble for him. She doesn't want Sam to try to change her, she likes her job, and it's putting her through law school. Barely blinking, Sam merely tells Laurie he's decided to become a good friend of hers.

The President's been woken at 3:35 A.M. Half-asleep and disheveled, he traipses down to the Oval Office, knowing he wouldn't be woken up in the middle of the night for any good news. Leo explains quietly that Morris Tolliver is dead. An air force transport with Morris, twelve other doctors, forty-two support staff, and a crew of five, exploded in midair 150 miles north of Tarsus on its way to Amman. Although they first thought the plane had been taken down by a Muslim terrorist, all evidence is pointing to Syria. The President is solid and calm.

BARTLET: I'm gonna call Morris's wife now and I'll meet you in the Situation Room. (pause) I'm not frightened, Leo. I'm gonna blow 'em off the face of the earth. With the fury of God's own thunder. (beat) Get the commanders.

A PROPORTIONAL RESPONSE

Josh barely steps into the West Wing lobby when he's intercepted by Donna. The sun wouldn't rise over the White House without some new crisis looming up during the night, and this time, Donna tells Josh C.J.'s looking for him. Is it possible there's a situation with Sam and a woman and C.J.'s not being let in the loop? Once the penny's dropped, Donna asks Josh if he's going to go hide in his office. No, Josh says, he's going to *go* to his office and devise a strategy. "But if C.J. calls," he adds, "I'm at the dentist." He heads for asylum behind his office door, and C.J. stares at him from his desk. "Wow, are *you* stupid," she retorts.

C.J. wants the details about Sam and Laurie and knows Josh is her man. Josh immediately jumps to Sam's defense, arguing that he didn't do anything illegal or immoral or unethical or suspect, and C.J.'s overreacting. "As women are prone to do," C.J. says.

JOSH: You know what, C.J., I really think I'm the best judge of what I mean, you paranoid Berkeley shiksa *feminista*. (beat) Whoa, *way* too far.

C.J.: No, no. (beat) Well, I've got a staff meeting to go to and so do you, you elitist Harvard fascist missed-the-dean's-list-two-semesters-in-a-row Yankee jackass.

The discussion's not over. C.J. catches up with Sam later, and she gives him the bottom line about his relationship with Laurie; if she figured it out, others can. Sam thinks it's possible that through him Laurie might start living life inbounds. C.J. doesn't want to hear about Sam's plans for reformation, she just cares what the relationship looks like to the public, and it doesn't look good. Sam's climbed on his high horse: he wants them to actually be good, not just look good. He resents the hell out of this conversation. C.J. takes the conversation away from the moral high ground— she should just be his first call. Not Josh. Not Toby. It's part of her job to protect Sam and the President.

C.J.: What this is about, Sam, is that you're a high-profile, very visible, much noticed member—

SAM: You just said three things that all mean the same thing.

C.J.: You won't let this out'a your teeth.

SAM: Can I go now, C.J.? 'Cause what I think this is about is you, once again, letting the family values cops win in a forfeit, because you don't have the strength or the guts or the courage to say, "We know right from wrong and this is none of your damn business."

C.J.: Really.

SAM: Yes.

C.J.: Strength, guts, or courage.

SAM: Yes.

C.J.: You just said three things that all mean the same thing.

With mixed emotions, having lost a close friend and a member of his military, the President has to decide how to respond to the attack on the air

Aaron Sorkin (Creator and Executive Producer)
I love off-screen characters. I have ever since I saw David Mamet's play *American Buffalo*. It's a three-character play and there is a very, very strong character that we never see named Fletch. We keep hearing about him. The guy is clearly very important to them. I just thought, God, Mamet wrote a four-character play where we only see three of the characters. It was in "A Proportional Response" that we first hear about Cashman and Berryhill. They are obviously high-ranking members at [the] State [Department].

force transport. He's barking orders at the military and scaring Fitzwallace with his talk about blowing up half of Syria. His nerves are taut, and he's snapping at the first lady, which everyone knows is a bad sign. He's tired of waiting to do something. Cashman and Berryhill are dragging their feet and it's been three days since they blew him out of the sky. Leo advises the President to widen his scope of reference in public to include all the citizens lost in the explosion, not just Tolliver.

In this atmosphere, Toby takes any threat against the President very seriously. When Sam reports that Congressman Bertram Coles said on the radio from Cromwell Air Force Base that Bartlet's weak on defense and he might not get out alive if he visited down there, Toby takes the congressman at his word. Joking or not, it sounds like treason to Toby, and he wants to bring Coles to the White House for questioning. Leo says you can't have people arrested for being mean to the President, but Toby's not satisfied.

A little while later, Toby walks in the direction of some reporters and inevitably, he's pressed for details about Coles's comment. Acting as though he's afraid to divulge too much, he says, "The

Secret Service investigates all threats against the President but the White House can't comment on such investigations." As he walks away, perhaps a slight smile creeps across his face.

In the Situation Room the chairman of the Joint Chiefs, Admiral Percy Fitzwallace (John Amos) has prepared three scenarios for the President for retaliatory action against Syria. Fitzwallace is calm and powerful and demands attention. As he discusses the obligations of a proportional response, Bartlet stops him and asks what the virtue of a proportional response is. There's an awkward silence; this is not a regular question on military strategy or briefing. Bartlet traces the development of a proportional response; they hit an airplane, we hit a transmitter, right? But the entire scenario is choreographed like an elaborate war dance and the targets are evacuated, so what's the point? Fitzwallace knows it isn't virtuous, it's just all there is. Bartlet demands to hear a different scenario in sixty minutes. He wants a *dis*proportional response, one that will bring "total disaster."

Meanwhile, Charlie Young (Dulé Hill), a very nervous young man who seems to feel out of place, is sitting in the Roosevelt Room trying hard not to be noticed. Josh doesn't give Charlie even a moment to be awestruck as he explains that he's vetting him for the job of President Bartlet's personal aide. It's a tough assignment with twenty-hour days, a lot of wait and hurry up, and it all involves some very important people. Charlie's confused because he applied for a job as a White House messenger, but Josh explains the woman in Personnel saw something special in Charlie and sent him over. They get so many qualified candidates for the job that they just go on gut. As he gets more comfortable in his surroundings, Charlie tells Josh he's not at college because he's looking after his little sister, Deanna. Their mother, a police officer, was killed in the line of duty five months before.

With evident reluctance, Fitzwallace presents Bartlet with a disproportional response scenario: the destruction of Hassan Airport. Fitzwallace says it's a staggering overreaction. "Five-thousand dollars' worth of punishment for a fifty-buck crime," he says. As the scenario plays forth in his mind, the

**Bradley Whitford
(Josh Lyman)**
Dulé Hill was such a joy to meet. My only fear for Dulé, and I keep telling him this, is he's such a young actor to have this experience. I just want him to know that it's not always like this. Boy, did his parents do a great job with him. He's tremendously positive and open. He's got incredible equilibrium. He's just terrific.

President asks for a cigarette. Someone slides him a pack; he takes one, lights it, and considers. He knows they can't hit the airport, so he gives the go-ahead to "Pericles-1." They'll hit two munitions dumps, an abandoned bridge, and the Syrian intelligence headquarters. "Fifty-buck crime," he mutters. "I honestly don't know what the hell we're doing."

Josh sits across from Charlie, accosting him with a slew of background questions. Sam comes into the room to hear Josh ask Charlie about his social life. Sam protests; all they need to know is if he'll come in early, stay late, and work efficiently and discreetly. Josh keeps at his line of questioning, asking about Charlie's friends. Sam interrupts to tell Charlie that Josh is asking if he's gay. Josh slams on the brakes and asks to see Sam outside. Sam's indignant that people are judging him. Toby interrupts their verbal war to tell them: it's happening: Bartlet's first military action.

Josh is duly impressed with Charlie, and reports his findings to Leo. His only hang-up in immediately hiring Charlie is that he's not wild about the visual of a young black man holding doors open for the President. Leo says *he* holds the door open for the President—they just need the right guy. Fitzwallace interrupts to ask Leo to sit down with the commander in chief.

FITZWALLACE: Tell him it's always like this the first time. Tell him he's doing fine.

LEO: He's not doing fine.

FITZWALLACE: Yeah he is. Kennedy once said, after he got to the White House, that the thing that made him sad was that he realized he was never gonna make a new friend. That's why presidents hang on to their old ones. You'll know what to say.

Leo shares Josh's concern about Charlie with Fitzwallace, but the chairman isn't worried. If Charlie's going to be treated with respect and paid a decent wage, then what does he care about appearances?

Words quickly become actions in the political arena, and Fitzwallace has ordered the air strikes. The world hasn't been told yet, but reporters are intuitive and are wondering why there's so much activity in the West Wing. One reporter, Danny Concannon (Timothy Busfield), explains that he urgently needs to speak with C.J. She thinks it's about the bombing but Danny's been a White House reporter for seven years and he doesn't need military action spelled out for him. No, Danny knows something else, that "Sam is going around with a three-thousand-dollar-a-night call girl." He doesn't have enough of a story yet but he's going

**Timothy Busfield
(Danny Concannon)**
I had done *A Few Good Men* on Broadway in 1990 and met Aaron doing that. Then I worked with Aaron at my theater in Sacramento . . . I directed some *Sports Nights*. I'm just a dear, dear friend of Aaron's. I was in his wedding. He called me one day and said there's a part of a reporter and maybe a possible love interest with Allison Janney. I hadn't read the script or read the scene, but I said, "I'm on a plane. Whatever you want me to do, I'll do." I came down and did one episode and that turned into eighteen.

Richard Schiff
(Toby Ziegler)

This ensemble is so talented and we understand what "ensemble" means. We come from theater, but a whole bunch of people come from Broadway and still don't know how to act their way out of their shoes. But a lot of us come from off-off-off Broadway where work was it. We didn't get any other reward except what happened on the stage and what happened in the process of rehearsal. So the process is important to a lot of us. I've always defined acting as what happens between people because I used to direct plays all the time and that's when I was affected. I was affected by the moments, which is the molecules moving between people. It's not, "Let me watch you, okay, now it's your turn." It's the tension and the movement of story that happens moment by moment. And we all understand that.

to ask around. Much to her own surprise, C.J. stands up for Sam, arguing that the White House doesn't get to judge Sam's friends and Danny's readers don't either. She asks Danny to back off. Danny agrees to drop it but warns that if he found out, other people will, too. And those people will put it in their pocket for later. In return for his discretion, C.J. gives Danny a ten-minute head start on the air raid.

The President is preparing to go on television from the Oval Office to tell the nation about the attack on Syria. In the chaos of planning and ordering the air strike, Bartlet has lost his glasses; he's been looking for them all day. Meanwhile, Josh has been giving Charlie a tour of the White House and they stumble into the Oval Office as Bartlet is ranting. Charlie, quietly observant of everything around him, nervously suggests where the glasses might be. Bartlet's too preoccupied to thank him. Leo sees how the scene is unfolding, and asks the President to step into his office. Without stopping to consider he's addressing the leader of the free world, Leo lectures Bartlet on being mad at people.

Bartlet confesses that what's eating him is his complete inability to protect American citizens. Where's the retribution? What the hell are they doing? Proportional response doesn't work: look at the marines in Beirut, in Somalia. Bartlet is fixated on reacting more fiercely, on going in hard, but Leo slaps him down. America's the only superpower left, so the President can conquer the world if he wants, but he'd better be prepared to kill everyone if he does, and he can start with Leo. American military responses are compromised, says Leo. "Of course it's no good. There is no good! It's what there *is!*" Bartlet says they'll just rebuild what we attack. "Then we'll blow 'em up again in six months!" says Leo. "We're getting really good at it." The two men stare at each other and after a quick moment, Bartlet laughs. Leo joins him slightly. They've diffused the tension, knowing the futility of the situation.

Just before Bartlet goes on the air, Leo briefs him about the other issues circulating the West Wing, namely, Bert Coles and Charlie Young. With his glasses safely back in his possession, Bartlet takes Charlie aside. The President just had the FBI director give him the details of Charlie's mother's death, and knows she was killed with "cop killer" bullets. Bartlet says they haven't had a lot of success yet but they're planning a big whack at trying to get them banned. Would Charlie like to come help try? He would. Just as Bartlet goes on the air, Charlie says to Josh, "I've never felt like this before." Josh smiles and says, "It doesn't go away."

FIVE VOTES DOWN

As the episode begins, Bartlet is speaking at a black-tie event in a hotel ballroom. The audience is comprised of Democrats who've paid five hundred dollars a plate to hear the President speak, and from the energy in the room, Bartlet's been giving them their money's worth. Bartlet knows how to work it, especially when he's preaching to his own choir. As Bartlet energetically discusses a vital gun control bill, word comes to Leo backstage that they've lost five votes. As Leo takes in the bad news, the President ramps it up for the final crescendo: We're going to win on Wednesday! As the audience stands and cheers, the band strikes up "Happy Days Are Here Again" and the President is taken out through the kitchen of the hotel by his Secret Service detail. After such an outstanding speech,

everyone's upbeat, although Toby thinks the President blew the D-section. On the down low, Josh informs C.J. they lost the five votes, and they're trying to find out who. C.J. keeps her composure.

The group brushes past event volunteers and hotel employees lining the corridors, all wanting to glimpse the President and be part of the excitement. Toby can't help asking Bartlet about the D-section. The President admits he gave it a little polish, right there on his feet. As they reach the motorcade, Charlie reminds Bartlet of the first lady's instructions, to take his back medication. Bartlet can imagine what her tone was. Three members of Josh's fan club shout out "We love you,

Josh!" C.J. rolls her eyes. "It helps not to know him." Chatting, debating, arguing, and laughing, the group gets to their cars and moves out. With hustle and bustle, energy and chaos, and fast-paced, breathless dialogue, it's the classic walk-and-talk.

Back at the White House, the mood of celebration is overshadowed by the intense need to win the vote on the gun bill. Now that they've publicly announced that the bill will pass, they have seventy-two hours to get it done, and it doesn't much matter how.

LEO: There are two things in the world you never want to let people see how you make 'em: laws and sausages.

The staff devises a strategy. They'll attend to the three defectors, Katzenmoyer, Wick, and O'Bannon, individually. Hoynes can deliver Tillinghouse, but Leo wants to exhaust every option before he depends on the vice president to save Bartlet. Mandy says that as a diversion, they can talk up the human interest aspect of their financial disclosure statements. Toby says he owns the tuxedo he's wearing, twenty-three dollars, and a 1993 Dodge.

Leo gets home after 2:00 A.M. His wife, Jenny (Sara Botsford), asks him where's he's been. Leo tries to explain the gun bill emergency, but Jenny cuts him off; she wants to know what could possibly change at two in the morning. As they argue, Leo notices a small gift-wrapped box. It's a gift for him, a wristwatch. It's their anniversary and he forgot.

Toby does, in fact, have more than twenty-three dollars in his pocket. He explains to Leela Radner (Jillian Armenante), a White House counsel, about a stock he bought last year, his first-ever foray into the market. Without lifting a finger or breaking a sweat, Toby turned his $5,000 into $125,000. Radner knows the story: 71 percent of the increase came after a Cal Poly professor testified before the Commerce Committee on Internet stocks. She also knows Toby arranged for the professor, his old college roommate, to testify. Radner asks Toby if he knows manipulating the market is a federal crime. He should have known $125,000 came with a few strings—should he talk to a lawyer? "You're talking to one right now," she replies.

Scanning the Financial Disclosure Report, Donna tells Josh he won the award for "Best Gift Valued Over Twenty-five Dollars": A $1,189 Vianatelli silk smoking jacket from Ms. Sarah Wissinger. He was also the runner-up with a $345 antique scrimshaw cigarette holder.

Leo knows he's in the dog house at home, and is arranging a silver service dinner to apologize to Jenny. He's ordered a Harry Winston choker to be delivered from New York and a violinist to

THOMAS DEL RUTH (DIRECTOR OF PHOTOGRAPHY)

I was particularly proud of the five-page walk-and-talk in [the episode] "Five Votes Down." The scene traversed three floors. It went through the kitchens and through the basements, and finally ended in a motorcade, all in one shot. I think that was probably the best continuous shot I have seen. All aspects of the production came together in a very harmonious blend. The performances were perfect. The staging was perfect. The energy of the actors was great. Everything worked beautifully and it was magnificent to see that happen.

ROB LOWE

You'll have to ask Tommy [Schlamme] how many takes it was. It was either in the twenties or the thirties. The steady-cam operator literally fell over from exhaustion when it was done. It's amazing in that we did that in a weekly television show. In a movie, that would be a staggering achievement.

JOHN SPENCER

As an actor, I adore walk-and-talk because I spent the first twenty years of my career onstage, and it's the closest to stage work in that there's no intercutting. So I like them, I find them very exciting.

ROB LOWE

They're very much like relay races. The baton has to be passed off perfectly each time. You need to have confidence in your other actors because lack of confidence is contagious, like seasickness. If you get the sense that somebody's off their game or they might not be there when you whip around that corner after you've just perfectly delivered your three pages of dialogue, even if all they have to say is "yes sir" at the right time, it's over. We all laugh that none of us wants to be the last person in an eight-page walk-and-talk.

play during dinner. Margaret (NiCole Robinson) declares he's spending too much money. Leo says Margaret can squeeze the life out of a nickel better than anyone, but Margaret shoots back: She's not making $40,000 a pop on the lecture circuit. Leo demands she stop reading the disclosure reports.

As he sets out to retrieve the votes that jumped ship, Josh proclaims he will kick ass. The congressmen want big concessions for their votes, but Josh is determined to play hardball. These people should be grateful the White House remembers their names. Leo gives Josh the green light.

Toby's stock windfall looks bad, and Sam advises him to hire a lawyer for precautionary measures. It's better to be on the offensive, and Sam's happy to help Toby after Toby supported Sam during the Laurie situation. Unable to let a good opportunity pass her by, C.J. sticks her head in Toby's office, says she's a little short for lunch, and asks Toby if he has a hundred and twenty-five thousand she could borrow.

Hunting for votes, Josh wants to reel in Congressman Katzenmoyer (Mark Blum), a forty-something man with the demeanor of an insurance salesman. Josh wastes no time asking if Katzenmoyer's constituents hunt quail with Uzis. Katzenmoyer tries to justify himself. He won his

district with just 52 percent of the vote, he needs to raise $10,000 a day for reelection, and is only getting $6,500. If the NRA targets him, he'll lose. He can't give them his vote, not right now. Josh argues that in two years, after the election, 55,000 more people will be dead.

> **JOSH:** Forgive my bluntness, and I say this with all due respect, Congressman, but vote "yes,"
>   or you're not even gonna be on the ballot two years from now.
> **KATZENMOYER:** How do you figure?
> **JOSH:** You're gonna lose in the primary.

KATZENMOYER: There's no Democrat who's challenging me.

JOSH: Sure there is.

KATZENMOYER: Who?

JOSH: Whomever we pick.

Josh paints a picture for Katzenmoyer. If he failed to cast his vote in favor of the gun control bill, the party would dig up a challenger and bring in Bartlet, whose popularity in Katzenmoyer's district is far-reaching. The moment there is a photograph of Bartlet endorsing a challenger, the congressman's finished.

> JOSH: President Bartlet's a good man, he's got a good heart. He doesn't hold a grudge. (beat) That's what he pays *me* for.

Josh isn't done kicking asses. He arranges to meet with Chris Wick (Jay Underwood), a Hollywood type who surrounds himself with aides and greets Josh with "dude." Josh kicks out the aides without blinking and tells Wick to "Shove it, dude, we're not in the frat house anymore." Josh continues on the attack: Wick has no idea what weapons are even banned in the bill but he's determined to stand in opposition just to prove a point. Wick says he's taken for granted, he's been in the House a year and he's had one photo op with the President. Where's the courtship? This one's easy, morals aside; Josh buys Wick off with a game of chess and a glass of brandy, photographers included. He has two of the five votes back.

Mandy and C.J. are cooing over the diamond choker Leo got for Jenny, and Sam kids Toby he should invest in a few of those. "There's literally no one in the world that I don't hate right now," says Toby. Leo has to choke down his pride to ask for Hoynes's help in turning Tillinghouse, but first he's going to try to convince Congressman Mark Richardson (Thom Barry) that his vote would be better spent on the other side.

Leo and Richardson take a walk. Richardson knows exactly what Leo is up to and he says he's voting no. The congressman wants to know what happened to the TEC DC-9 and the TEC 22, the Striker 12 and the Streetsweeper? Richardson tells Leo he didn't fight for them and that he's just interested in keeping the White House strong. Leo says if the White House isn't strong, he can't do anything. And a whole generation of African American men is being eaten alive. Richardson says the bill is a waste of money. He tells Leo if he writes a law that saves some lives, he'll sign it. Richardson advises Leo not to lecture him on being a leader of black men.

So Leo has to see Hoynes. Leo goes home for his dinner with Jenny first and sees a cab waiting. Inside, there's a couple of suitcases at the bottom of the stairs. Jenny tells Leo she can't do it anymore. It's not the anniversary, it's everything. Leo says this is the most important thing he'll ever do. Jenny asks if it's more important than their marriage.

> LEO: It *is* more important than my marriage. Right now, these few years, while I'm doing *this*, yes, of *course* it's more important than my marriage. I didn't decide to do this *myself*, Jenny, there were many discussions.

Jenny relays a message: Margaret called to confirm his nine o'clock meeting with Hoynes. Leo couldn't even make time to apologize for missing their anniversary. Leo swears he was only going to be forty-five minutes, but Jenny tells him to take his time, she'll be at the Watergate.

Unable to postpone the inevitable, Leo dutifully goes to see Hoynes. He's shaken up from the night's events; he's subdued and distracted. Somewhat concerned for Leo, Hoynes assures him he'll deliver Tillinghouse, no problem. Switching gears, he asks Leo, "When was the last time you went to a meeting?" Leo's puzzled: Hoynes explains he goes once a week in a basement office at the Old Executive Office Building. With three senators, two cabinet secretaries, a federal judge, and two agency directors. All our people. It looks like a card game, and maybe Leo should go and reconnect with himself once in a while.

Josh is in more hot water over the disclosure report. Mandy tells him he received the gifts from Sarah Wissinger on July 3, and he and Mandy broke up on July 9. A mere coincidence? Josh assures her they weren't presents to say thanks for the rollicking time in bed. Meanwhile, Leo is avoiding questions, telling everyone that last night with Jenny went great.

The staff is congregating in the Oval Office when the President comes in dressed like he's about to go fishing and spouting nonsensical advice. It's clear Bartlet's on another planet. C.J. asks if he took any of his back pills, the Vicodin or the Percocet? Bartlet asks, "I wasn't supposed to take both?"

Considering his boss's mental state, Sam decides this is a good time to bring up Toby's stock windfall. Helpfully, Mandy says Toby could resign, but Sam suggests that to avoid even the appearance of impropriety, Toby should cash out on the stock and reduce his salary to one dollar for a year. After complimenting Toby on the beauty of his name, Bartlet declares Sam's idea perfect. Everyone in the room approves, except Toby says he feels like he got screwed with his pants on.

As promised, Hoynes pays a visit to Cal Tillinghouse (Michael McGuire). The congressman says he's voting his conscience. With 240 million guns floating around in the United States, he wants his wife and daughter to have the protection of one. *He* wants one himself. Tillinghouse tells Hoynes that congressmen are annoyed at being bullied by the White House and they want retribution. Hoynes looks smugly satisfied at this response, and explains that's why he wants Tillinghouse to vote yes. And he might want to mention their talk to his colleagues.

TILLINGHOUSE: Tell me something: what's in it for me?

HOYNES: Right now?

TILLINGHOUSE: Yes.

HOYNES: Nothing.

TILLINGHOUSE: Then why am I handing you a personal political victory?

HOYNES: Why?

TILLINGHOUSE: Yes.

HOYNES: Because I'm gonna be the President of the United States one day and you're not.

As the staff watches the news on television, they learn the bill passes by one vote. However, the atmosphere of the West Wing is glum. Newscasters are crediting Hoynes for the White House victory, and with their work and sweat fresh in their memory, the staff is incredulous. Josh shoulders the blame; he knows he pissed the congressmen off and they're getting him back by giving Hoynes the curtain call. Leo says they got what they deserved for their hubris. But hey, they won.

Against his will, Josh knows he needs to congratulate Hoynes on his victory with the gun bill. Josh admits it's a crappy law, but that Hoynes had a good day. Hoynes knew how it would play out. "Welcome to the NFL," he says to Josh.

As the day comes to a close, Leo makes his way through a corridor at the OEOB. An undistinguished-looking door is being guarded by a Secret Service agent. Leo tells him he's there for the card game, and the guard allows him in.

Aaron Sorkin

I'm in AA. AA meetings are open to the entire public. You and I can go to any one we want right now, except for some. There are secret AA meetings for commercial airline pilots for reasons you can understand. There are secret AA meetings for judges, for surgeons, and things like that. The thought occurred to me, I wonder if there's such a thing as a secret AA meeting for very high-ranking government officials? This is how it would be if a couple of cabinet members, the chief of staff, and the Vice President of the United States were all recovering alcoholics. They wouldn't be able to go down the block to the Salvation Army and have an AA meeting there. It would be at eleven o'clock at night, in the basement someplace, there would be a Secret Service agent outside the door, and it would have to look like a card game. I simply wanted to show that, so I gave it to Leo. Little did I know I was going to be able to get any number of stories out of it.

CREATING
THE WEST WING

Aaron Sorkin

I suppose if you had to trace it back someplace it was that my first draft of *The American President* was about three times as long as a movie is supposed to be. There were many more stories in it other than the story of the President and the lobbyist and their romance. I thought, you know, I never really did get to tell the stories about the senior staffers that I wanted to tell. When John Wells came around and said, "Would you be interested in writing a television show?" I thought, boy, I'd be interested in writing this television show. That's how it started.

Thomas Schlamme (Executive Producer/Director)

I think Aaron works from a very emotional place. I'll try to find the moment in the whole piece that I believe, true or not, that is an image or a line Aaron had in his head which is why he wrote the whole script. It's not even something that I talk to him about. It helps me because it's an emotional truth and there's no one way to interpret it. That's my job, to direct his material. It will be processed through who I am too. That's what the actors and directors are. We are the interpretive artists in this. We are interpreting what he has created.

John Wells (Executive Producer)

NBC bought it, expressing some real concerns about the political arena. He [Aaron] wrote it and they didn't want to make it. They didn't think a political show could work. In their defense, political shows hadn't worked. They were very nervous about proceeding. It wasn't going to be an inexpensive show to do. We spent a lot of time talking about it. It took about a year and a half but we eventually got them to agree to make it.

Llewellyn Wells (Producer)

Once we did the pilot we felt confident that NBC would pick it up. And they did, originally, for thirteen episodes. Then the job becomes, how do we now take this concept that was designed to make a big splash for a pilot into a series? Once you delve into making a TV series it really is a very unique brand of organized chaos. You have a certain schedule you have to keep. The script has to be written and then produced, then film edited and delivered to the network, and aired. And in very short order, compared to other types of filmmaking.

You work with Aaron and his writing and research staff to discover what it is they have in mind and talk about what you can and can't feasibly do. You try to put very few limits on that. All of us who work on the production have the attitude that Aaron and Tommy should be able to dream up and create whatever they want. It's not our job to say no, but to say how. Which isn't always the process on television. Then again, this is a unique show.

Martin Sheen

They ask, "What's the reason for the success of the show?" In two words, "Aaron Sorkin." He's the reason. And no one involved in the show that knows what the show is disputes that one iota.

Richard Schiff

Aaron is very open to ideas, to reworking his words. But you have to understand that he writes poetry and he writes music. If you come up with an alternative, it better be in meter. Don't vernacularize the language and don't make it slang because it's not what he's writing. He's writing music. You have to replace music with music that's better or at least equal to what he's come up with.

Janel Moloney (Donna Moss)

One time I asked Aaron what he did on the weekend and he motioned like this [motions like typing]. I didn't see this as typing. I saw this as playing the piano. So I said, "Oh, Aaron, I didn't know you played the piano."

Dulé Hill (Charlie Young)

I guess for me it helps because I come from tap dancing and musical theater. It's all about rhythm. When I'm tap dancing, everything you do is in rhythm. I mean, our life is in rhythm as it is. That's how I approach my life. But Aaron Sorkin's work is definitely a rhythm. It goes. It's very musical. It flows.

Rob Lowe

There's always a build. There's a rhythm. There's a certain tempo. There's a meter. With Aaron's stuff there's usually only one way to play it great and a lot of other ways to play it very well. Aaron Sorkin has the ability to lay in exposition as quietly and gently as a leaf falling on a lake.

Aaron Sorkin

I do have a music background and I love music. Words, when they're spoken for the sake of performance, are music. They have rhythm. They have tone. They have pitch. They have all the same properties of music. When I began to develop a love for theater it was because of the sound of dialogue much more than plots or stories. I just love the sound and the rhythm of dialogue and I wanted to imitate that somehow.

I think about the music of one line; of an entire scene or an entire episode which will follow the patterns of movements in longer pieces of music. There'll be an *adagio* and there'll be an *andante*, where people are talking very fast. There'll be an aria and there'll be pauses and rests as it is in music. Now you have to marry all that to a story that you're telling. But the sound of it is terribly important.

The cast will be driven to distraction by my saying, "You're leaving out a beat in that measure. Actually, there's an 'and' there and if you leave that out, it's like taking a note out of a measure in 4/4 time that now only has three beats in it. It's just going to sound wrong." But they're fantastic about it.

Thomas Schlamme

Aaron writes musically. In some ways, what I'm trying to do visually is follow the orchestra a little bit. I've got the score. There's movement at a certain point and I can feel the movement when I'm reading it. It might even be a scene where it's stationary. I'll start to feel that there needs to be movement here and then it needs to come down and settle and rest.

In the pilot, specifically, I felt like when we come down with that first big downbeat, there's just activity. The whole orchestra's tuning up. It's just going all over the place. At the end, I wanted it to be so simple. The whole last act is people just sitting and talking. The President comes in, makes one circle, goes into his office, everybody stands absolutely still while he talks, and then they leave. That was all somewhat designed and became the palette for the show.

You can watch the shows and watch how act one, act two, act three, and act four evolve themselves. And where I start to feel, in the middle of the show, "I need some movement here." I don't just mean walk-and-talks. It can also be done with the camera. But I know that's what it takes. I sometimes feel like I'm reading a piece of music. It's kind of there and I'm not even aware I'm doing it.

Martin Sheen

Tommy is the glue between each one of us. Tommy has this really unique talent and honesty, he has a great honesty about what works. We can be down here doing a scene and acting up a storm, impressing everybody, and just knocking 'em dead. And if Tommy comes in and says to any one of us, "Um, may I suggest this?" *Boom!* There's no hesitation on anyone's part.

You need a Tommy Schlamme to keep you honest, so you don't get full of yourself. You know that phrase, with all this praise and success, you have to remember: "the higher the monkey climbs, the more he shows his ass." You gotta be really careful.

John Spencer

Tommy's my hero. He's a true artist. He's inspiring because he comes from such a place of artistic passion and excitement. And it's contagious. On a tired day you can hook into it and Tommy can give you energy that you didn't know you had. Whenever I have an artistic problem he's the first person I seek out for an opinion or advice. I just have total respect for him as an artist and as a man.

Janel Moloney

It's funny, because if Tommy comes into the room, or if Aaron comes into the room, you can see everyone just kind of zooms in around them, and it's not just because they're our bosses. We enjoy each other. Every night we have off, all of us are out having dinner and just absolutely laughing our heads off.

Bradley Whitford

Any one of these scripts, I'd happily do as a play for months. It would be a lot easier for us all if Aaron was not as good a writer.

Thomas Del Ruth

I wanted to play the dramatic elements along with the comedic elements in one cohesive whole. That's why the show has a great deal of depth of shadow. To me there's a subtext about the shadowy side of government which we, the public, don't always know about. The inability to peer into the shadows and see exactly what's there all of the time heightens that sense of drama.

The show also needed to have a certain kinetic feel to it, an energy. Since I had done *ER*, I was familiar with working with a fluid camera, one that would progress from one scene to another set, another set, another set on the move. I was used to lighting that kind of a set. I used these hot lights that were in the ceiling that punctuate the actors' heads as they pass underneath them. Even when they're going relatively slowly it gives the audience the impression that they're flying at hypersonic speed. Combined with the rapid-paced dialogue and throwaway lines of substance made for a very compelling pilot.

Aaron Sorkin

There are so many writers that I love, both dead and alive. It should go without saying I'm a fan of Shakespeare, and Tennessee Williams, and Eugene O'Neill, and Chekov. I'm a great fan of David Mamet, who also knows a thing or two about music and rhythm in his writing. I'm a great fan of Paul Attanasio, one of my contemporaries who had *Gideon's Crossing* on TV and has written the films *Quiz Show* and *Donnie Brasco*—some great movies. I don't need to say Arthur Miller's one of my favorite writers.

I'm a great fan of Garry Trudeau. I love *Doonesbury*. Two things I think I've copied from Garry Trudeau. I don't know how long he's been writing *Doonesbury* now, but it's over twenty-five years. Over that time, he's populated his world with all kinds of characters, so now any story he wants to tell, he can reach back to a character he had four years ago and bring him in.

The other thing Garry Trudeau does with jokes is, comic strips are in four frames and most comics will put the joke with the punch line in that fourth frame. He'll put it in the third frame and have a kind of blow off, a line like "I'll say," or "You bet," or "That's what I thought." What it does, it takes some of the edge off the joke itself and makes it more conversational and actually makes it funnier. It's something I try to do on the show, too. I bury the joke in a conversation and throw it away.

I feel our White House was Camelot, but with a shadowy subtext. So I wanted to bring forth a golden, Romanesque kind of quality. To give it a rich depth of color and cohesive palette of warm tones that would enhance the viewers' experience. So we went all out in choosing colors that were in the warm tones, the yellows, the oxblood reds, the golden tones.

Aaron Sorkin

You start out where it's a huge deal that the network has said, "Yes, I'm going to give you money. Write the pilot." And then it's a huge deal when the network says, "Okay, we're going to make the pilot." It's a huge deal when they say "We're going to pick up the show." Then the pickup after thirteen and the second season order.

To show you how far we've come from that, at the end of our second season NBC forgot to pick us up. They just forgot to tell us. Scott Sassa [President, NBC West Coast] was at the wrap party. I had just turned in the final script and he was talking about how wonderful it was. He saw a cut of the show and said, "It's just terrific. I can't wait to see what we can do for the third season premiere." I said, "Scott, since you brought it up, you haven't picked us up yet." He said, "Okay, well, I'd be optimistic."

The job stays the same, every week. Writing episode forty-four, I still feel the same way as I did writing episode two. I'm terrified. I have no ideas. I'm certain this is going to be the one where I put the script on the table and people are going to go, "Oh." I want to nail it. When it works we still all jump up and down.

THE CRACKPOTS
AND THESE WOMEN

On a crisp, cold autumn night, the Secret Service stands guard discreetly as the senior staff plays a pickup game of three-on-three basketball outside the White House. It's game point and the President won't concede. Toby's not afraid to resort to trash talk and tells the President there's no shame in calling it quits.

TOBY: This is perfect, you know that? This is the perfect metaphor. After you're gone and the poets write *The Legend of Josiah Bartlet*, let them write you as a *tragic* figure. Let the poets write, "He had the tools to be a leader of men, but the voices of his better angels were shouted down by his obsessive need to win."

Refusing to be beaten, Bartlet brings in the reinforcements, namely, a towering ringer called Rodney Grant. Toby rolls his eyes—this is like the time he was playing doubles tennis with C.J. in Florida and the President introduced his new partner, Steffi Graf. Bartlet assures them that Mr. Grant is on the President's Council on Physical Fitness. As Grant swats away shots righteously, Toby recognizes Grant as a member of Duke's Final Four team. Toby tells Charlie to guard the new guy.

Donna is prepared to divulge the dirt on a new Romeo she met, but Josh isn't interested in the revolving door of local gomers she sees. Shut down, she goes back to business: Leo wants him to see someone from the National Security Council, and C.J. wants him to read an article in *The New Yorker* about smallpox.

Much to the chagrin of the staff, Leo announces the anniversary of Big Block of Cheese Day honoring President Andrew Jackson, who kept a two-ton hunk of cheese in the main foyer of the White House for any and all who might be hungry. Leo says Jackson wanted the White House to belong to the people. In this spirit, Leo asks senior staff to meet with organizations who wouldn't

Richard Schiff

We were playing basketball in front of the White House, and the prop guy said, "Do you want to wear a sweatshirt from your college?" It made complete sense to me that Toby went to CCNY. I said, "I want an old CCNY from twenty years ago. I don't want a new one." They called the college and they had to look at the script to approve it because they had never heard of *The West Wing*. And then I was wearing the City College, CCNY, sweatshirt, cut off and old, playing ball.

It got around that Toby from *The West Wing* went to City College. The college called me and asked if I'd like to come back and give a speech at the honors convocation. I wasn't an exemplary student by any means, so I asked, "Why on earth would you pick me?" I went back and I gave a very long speech on my whole experience at City College. It was the most important thing I'd ever written. It was a very moving experience for me. That link between Toby and Richard was really important because it reconnected me to my college, which I hadn't been back to in twenty-some-odd years.

ordinarily get access. Josh says it's "Total Crackpot Day," which earns him a slap on the head.

As the staff disperses to see their assigned groups, Leo pulls Josh aside. He introduces Lacey (David Fabrizio) from the National Security Council, who gives Josh a laminated card like a bus pass. His heart rate quickens as he reads his instructions in the event of a nuclear attack. The NSC has to get select people up in Air Force One or in an underground shelter as fast as possible. Josh asks, "And my staff comes with me, or they have separate . . ." Lacey shakes his head. They don't get to go. Josh is stunned.

Bartlet is prepping for a press conference and Toby wants him to discuss gun control and the recently passed bill. Bartlet blows off the suggestion, as he will if he's asked any questions about guns. The bill was popular— they shot up eight points after it was passed. Toby says he hopes "none of our new fans are among the thirty thousand people this bill won't protect from a gun this year."

The Big Block of Cheese Day appointments are arriving, and Leo insists everyone keep them. So instead of working on briefing questions with the President, Sam gives his ear to a guy who wants the government to concentrate on the existence of UFOs. Josh turns his attention to smallpox. While it was eradicated in the fifties, countries like Iraq, Syria, Korea, and China have stockpiles of it.

The President cheers up when he hears his daughter, Zoey, is coming to dinner. She's in town looking at student housing for Georgetown, and in celebration Bartlet is making a batch of his famous chili. Enthusiastically, he invites the entire staff to attend, but gets a lukewarm response. Bartlet tells them to look at the big seal on the carpet, then back at him. He asks them again and they're much more excited.

Toby doesn't want the President attending a fundraiser Mandy's arranging at a Hollywood mogul's house. The President is due to give a speech about violence in

the media twenty-four hours before the party and Toby declares they can't admonish Hollywood one day and take their money the next. "Why not?" asks the President. He says the problem with the movies is not that they're violent, it's that they suck, and if people didn't go, they wouldn't be made. Problem solved. Toby flips one hundred and eighty degrees and argues that it's a hose job, the target is ridiculous, and coming at Hollywood with a list of things that are un-American might sound "eerily familiar."

BARTLET: Do I look like Joe McCarthy to you, Toby?

TOBY: *Nobody* ever looks like Joe McCarthy, Mr. President, that's how they get in the door in the first place.

Josh can't take his mind off the laminated NSC card burning a hole through his wallet. He takes his thoughts to Sam, asking how he felt when he received the card. But when Sam asks, "What card?" the blood drains from Josh's face. He's one of the select few, and the rest of the staff merely gets to fend for themselves in the face of a nuclear disaster.

In the spirit of Cheese Day kindness, Mandy goes to Toby to discuss the fund-raiser, but Toby doesn't want to hear it. Rebuked, she gives up kindness and announces she's glad David Rosen passed on the Communications job, Toby really deserved it. Feeling as though he's been slapped, Toby pulls C.J. out of her cheese meeting about a wolves-only roadway. He'd asked her before if he was Bartlet's first choice and C.J. called him a "paranoid noodnik," but now he's asking her again. C.J. dismisses him; she's never heard anything about David Rosen. Switching gears, Toby asks C.J. for help with the gun issue. He feels like the kid in class who waves his hand furiously but never gets called on.

Josh is noticeably absent from the speech run-through. Donna makes the excuse that he's at the dentist but he's really gone to see his therapist, Stanley Maxwell. Maxwell says he hasn't seen Josh in ten months, why has he come now? Josh mentions he read this article about smallpox. And he can't get "Ave Maria" out of his head, a song that his sister used to play over and over. Maxwell asks if he means his sister who died? "Yes," Josh says, "Joanie." He admits what this is really about—he was thrown off when he got the NSC card, and more disturbed to learn he was the only one of his friends who got one. Josh continues, "Joanie and Toby and C.J. and Sam were . . ." Maxwell interrupts him. "Joanie?" Josh stumbles over his words, mumbling that he can't talk about the card, and he tries to leave.

Maxwell soothingly mentions that Josh never told him how Joanie died. Josh shrugs his shoulders, claiming it's not a big deal. She was baby-sitting for him and there was a fire, a popcorn maker or something. Maxwell repeats that the house caught fire. "Why aren't *you* dead?" Josh's memories of the night are vague, but he knows he ran out of the house. "You were just a little boy, Josh. That's what you were supposed to do." Maxwell gently chides Josh that this is *not* not a big deal.

Later, Josh is back in his office, sitting alone, and listening to Schubert's "Ave Maria." C.J. comes to fetch him for the chili party but his mood is far from enthusiastic. Josh confides in C.J. about the card he got from the NSC and that he knows C.J., Sam, and Toby didn't get one. C.J. realizes this knowledge has been hanging over his head and upsetting him and says, "You're really very sweet sometimes." C.J. casually tells Josh, of course they don't want her and the other guys. They're not going to need a lot of press releases or speeches after the bomb goes off. What Josh is most worried about is that the end of the world is not going to come with the red phone and nuclear bombs. It's going to be something like smallpox. If a hundred people in New York get smallpox it's going to make HIV look like the cold season. He says there are only seven doses of vaccine in this country. C.J. tells him to come have chili and repeats herself: He really is very sweet sometimes.

In the residence, Bartlet is having a good time at his chili party and he's trying to make sure everyone else is too. Toby has a lot hanging on his mind, though, and finally concedes to the President that their professional and personal relationships have hit a rough patch. Bartlet agrees with that. Toby ventures that he's been irritating the President, and Bartlet agrees with that too. Toby asks what's really been on his mind: if David Rosen was Bartlet's first choice for the communications director. Bartlet admits he was, but Rosen turned him down. Thank God.

> **BARTLET:** I couldn't live without you, Toby. I'd be in the tall grass, I'd be in the weeds. I know I disappoint you sometimes. I mean, I sense your disappointment and I get mad 'cause I know a lot of times you're right. You're not the kid in the class with his hand raised and whatever it was you said to C.J. You're a wise and brilliant man, Toby. Don't ever wait for me to call on you.

Josh sees Zoey Bartlet (Elisabeth Moss) and introduces Charlie to her. They seem to get along well, although Charlie keeps calling Zoey "ma'am."

The President, Leo, and Josh look around the room. Bartlet says he loves seeing colleagues having a good time together. Bartlet says he can't get over these women. There's C.J., who's "like a fifties movie star. She's so capable. So loving and energetic." He points out Mandy, going at it toe-to-toe with Toby. And look at Mrs. Landingham, who lost her two boys in Vietnam and hasn't missed a day of work in fourteen years. He says look at Donna, Cathy, and Margaret. Look at Zoey.

Josh admits there's something that's been troubling him. He says he serves at the pleasure of the President, but he can't keep his NSC card. Josh takes out his wallet and carefully removes the card. He says he wants to be a comfort to his friends in tragedy and to celebrate with them in triumph. Josh wants to be able to look them in the eye. He wants to be with his family, his friends, these women.

Bartlet smiles and quiets the room. He says the first lady is in Pakistan, he's not sure why, but Zoey is here and starting Georgetown before medical school and a life of celibacy. He says there's always one or two converts on "Big Block of Cheese Day." He wonders if it's C.J. and her wolves, or Sam and his UFOs. He asks what the next challenge will be. Smallpox has been eradicated once and, Bartlet says, "Surely we can do it again."

MR. WILLIS OF OHIO

I t's a late night in the White House, and the senior staff is playing poker. C.J. deals seven-card stud but President Bartlet is distracted. He's insisting on mining his inexhaustible reserve of cerebral trivia. He says there's only one fruit with seeds on the outside (the strawberry). There are fourteen punctuation marks in standard English grammar.* There are only three words that begin with the letters "dw." "Dwindle," says Sam. "Dwarf," says Toby. He wracks his brain for the last. With a nudge from the President, he dredges up "dwell." As Bartlet wins the hand and the game breaks up, the Secret Service calls a security alert. The building is

*The fourteen punctuation marks in standard English grammar are period; comma; colon; semicolon; dash; hyphen; apostrophe; question mark; exclamation point; quotation marks; brackets; parentheses; braces; and ellipses. Toby knew the last seven.

not secure and everyone stands right where they are until the all-clear is given. Mandy declares this never happened at her last job.

As a new day dawns on the West Wing, Toby calls out to the communications bullpen for a copy of Article I, Section 2. "Of what?" Bonnie (Devika Parikh) asks. "The Constitution," Toby says dryly, as if it could be anything else. Undiscouraged by her apparent uselessness in this situation, Bonnie asks if it's still in print. Toby says if Amazon.com doesn't have it, she can go bust it out of the glass-encased display in the Archives.

Over the phone, Sam is saying the President will veto the Commerce Bill if it prohibits using sampling data in the 2000 census. As he hangs up, C.J. sidles up: she likes the way Sam said that. And he's looking good these days. Sam's not convinced of her sincerity, and C.J. fesses up. She says she doesn't quite understand the census. Any of it. She's been commenting about the bill to the press for three weeks, but she's been faking her knowledge the whole way.

Donna's waxing philosophical, and proposes to Josh that the root of all politics is economics. In terms of the budget surplus, she's right in thinking the Republicans want to give it back in tax relief, but we don't. No, says Josh, we're Democrats, we want to spend it. Donna demands her money back.

The staff is perusing the latest Appropriations Bill, which includes such allocations as $12 million

for an Appalachian Transportation Institute and $2 million for a volcano monitor in Alaska. Mandy reports they're looking at three swing votes on the Commerce Committee. If the committee drops the sampling prohibition, the Appropriations Bill passes the President and Congress without a problem. The swing votes are the key: two of the three are Gladman and Skinner, and the third is the late Congresswoman Janice Willis's husband. Toby presumes Mr. Willis will do what he's told. He predicts that they can be brought around quickly—everyone wants to get out of town for the three-day weekend.

Ron Butterfield (Michael O'Neill), part of the President's Secret Service detail, briefs Bartlet about the security breach. A mentally unbalanced woman in her forties got onto the White House grounds, brandishing a gun.

Aaron Sorkin

I think we're all very flattered when we hear that the show illuminates certain things. We hear it from high school history and social studies teachers. We hear it from the politicians themselves. We hear it from people who lead certain causes. Whether it's on drug policy, or the census, or AIDS in Africa, or the death penalty, or what have you.

We're delighted when we hear that, but it's not our goal. Our goal is the same as David Kelley's goal on *The Practice* and *Ally McBeal* and John [Wells's] on *ER*, and Steven Bochco and David Milch's on *NYPD Blue*. It's simply to captivate you for an hour and when the hour's over make you feel like, That was worth it. I had a good time and I want to watch again next week. We are storytellers first and last. If we do something else, well then, that just speaks to the power of storytelling.

Bartlet remains calm until he hears she wasn't after the President, her target was Zoey. Leo has been meaning to tell the President about Jenny leaving him but knows this isn't the time. He's afraid of how his old friend will react. The burgeoning emotional crisis might prove too much for Bartlet to handle.

Determined to push the Commerce Bill through, Toby, Josh, and Mandy are elucidating the administration's case to Gladman, Skinner, and Willis in the Roosevelt Room. The pork-stuffed Appropriations Bill is 7,000 pages long and weighs fifty-five pounds. If the anti-sampling amendment is attached, a bill that size is sure to get stuck in the system for a long time. It's the standard political game: a combination of chess and chicken. One of the players is a rookie, Congressman Joe Willis (Al Fann), a quiet African American man in his fifties. Mr. Willis, a former social studies teacher, only took his wife Janice's seat a month before, and he still appears to feel out of place in his surroundings. Toby tries to put everyone on the clock, saying he's sure they want to get home for the weekend. Mr. Willis interrupts, saying he's in no hurry. They should take their time.

As their cronies hammer the congressmen, Sam schools C.J. on the census. He explains that government representation is based on population, so there needs to be an accurate count of who's being represented. Every ten years, the Census Bureau goes door-to-door, performing an elaborate head count. The process takes 950,000 people and costs nearly $7 billion.

In the Roosevelt Room, the argument turns to the inherent flaws of the census: it always undercounts people in the inner city, recent immigrants, and the homeless. In 1990, eight million people, mostly black, were excluded or missed completely. Sampling, on the other hand, would be much more accurate and would cost four billion less. But it's unconstitutional, the congressmen protest. Toby saw that coming.

Donna is stubbornly fixated on the idea of asking for her money back now that there's a budget surplus. Josh suggests he wants to take her share, put it with everyone else's, and pay down the debt and endow Social Security. Donna shrugs her shoulders—she'd rather have cash to buy a DVD player.

JOSH: One of the problems is that the DVD player you buy might be made in Japan.
DONNA: I'll buy an American one.
JOSH: We don't trust you.
DONNA: Why not?

JOSH: We're Democrats.

President Bartlet, concerned that Charlie has no extracurricular or personal life, asks Josh to take his aide out for a beer. Like a father, Bartlet offers to give Josh some spending money but he realizes he doesn't carry cash anymore. Josh plans for him and Charlie to "speak as men do." But his plot is thwarted when Mallory and Zoey ask to come along. Mallory tells Josh to bring Sam, assuring him it's not a booty call. C.J. hops on the bandwagon as well.

> **JOSH**: The President's daughter, the chief of staff's daughter, a Georgetown bar, and Sam. What could possibly go wrong?

In his meeting, Toby says the constitutional article is arcane regarding sampling measures, unable to be the basis of modern judgment. Toby produces a copy of the Constitution with a flourish and Mandy reads Article I, Section 2. It mandates that representation and taxation are apportioned by population. Ahead of a Supreme Court ruling, this is the provision the opponents of sampling say will render it unconstitutional. He persuades Mr. Willis to admit that he knows the exact wording of the article, that government shall count free persons and "three-fifths of other persons"—slaves. Toby says, "They meant you, Mr. Willis, didn't they?" Gladman and Skinner want to wind up the meeting before tension mounts too high to handle, but Mr. Willis informs them he's changed his mind. He'll vote to drop the census amendment until the court rules on whether sampling is constitutional.

> **TOBY**: I was wondering, what changed your mind?
> **MR. WILLIS**: You did. I thought you made a very strong argument.
> **TOBY**: Thank you. (beat) I'm smiling because . . . well, around here the merits of a particular argument generally take a backseat to political tactics.

Toby can't lie to the man's face—he took advantage of Mr. Willis and his naïveté in politics. Sampling *is* partisan, and if they sink to using it for the census, what will stop them from using it for elections? But Mr. Willis is content with his decision, it is likely to be the only vote he makes in the House.

Leo gathers the courage to tell Bartlet of his pending divorce, and his

Martin Sheen

I remember I was pushing for sons for the President. Aaron said, "No, no, no. These guys are your sons." I said, "Oh, they're a little old, aren't they?" But I see his point. Bartlet really is a very strong father figure. The great humanity. The heart he has. And the interplay. He loves to have fun and play these awful word games, geographical games, and Latin. He loves to show off and trap them. Mind you, I don't play chess.

friend's reaction is as anticipated. Bartlet asks to speak to Jenny himself, to smooth things over. He wonders why Leo waited so long to break the news, and Leo admits that he feared the President would garner the blame for the split. From the sag in Bartlet's posture, it's clear he does feel the weight of responsibility on his shoulders.

Meanwhile, at a Georgetown hangout, the gloves are off for the office night out. Mallory kids Sam about his "special friend." Zoey interjects, "The hooker?" Sam nearly spits out his drink, interrogating Zoey and Mallory about their knowledge of Laurie. More importantly, do their fathers know? Each says that they don't. Yet. Laughing, Zoey goes up to the bar, leaving her panic button behind.

At the bar, four college guys surround Zoey and start to harrass her, unaware of who she is. Charlie notices the scene they're making and comes to Zoey's aid but immediately the guys start in with racial slurs. Sam jumps up when he notices what's going on, and he and Josh move toward the bar in hopes of cooling some tempers. Josh calmly tells them they don't know it yet, but they're having a pretty bad night. One frat boy wants to know who's gonna give it to them. As he speaks, the Secret Service charge in and cave in their world. The frat guys are thrown facedown against the bar. Zoey is whisked out the door by two agents. Charlie stands by, watching the guys being frisked, stripped of all their pride.

> **FRAT GUY #1:** I'm not done with you, Sammy.
>
> **CHARLIE:** My name's Charlie Young, jackass, and if that bulge in your pocket's an eight ball of blow, you're spending spring break in federal prison.

When he hears about her evening, the President has to give Zoey the lecture he's obviously rehearsed in his head many times. Zoey tells him she's entitled to a normal life. Bartlet brushes her demand off; he's worried about getting shot, sure, but that's nothing compared to his constant fear of what might happen to her. Her

spontaneous charades scare the hell out of the Secret Service and her father. He outlines what happens in his nightmare: Zoey gets dragged out of a party where she is innocently hanging out with friends. She's kidnapped and spirited out of the country, and the United States is held up for 460 prisoners in Israel that they won't release because Israel doesn't negotiate with terrorists. At that point in the nightmare, Bartlet says he's no longer the commander in chief, he's "a father out of his mind because his girl's in a shack in Uganda with a Luger to her head." He wants her to have a life, but she has to be careful.

Making his amends, Bartlet goes to Leo's office and apologizes to him for his rather self-centered attitude toward the divorce—he truly wants to help his old friend through this. On a lighter note, Josh, Sam, and Charlie are going to be severely reprimanded for their night out on the town. Josh is sure he could have taken the two guys on the left. Donna has bought Josh a sandwich. She tells him she'll keep his change and invest it for him. After all, he's not to be trusted with it.

At their next poker game, Josh confesses to the President that Charlie didn't even blink before putting himself between Zoey and danger. Toby shifts the mood, exclaiming that he met a good man in Mr. Willis. "He didn't mind saying, 'I don't know.' " Bartlet says, " 'I don't know' and 'What do *you* think?' are two phrases that could fit nicely into all of our vocabularies." Toby watches on the television coverage as Mr. Willis of Ohio votes "yea," and he smiles.

THE STATE DINNER

s the White House prepares to play host to the president of Indonesia at a state dinner, multiple crises are brewing. Hurricane Sara, a class-four storm system, is heading for Georgia and the Carolinas. Teamsters have voted to strike, and once the Taft-Hartley Act expires that evening, they will stage a walkout.* And in McClane, Idaho, law enforcement has surrounded a farmhouse containing anywhere from eighteen to forty survivalists. They're armed, kids are inside, and the FBI has decided it's a hostage situation. Crises aside, the press is most interested in asking C.J. about the fabulous world of fashion on showcase at the dinner.

*The act, officially the Labor-Management Relations Act, dates from 1947. The union or the employer must, before terminating a collective bargaining agreement, serve notice on the other party and on a government mediation service. The government was empowered to obtain an eighty-day injunction against any strike that it deemed a peril to national health or safety. The act takes its name from its sponsors, Senator Robert Taft and Representative Fred Hartley.

The West Wing staff works frantically: Josh needs Donna to find an interpreter for a meeting with an Indonesian deputy, Rahmadi Sumahidji Bambang. Leo summons the truckers and management and gives them until midnight to resolve their conflict over hiring practices. Sam is concentrating on creating the dinner toast with Toby, and Mandy will monitor the Idaho standoff. Josh doesn't think it's a job for a political consultant, but Leo doesn't have time for games tonight: she's to keep her eye on the hostage situation.

The President sits through an excruciating photo session with his Indonesian counterpart, President Siguto. As they face dozens of photographers, surrounded by aides and Secret Service looking on, Bartlet tries to engage his guest in chitchat. They're serving salmon. President Siguto doesn't like salmon. Yo-Yo Ma is going to play. Siguto is unmoved. Bartlet shares his concerns and frustration with Leo.

Patrick H. Caddell (Consultant)
Aaron wanted that whole dinner to be one crisis after another. We were doing the foreign policy thing where we insult the Indonesians and so forth. Then he said, "I want three things. I want some kind of natural disaster, I want some kind of strike that Bartlet has to deal with, and I want some episode like a hostage situation."

BARTLET: I can't decide whether that man is boring or rude, but he's one or the other.

LEO: I'm sorry to hear that.

BARTLET: I mean, I'm in there trying to picture how this guy could campaign for something and win. Then I remembered, we usually rig the election.

It might be that President Siguto's ears are burning as Toby proposes his toast to Sam. Dispensing with the usual platitudes, he asserts, "I don't think we should remind people how friendly we were with dictators who oppressed their people while stealing their money." Toby tells Sam to toughen it up: it's dinner, but it's still hardball.

As their media consultant, Mandy's job is to predict the PR implications of the developing crises, and she foresees disaster at the siege. She tells Josh the reason the FBI knew the survivalists possessed illegal weapons is because they sold them to them. Furthermore, there are crossed wires in Idaho, so it's not clear who's running the show. Miscommunication can have devastating effects. Meanwhile, Leo works to start the flow of communication between the two sides of the trucking dispute, but to no avail. Silence reigns in the Roosevelt Room.

At another photo op with Siguto, Danny Concannon questions Bartlet about the presence of protesters across the street. Neither the President nor C.J. are aware of any protesters, but they'll check into it. Danny drops a hint, clearly enunciating as he says, "Vermeil." C.J. reiterates that she'll cover it at the next briefing. When Danny is safely out of earshot, C.J. asks Carol to go research vermeil; she needs to know what it is.

C.J. learns that vermeil is gilded silver, and the White House has a large collection of it. The small band of protesters objects to its presence in the virtual seat of democracy, viewing it as a relic of tyranny because Louis XV owned a lot. C.J. reprimands Danny for asking about the protest; had he kept his mouth shut, no one would have known that six people were protesting across the street. Danny shirks the blame by asking C.J. what she's wearing to the dinner. His paper doesn't really care, but he does.

Sam meets Laurie for lunch, and while he clearly wants to talk to her, she's trying to study for a test. She looks up from the books long enough to ask Sam if he's afraid to be seen with her. Sam says he isn't. He asks if she's working tonight. She is, but she doesn't know where she's going. The guy calls, tells her what to wear, and the rest is a surprise. The name of the game is discretion, and Sam says her night job stinks.

At an Oval Office meeting about the hostage situation, Mandy suggests using a negotiator when everyone else, the FBI included, wants to take the farmhouse by force. Mandy argues that if they raid, the next day's front page will show a screaming woman running out of a burning house with a baby in her arms. Her point is well taken and the President decides to go with Mandy's negotiation plan. She seems utterly surprised she won out.

Fending off any questions regarding what appears to be a huge military mobilization out of Norfolk, Leo explains to the President they're clearing a battle carrier group away from the path of the hurricane. Charlie pulls Josh aside and asks him to find out if his grandparents are safe. They live in a little house off the coast of Georgia.

As the storm closes in around Washington, the staff anxiously waits for news. The lull is eerily quiet. The FBI negotiator in Idaho has been in the house two hours; the teamsters are still hashing out hiring procedures with management; Donna is out of luck with her translator. Indonesia is home to 583 languages: her guy speaks Javanese and Mr. Bambang speaks Batak. After much searching, she finds someone in the kitchen who can translate Batak into Portuguese for their translator to render into English.

The reception preceding the state dinner is swarming with elegant people. Abbey Bartlet (Stockard Channing), the first lady, is the center of attention. Both stunning and likable, she puts people at ease, even on this stuffy occasion. As she not-so-discreetly introduces C.J. to an unmarried cardiologist, C.J. asks the first lady about the vermeil collection. Abbey's not embarrassed by

its tarnished history. It's our history, she says.

At the dinner, Leo introduces Toby, Josh, and Sam to Carl Everett, a man who's raised a sizable amount of money for the party in the Midwest. Without using so many words, Leo wants Everett to be schmoozed. Everett introduces his date, the very beautiful and very nervous Laurie. Sam plays it cool, but says there are to be no pictures of Everett's date with the President.

Each of the day's crises are coming to a head. Charlie's grandparents are safe, but Hurricane Sara's headed out to sea, straight toward the newly positioned fleet, which could be catastrophic. In Idaho, the FBI has recaptured the house, but in the chaos, the negotiator was shot and is in critical condition. As the carrier group and its crew of 12,000 sit waiting for the hurricane to crash upon them with the fury of Mother Nature, the FBI negotiator enters surgery. There is nothing for the President to do but wait at the dinner for news.

Toby's meeting in the White House kitchen with Bambang resembles a three-ring circus and looks like it could last for hours. Three languages float off the tongues of the interpreters, and Toby asks Bambang for a favor, the release of a friend of his imprisoned for antigovernment activity in Indonesia. With his ears ringing, Bambang admits he speaks perfect English. But he believes the dinner toast was despicable and humiliating, and he knows who wrote it.

> BAMBANG: Mr. Ziegler, does it strike you at all hypocritical that a people who systematically wiped out a century's worth of Native Americans should lecture the world so earnestly on human rights?
>
> TOBY: (pause) Yes, it does.

With that, Bambang tells Toby to go to hell.

Danny Concannon has heard rumors of the siege in Idaho and asks C.J. about it. Without waiting for a response, he tells her she has on a nice dress.

C.J.: When you flirt with me, are you doing it to get a story?

DANNY: No.

C.J.: Why are you doing it?

DANNY: I'm doing it to flirt with you.

C.J. accuses Danny of saying she's too friendly with the press. You are, he says. But he's still flirting with her.

Carl Everett is willing to take advantage of the schmoozing; he knows Sam gets a lot of face time with the President and suggests they form a mutual bond. Eyeing Laurie, Sam says he costs $500 an hour. The meaning and intent is lost on Everett, but Sam clarifies—he costs $500 an hour in the private sector, and the White House is pretty rigid on people taking on private clients. Everett quickly makes an escape, and, without considering the consequences, Sam offers Laurie

$10,000 not to go home with Everett. She looks at Sam with a mix of affection and sadness, but returns to Everett when he calls.

In the Roosevelt Room, the Teamsters and management have failed to come to an agreement. As the deadline draws near, President Bartlet gives each side five minutes to present its case, standing as if appearing in court. Bartlet, a Nobel Laureate in Economics, listens for a while before declaring that none of them knows what they're talking about. He threatens that at 12:01, he'll use his executive power to nationalize the trucking industry. Management protests, but Bartlet argues that Truman did it in '52 with the mines, and he'll take his chances with the Supreme Court. And he'll ask Congress to give him the power to draft truckers into the military. Leaving the room, Bartlet tells the open-mouthed teamsters and management that they have forty-seven minutes to do a deal.

Mrs. Bartlet finds her husband. She knows the evening's turning out to be a rough one.

> ABBEY: I've found that one of the things that happens when I stay away too long, is that you forget you don't have the power to fix everything. (smiles) You have a big brain and a good heart and an ego as big as Montana. (laughs) You do, Jed. (beat) You don't have the power to fix everything. . . . But I do like watching you try.

As Hurricane Sara transforms the ocean into a giant whirlpool, the President tries to reach the fleet commander on the USS *Kennedy* to hear how they are weathering the storm. The only answer they can get is from Signalman Third Class Harold Lewis, a radio man aboard the *Hickory*, a maintenance ship. Lewis reports 80-foot seas and 120-knot winds. There's a fire on board and no lights. The President says he'll stay on the line as long as the radio works. "Just hang on."

Lyn Elizabeth Paolo
(Costume Designer)
We had to fit Stockard only an hour before she went to the set. So we had the famous cleavage dress, which Stockard loves, but the rest of America was very upset because the first lady should not have cleavage. We got more letters about that dress than anything else.

Stockard Channing
(Abbey Bartlet)
When I made my first appearance I was wearing something with a lot of décolletage. There were a lot of letters saying, "How dare she," while others said, "How great." Her style is very womanly. Even though I wear suits all the time. I've got long hair and it's not in a serviceable bob. I like that she's got a little verve to her. That's a great balance to her intelligence.

ENEMIES

It's 1:30 in the morning as the President sits in the Oval Office lecturing Josh on another one of his pet passions, America's national parks. Josh's body language says he's heard enough but the President's having fun. Not only can he name the parks, he's visited all fifty-four. Bartlet warns Josh if he's any less deferential and any more uninterested, there's a chance he'll get an oral guided tour of each one right then and there.

JOSH: You're quite a nerd, Mr. President.

BARTLET: Really.

JOSH: Yes, sir.

BARTLET: I assume that was said with all due respect.

JOSH: Yes, sir.

The morning dawns early for the West Wing, and the talk of the office is the banking bill, which appears to be in the bag. The President excitedly tells C.J. they beat the banking lobby and advises she should talk it up to the press. Over breakfast, Mallory congratulates her father. Leo asks about Jenny but Mallory refuses to be her parents' middleman, and suggests he call her and ask her himself. With no reconciliation in sight, Leo gives his daughter his and Jenny's opera tickets.

In the Roosevelt Room, Vice President Hoynes commences a cabinet meeting, in the President's absence. Mounting his high horse, Hoynes says their first goal must be to find a way to reconcile the White House ties with Congress, to reach out to the House and Senate. Hoynes stops abruptly when the room comes to its feet, hailing the President's arrival. Bartlet slyly asks the stenographer Mildred what he's missed. She repeats what Hoynes said and Bartlet stares him down, "You don't think our first goal should be finding a way to best serve the American people?"

In Toby's office, Toby and Sam are running a fine-tooth comb over a speech. Josh comes in and asks if they're hearing anything on the banking bill, because he has. Approaching C.J. in her office, Danny fishes for some gossip; he's heard the President roughed up Hoynes at the cabinet meeting. On the record, nothing happened, C.J. says. Off the record, yes it did. Back on the record, Danny asks C.J. out for dinner. She says she can't go.

Still searching for a story, Danny takes his gossip to Hoynes. The vice president is talking to reporters about the robustness of Internet stocks. He denies anything happened at the cabinet meeting, but from the widespread story, C.J. knows there's a leak.

With her father's tickets in hand, Mallory asks Sam if he wants to join her for the Beijing Opera at the Kennedy Center. Sam asks her if it's a date, and Mallory answers a firm no. "There will be, under no circumstances, sex for you at the end of the evening."

SAM: If you hadn't come along with your offer of Chinese opera and no sex, all I'd be doing later is watching Monday Night Football, so this worked out great for me.

Lacking insight into the mind of an overprotective father, Sam tells Leo about his date to the opera. Unconvincingly, Leo says he's fine with Sam and Mallory pursuing a social relationship, someone should use the tickets.

C.J. is on a mission to find the source of the cabinet meeting leak of the Hoynes story. She goes directly to the horse's mouth, Hoynes himself. He tells her he didn't talk to Danny and if she's implying he did, she's being ignorant and insulting. No matter what she thinks of him personally, Hoynes reminds her he represents the Office of the Vice President.

Josh's concerns weren't unfounded, because the banking bill is encountering a few bumps on the way to Congress. Josh wasn't hearing things. He informs Toby that Broderick and Eaton have added a land use rider that would allow strip mining in the Big Sky Federal Reserve. The addendum comes as a total surprise, so when C.J.'s asked about it at a press conference, she's blindsided. After the briefing, Danny ventures that the question came as a complete shock. Undaunted by her glares, he asks C.J. out again. And again, she says no.

The staff has different ideas on how to respond to the rider. Bartlet is incredulous. Why are these two guys screwing up the bill? Toby explains that it's retaliation for the campaign. Bartlet asks what he did. "You won," says Toby. Sam would swallow the rider for the sake of the bill. It's a good bill, the reserve is just a bunch of rocks, and electorally there's not much to lose. But Josh has his

ego in full gear, and proposes a veto. Toby hops on board. It would demonstrate their unwillingness to be held hostage by two members of the Banking Committee who just want to be a thorn in the President's side. When Toby and Josh get geared up for this kind of thing, it's hard to move them. Bartlet is roused by their determination: "I don't like these people, Toby. I don't want to lose."

Now that Leo's let the President in on his deteriorating marriage, he has to live with his boss's unsolicited advice. Bartlet, who lives among women, explains that Mallory's annoyed because Leo ignored her mother and made her cry. Leo's not in the mood for pep talks and explanations. When Charlie tells him that tomorrow is the deputy transportation secretary's fiftieth birthday, Leo asks Sam to draft a letter of congratulations before he leaves for the opera. Meanwhile, C.J. can't get Danny to loosen his bite on the Hoynes story. Mandy suggests she trade him something—half an hour alone with the President on the record. Danny takes the offer.

When Mallory, looking fantastic, comes to get Sam for their nondate, he's slumped over his computer, still polishing the birthday letter. The President had glanced over a draft and asked him to revise it. Mallory doesn't understand what's going on. Sam's written large parts of stump speeches, Bartlet's acceptance speech, the Inaugural, the State of the Union, and now he's writing a birthday card? Sam makes her wait while he fiddles with the writing. She thinks Sam's chickening out and it makes her crazy.

As she waits for the final version of the birthday card, Mallory realizes she's been set up by her dad. She calls him an "addle-minded Machiavellian jerk." Leo confesses. He wanted to show Mallory how inflexible his job is, asking her to stop blaming him for what's happened with her mother. Bartlet joins them, and clearly he's a co-conspirator. He runs down the checklist of Leo's day: intelligence briefings, meetings with Senate Democrats about funding for the army, meetings with counsel, security briefings, and so on. A light day, he says. Bartlet tells Mallory to give her father a break.

When the President takes his leave, Mallory and Leo patch up their misunderstanding and mistaken emotions. Mallory suggests they go out for coffee and dessert and invite Sam as a gesture of peace. Leo fesses up to Sam and apologizes for plotting against him. He admits Sam's first draft was fine, but as the resident perfectionist, Sam wants to nail it. Mallory tells Sam, "You are so exactly like *him*."

Hoynes requests to see Bartlet to straighten out the awkward situation during the cabinet meeting. C.J.'s already told Bartlet she's sure the stenographer was the source of the leak, and the story's dead. Hoynes clearly has something he wants to say to Bartlet but he's almost out the door before he turns around.

John Spencer
It's a handful being the chief of staff. I'm very impressed with Leo for carrying it off as well as he does.

> **HOYNES**: Where in our past, what'd I do that makes you treat me this way?
>
> **BARTLET**: John—
>
> **HOYNES**: What'd I ever do to you but deliver the South?
>
> **BARTLET**: (pause) Really?
>
> **HOYNES**: Yeah.
>
> **BARTLET**: You shouldn't have made me beg, John. I was asking you to be the Vice President.
>
> **HOYNES**: Due respect, Mr. President, but you'd just kicked my ass in a primary. I'm fifteen years younger than you are and I've got a career to think about.
>
> **BARTLET**: *Then don't stand there and ask the* **question**, *John!* (beat) It weakened me right out of the gate. (beat) You shouldn't have made me beg.

John Wells
(Executive Producer)

An aspiration of the show is the idea that people who choose government service, or public service, are not suspect. They are, in fact, sacrificing their chance to make more money and have better career opportunities to try and make a difference. The people we've met in Washington are genuinely committed to trying to make the world a better place.

Without another word, Hoynes leaves.

The hours have brought no resolution to the banking bill. Mandy is still fighting to accept it, rider and all. She tells Josh a tie is a win, but he doesn't know how to back off his pride. Crankily, he tells Donna to hurry up with the information he wants. Donna says she's doing her best, but the files are antiquated. *Eureka!* He rushes to Toby and Sam, ranting about the Antiquities Act, which says the President can designate any federal land, like the Big Sky Federal Reserve, to be a national park. Josh goes to tell the President. Toby and Sam leave Josh to it; they're now both hooked on nailing the birthday greeting.

Josh tells the President his idea. Bartlet loves it, though he knows Big Sky National Park will just amount to a bunch of rocks.

JOSH: I'm sure that someone with your encyclopedic knowledge of the ridiculous and dorklike will be able to find a tree or a ferret that the public has a right to visit.

Abruptly, Josh changes tactics. He tells Bartlet, "We talk about enemies more than we used to." He just wanted to mention that.

THE SHORT LIST

Josh is in his office with a phone pressed to his ear, a smile playing on his lips. In the corner, C.J.'s listening in on an extension, and her expression belies the excitement for what they're about to hear. Josh gets confirmation and hangs up, ecstatic. Not even the tremendous thumping and banging coming from somewhere right above his office can divert him from his triumph. He rushes into the halls to tell everyone the news.

MRS. LANDINGHAM: Is it done?

JOSH: That depends on your answer to this question, Mrs. Landingham: Who da men?

MRS. LANDINGHAM: Excuse me, Josh?

JOSH: Um . . . who da men?

MRS. LANDINGHAM: (pause) *You* da men?

JOSH/TOBY/SAM: (in triumph) We da men!!

LEO: You got yourself a Supreme Court nominee, Mr. President.

BARTLET and LEO shake hands.

BARTLET: This is huge.

JOSH: Yes, sir.

BARTLET: Which one of you is the man?

TOBY/JOSH/SAM: I am.

As the excitement dies down, Leo lays out the plan. In four days there'll be a ceremony to parade the nominee and Toby will ensure there are no slipups or leaks. They vetted the guy for two months but Toby says they'll vet him again. Giddily, Josh walks back to his office, where the banging continues, getting even louder. Just as he announces that Peyton Cabot Harrison III of Philips Exeter and Princeton, a Rhodes Scholar, editor of the *Harvard Law Review* and dean of Harvard Law School is a lock, a chunk of Josh's office ceiling falls onto his desk.

The celebration of the Supreme Court nominee is not far-reaching. The President realizes this when he places a courtesy call to the outgoing Justice Joseph Crouch (Mason Adams). Even by the

standards of the Supreme Court, Crouch is years past retirement, and clearly believes he's earned the right to speak bluntly. Crouch assumes Bartlet has chosen Harrison, which Bartlet won't confirm or deny, but what about Mendoza? Bartlet acknowledges that Mendoza was on the short list, but Crouch calls his bluff: it was just for show. Crouch admonishes Bartlet for always leaning toward the middle of the road in his administration. Crouch pushed back retirement until a Democrat was elected to office, but got Bartlet instead. He wants the President to think about Mendoza.

The President's used to having the upper, more experienced hand in conversations, but Crouch keeps shutting him down. Bartlet says they will consider Mendoza for the next seat but Crouch says he won't get the chance, because he'll lose in three years. He reminds Crouch he has to contend with "an opposition Congress, powerful special interest groups, and a bitchy media." So did Truman, Crouch retorts. Bartlet says he's not Harry Truman. Crouch tells Bartlet he needn't point that out. Bartlet's had enough of this whipping, so he reminds Crouch it's Dr. Bartlet, and says pointedly, "Let's go start your retirement."

Sam notices on Toby's television that Congressman Peter Lillienfield is holding a press conference. It's clear he sounds off a lot and Toby's not at all interested in hearing the man preach from his soapbox. "Gone are the days of the best and the brightest," Lillienfield begins, waxing poetically. He then says the White House is staffed by Ivy League liberals and Hollywood darlings, one in three of whom smoke marijuana or snort cocaine regularly. Toby's eyes move up to the screen—he's interested now.

It's now open season on the White House, and the West Wing has to figure out how to respond to the unsubstantiated claims. Josh says Lillienfield's a featherweight, they should deny the allegations and move on. C.J. knows it's not as easy as that. If she tells the press that none of the 1,300 White House workers are drug users, and it turns out three of them find recreational drugs to be a fun habit, then she's a liar. Leo says to report that they're looking into it, and then tells his staff to look into it on the double. Mandy thinks they could end the scandal fast by drug testing the White House staff, but Josh is adamant there'll be no testing. He's indignant that Toby wants him to investigate the story at all.

TOBY: This isn't the time, Josh, we're takin' water over the side—

JOSH: I'm not in*different* to that, but there's a principle—

TOBY: No, there's not! Not this week! We've been doing this for a year and all we've got is a year older. Our job approval's at forty-eight percent and I think that number's *soft*. I'm tired of being the field captain for the gang that couldn't shoot straight! We're getting this done. (pause) What do *we* know/what do *they* know. (pause) You can start with me if you want.

Regardless of the developing crisis, the staff doesn't lose faith in good news; it had been looking like Harrison was a lock with unanimous committee approval and ninety votes in the Senate. All the same, Bartlet requests a brief on Mendoza from Toby, so he is prepared to answer any questions about Mendoza and his qualifications for a Supreme Court Justice. He wants to show that Mendoza wasn't placed on the short list for appearances.

Sam is reading Harrison's old papers when he gets a call that diverts his attention. The voice on the other end of the line yields information about Harrison and it's not good. Sam rushes to Toby with a copy of an "unsigned note," a scholarly document prepared by members of the *Law Review* and published anonymously. Sam recognizes Harrison's style, and he and Toby know they must inform Bartlet of the development.

Josh is struggling to make sense of Lillienfield's motivations. Lillienfield sits on the House Government Oversight Committee that controls the White House budget, and he would have access to all staff background checks. Brainstorming, Josh asks Donna if she knows anyone on the staff who uses drugs. She says she does. Josh asks if she wants to tell him who. Donna says she doesn't. Josh says good, she should consider herself interviewed.

> **JOSH**: I've looked at your records.
> **DONNA**: I know.
> **JOSH**: You gotta learn that no parking means no parking.
> **DONNA**: The thing is, sometimes I can't find a space.

Mandy and Josh continue to butt heads about the legality and necessity of drug tests. Mandy says not only would the gossip be extinguished, but they'd end up with a drug-free White House to show the world. Josh points out you can't force people to incriminate themselves for the sake of hushing an unflattering story. Mandy just wants him to talk to whoever it is he talks to.

One of these people is Danny Concannon. Danny tells Josh that Lillienfield is a jackass but he's not stupid; he must have a bite and now he's after someone. In a gesture of thanks, Josh gives Danny some unsolicited advice. C.J. likes goldfish.

Danny continues his barrage of C.J. Trying to keep a lid on the story, she told the press corps Lillienfield has offered no evidence and no one has been subpoenaed. Danny said she blundered by being the first to say "subpoena." Why challenge Lillienfield to produce evidence that could bring harm to the administration? Then he asks C.J. to watch the Knicks game with him.

Sam's the bearer of bad news: their princely nominee wrote a paper at Harvard that argues that privacy is not a right guaranteed by the Constitution. Toby rationally says they can't necessarily hold a fifty-five-year-old man responsible for something he wrote when he was twenty-six, but

Sam knows they won't get the chance to hold him responsible if they put him on the bench. The issue will come up, guaranteed. Bartlet tells Sam he wants to see Harrison first thing in the morning. And then he announces he wants to meet Mendoza.

Josh has figured out who Lillienfield is after. With his pride in his pocket and a great amount of courage in his heart, he goes to see Leo.

JOSH: Leo, you know the worst-kept secret in Washington is that you're a recovering alcoholic, right?

LEO: (pause) I had a hunch.

JOSH: Leo, you're a Boston Irish Catholic and back there and back then a drinking problem wasn't a problem. This isn't what he's going for. Were you into something that maybe wasn't so acceptable?

LEO: (beat) Pills.

JOSH: Were you ever in treatment?

LEO: Sierra-Tucson. Six years ago.

JOSH: Leo—

LEO: Records kept by these facilities are confidential, Josh.

JOSH: He's got 'em.

After a moment, JOSH reaches over and puts a hand on LEO's knee . . .

JOSH: You're Leo McGarry. You're not gonna be taken down by this small fraction of a man. (beat) I won't permit it.

The instant Harrison (Ken Howard) sits down in the Oval Office, Bartlet asks him if he wrote the unsigned note. Unabashedly, he says he did. The President introduces Sam and Toby. Before the meeting, Toby's still inclined to give him the benefit of the doubt. They hold a seminar. Harrison explains that for litigation purposes, the Constitution has to be interpreted strictly according to the text and it doesn't mention a right to privacy. His explanation doesn't sit well with

Sam, who believes the Framers didn't intend the Bill of Rights to limit rights. In fact, many people were against codifying a bill of rights. In 1787, a member of the Georgia delegation said:

SAM: "If we list a set of Rights, some fools in the future are going to claim that the People have only those rights enumerated and no more."

HARRISON: Were you just calling me a fool, Mr. Seaborn?

SAM: I wasn't calling you a fool, sir, the brand-new state of Georgia was.

Pompously, Harrison starts objecting to the questioning. He finds it rude and disgusting, and unable to adequately defend himself, he hops on the offensive. The White House needs him as much as he needs them, Harrison threatens. The ninety Senate votes, a seven-to-ten-point poll bump. "I was courted. And now you have me taken to school by some kid." Bartlet says he gave Sam leave to take him for a ride. Harrison leaves in a huff. Sam says they should put him on a bus but Toby wonders if it's wise to send home a guaranteed confirmation.

SAM: It's the next twenty years. Twenties and thirties it was the role of government. Fifties and sixties it was civil rights. The next two decades are gonna be privacy. I'm talking about the Internet, I'm talking about cell phones, I'm talking about health records and about who's gay and who's not. Moreover, in a country born of the will to be free, what could be more fundamental than this?

The room rings with a new sentiment: bring on Mendoza.

Danny Concannon has heeded Josh's advice and approaches C.J. armed with a goldfish in a bowl. C.J. admits he was right: every paper except Danny's leads with her saying "subpoena." She stops for a moment; why's he holding a goldfish? Danny says Josh told him she liked goldfish. C.J. breaks up laughing—she likes the *crackers*. But she'll keep the fish.

Mandy and Josh debate the merits of Mendoza and Harrison. She says Mendoza would be a great justice, but he's going to be a lousy nominee

who'll have to explain his position on same-sex marriages and free speech. She draws up a comparison to Harrison: Mendoza went to P.S. 138 in Brooklyn, CUNY, and the New York Police Academy. Yes, Josh says, then he worked in the NYPD and was an assistant DA who put himself through law school. He says, "If you don't think that's America's idea of a jurist, then you don't have enough faith in Americans." Clearly Josh would have taken Mendoza any day.

Leo gives the President a heads-up about what Lillienfield has discovered.

BARTLET: Did you have a drink yesterday?

LEO: No, sir.

BARTLET: That's all you ever need to say to me.

LEO: You know it's gonna make things very hard for a while.

BARTLET: You fought in a war, got me elected, and run the country. I think we all owe you one, don't you?

Mendoza (Edward James Olmos) is in the Oval Office, unaware of why he's been called there. Toby has one question for him. Absent details or special circumstances, what would Mendoza say of someone being fired for refusing to take a drug test on the order of the President? Mendoza says regardless of circumstance or who ordered the test, it would be an illegal search. Toby is sold. The President tells Mendoza he's going to nominate him as an associate justice of the U.S. Supreme Court. Mendoza, shocked and stunned, accepts. The nomination process will be a dogfight. Let it begin.

CHARLIE YOUNG
DULÉ HILL

It's easy to trace the network of relationships that brought the staff of *The West Wing* together. Leo McGarry is the nexus. Leo had the history with the candidate. He knew Josh Lyman through Josh's father. He'd also worked with Josh's friend Sam Seaborn on the Whitaker campaign. The career campaigner Toby Ziegler would have been known to Leo from around Washington and Toby is the guy who reeled in C. J. Cregg. The maverick Donna just latched onto Josh, but Charlie Young got his job because of the excellent instincts of a faceless personnel executive named Miss DiLaguardia.

Charlie's efficiency and intelligence were immediately apparent and not just because he intuited where the President had left his glasses during his first visit to the West Wing. Two years on, Sam finds out that Charlie will be halfway to a college degree with his high school credits. Miss DiLaguardia was just the first to notice that Charlie's got some game.

There was no time given over on the show to watch Charlie get up to speed with his job. It can be presumed that Charlie was thrown in the deep end and didn't sink. On the other hand, Dulé Hill had someone with firsthand experience of the job show him the ropes.

Dulé Hill

Early on, in my first month of being a part of the cast, Dee Dee Myers arranged for me to meet Kris Engskov. He was Bill Clinton's body man at the time. On my first trip to D.C., he came over to the hotel and we sat down to talk for a couple of hours. I was able to realize how similar Hollywood and Washington are in many ways. They are very much into themselves.

Kris took me on a journey of what he goes through each day and some situations that have happened. I realized how important the character was. Before, I always looked at him as an assistant. He is an assistant, but it's different from being an assistant to, say, the head of Warner Bros. or the head of NBC. There's a lot more at stake. You interact with powerful people. He was telling me that a lot of heads of state know him by his first name. When he said that, it really dawned on me, wherever the President is, he's there. The things he's heard, documents that may have passed through his hands. He's one of the very few people who can call the White House and say "Put me through to the President," and they will. His job is to make sure that the President—the most powerful man on Earth—does what he's supposed to do.

When Charlie started to date his boss's daughter he ran the obvious danger of mixing business and pleasure. But no matter what the outcome of Charlie's romance with Zoey, the bond with

Bartlet looks sure to remain, provided Charlie is able to negotiate the legal minefields ahead without economizing on the truth.

Aaron Sorkin

Charlie's a great character and Dulé is a very, very special young actor. First of all, he's been working in show business, I think, longer than Martin Sheen has. I was really looking forward to that character coming in, in the third episode, "A Proportional Response." I felt even luckier when we found Dulé. He can truly say more with his eyes than most actors can with a script. He also is a son to Bartlet and a friend to the rest of the group. His relationship with Bartlet did come along as a result of dating Bartlet's daughter.

Dulé Hill

I think it was a great idea by Aaron to explore it because it put interracial relations on the highest level under the public eye. And it was fuel to the fact that the President wanted to take Charlie in as a son. It culminated when the President gave Charlie the knife in "Shibboleth." He gave me a family heirloom. His father passed it on to him and now he's passing it on to me. I'm like a son he never had.

Dulé Hill

For me it was the realization of a dream. I had been trying to get on television for ten years, since I was fifteen years old. To finally make it on and with a show such as this, I couldn't ask for anything better. It was definitely worth the wait. Before I even went in and read for the show, I was able to see the pilot. I was amazed. I couldn't believe that something of this caliber was going to be on TV every week. I really wanted to be on it.

IN EXCELSIS DEO

Filled with miniature evergreen trees, poinsettias, and brilliant white lights, the White House is brimming with Christmas spirit. Famous guests are arriving in droves: José Feliciano is dropping by along with Sammy Sosa, and Al Roker has signed on to don a big red suit and be Santa.

Toby could care less about any of it. Even a call from the D.C. police isn't going to spoil his holiday mood, because he has shunned the idea of a holiday mood. He is summoned to go to the Mall to identify the body of Walter Hufnagle, who was carrying Toby's business card in his pocket when he was found near-frozen on a bench. Toby doesn't know the deceased, but he recognizes Hufnagle's

coat as one he'd recently donated to Goodwill. The body bears a tattoo of a marine battalion—the Second of the Seventh.* Hufnagle was a veteran of the Korean War, but as a homeless man, his body's not a priority to the D.C. police.

In the Christmas spirit of giving, Donna gives Josh a list of Christmas gift suggestions: "Ski pants, ski boots, a ski hat, ski goggles, ski gloves, ski poles . . . I'm assuming you already have skis?" Donna shakes her head and tells him to flip to page two of the list.

Margaret is making Leo sign Christmas cards, and he's complying with the enthusiasm of preparing to have a tooth filled. Welcoming any distractions, Leo takes a briefing from Josh. He reports that Lillienfield is waiting until after Christmas to move on the drug accusation and suggests a preempt. Moving on, Josh alludes to the rumors of Sam's evolving friendship with Laurie, and suggests he talk to her. Leo is emphatic: "No. We don't *do* these things." Leo mentions a gay high school senior in Minnesota who's in critical condition after a gang of thirteen-year-olds stripped him, tied him to a tree, and pelted him with rocks. With a sigh, Leo says they'll have to revisit hate crimes legislation. C.J. can send up a trial balloon at a briefing to gauge reaction before the administration gets in too deep.

Donna's heard through the grapevine that something's going on with Leo. She encourages Josh to help him somehow, just as Leo would do if he was in trouble. Josh doesn't need convincing—he still has preemptive strikes against Lillienfield on the brain. Meanwhile, Toby is on the phone trying to find out more information about Hufnagle. He's missing a few of the puzzle pieces—all he knows is that Hufnagle is a homeless Korean War vet who died of exposure on the Mall. In a moment of compassion, Toby's asking whether the man's family has been notified, whether any funeral arrangements have been made.

President Bartlet is in his element as he meets a group of schoolkids in the lobby. He's good-naturedly joking around with them when Charlie pulls him aside. The gay student in Minnesota,

*The Second Battalion of the Seventh Marines was activated January 1, 1941, at Guantanamo Bay in Cuba and saw extensive action in the Pacific. It was reactivated August 17, 1950, at Camp Pendleton, California, and assigned to the First Marine Division, the Fleet Marine Force. In September 1950, it was deployed to Korea, where it remained until 1953. It participated in action at Inchon, the Chosin Reservoir, and the East Central and Western Fronts. The Second of the Seventh also saw action in the war in Vietnam and Desert Storm.

Lowell Lydell, has died. Afraid of diving in too deep, Sam asks C.J. to keep her foot off the gas on hate crimes.

Abruptly, C.J. asks Sam what his Secret Service codename is. He says it's "Princeton."

c.j.: Mine's "flamingo."

sam: That's nice.

c.j.: It's not nice.

sam: A flamingo's a nice-lookin' bird.

c.j.: A flamingo's a *ridiculous*-looking bird.

sam: *You're* not ridiculous looking.

c.j.: I *know* I'm not ridiculous looking.

sam: Any way for me to get out of this conversation?

From the way he creeps into Sam's office and closes the door, it's clear Josh is scheming. Josh wants to know if Laurie would release the names of any Republicans she may have come across in a professional capacity. Sam is hesitant to drag his friend down, but when he learns that Lillienfield is threatening to expose Leo, he relents and offers to call Laurie. "We owe Leo everything," Josh pleads.

Charlie has noticed that Mrs. Landingham seemed a little depressed in the face of cheer. She explains she gets that way on the holidays because she misses her twin boys, Andrew and Simon. Candidly open about her private life beyond the White House, she tells Charlie that they did everything together. They went to medical school together and got drafted at the same time. They wouldn't defer to finish school, though she and their father begged them to. Mrs. Landingham says they went to Vietnam as paramedics and four months later they were killed at Da Nang together, Christmas Eve, 1970.

mrs. landingham: You know, they were so young, Charlie, they were your age. It's hard when it happens so far away, you know, because with the noise and the shooting, they had to be very scared. And it's hard not to think that right then they needed their mother. (pause) I miss my boys.

Kathryn Joosten (Mrs. Landingham)

I have two sons. Fortunately, they're both alive. I lived through the Vietnam War. I had brothers that were in Vietnam. I remember families who lost loved ones. As a matter of fact, my sons were both a little disturbed by the scene. They didn't like the idea of their mother talking about them being dead. They're close but they aren't twins. And so it was very easy to relate to that storyline because it couldn't be that far from the truth.

The Christmas spirit is contagious, and the President wants to do some Christmas shopping at a rare-book store. Mandy enthusiastically seconds the motion, seeing it as a good press opportunity, but the President is more concerned with having fun. He asks if Josh wants to join them, and knowing the argument is futile, he jokes, "An hour with you in a rare-book store? Couldn't you just drop me from the top of the Washington Monument instead?"

After the Secret Service seals off the tiny bookshop, Bartlet wanders around like a child in a candy store. He lovingly handles a copy of *The Fables of Phaedrus* from 1886. It's a first-edition red leather label with gilt lettering and an engraved frontis. Josh warily eyes a book titled *The Adventures of James Capen Adams, Mountaineer and Grizzly Bear Hunter of California,* and announces he'd eat it before he'd read it. Oblivious to Josh's pain, Bartlet is trying to persuade Leo to come to Manchester for Christmas to spend it with family and friends. Leo declines; with Lillienfield hanging over his head, he's going to have to think about an "exit strategy." Bartlet assures him it will be fine.

Toby can't shake the vision of Walter Hufnagle's body on a bench at the Korean War Veterans Memorial. He gets directions to a homeless shelter and finds Hufnagle's brother, George. Toby explains that his brother Walter has died, and because he received a Purple Heart in Korea for his valor, he's entitled to a proper military funeral and burial. Toby offers to arrange the service and asks George if he'll be in the same place the next morning, Christmas Day.

Danny Concannon proves to be a persistent Casanova. He's made a list of reasons C.J. should go out with him. C.J. rebukes his efforts with a catalog of why she shouldn't. He presents her with a Christmas present: food for her goldfish.

Leo reminds C.J. to dial down the rhetoric on hate crimes, but C.J. can't help thinking of Lowell Lydell and his last moments before death. "They made him say Hail Marys as they beat him to death." Although he's sympathetic to the family, Leo's not sure it's right to legislate how citizens should think. C.J. disagrees but respects her boss, and instead offers to cook for Leo at Christmas. This year, he thinks he'd rather be alone.

Laurie opens her front door, fresh from the shower, to find Josh and Sam with slightly pained expressions on their faces. Laurie says she doesn't have a lot of time. Sam circles around his point but Laurie cuts to the chase. They want to know if she'll give them the names of her Republican clients who like it "kinky." Sam tries to explain: their colleague is in trouble and they need some firepower . . . . He trails off. Laurie's ire is palpable.

Timothy Busfield
It's a relationship that's riddled with ethical conflicts. Aaron stretched that out and let that be very flirtatious and fun. What happened, which you really can't ever anticipate, is that Allison and I love playing together so much. We both jumped at that opportunity and we got along so well. We're both just so tickled whenever we see each other.

JOSH: I couldn't be any less interested in your indignation right now. A man has left himself open to the kind of attack from which men in my business do not recover. If our tactics are less than civilized, it's 'cause so are our attackers. In any event, I don't feel like standing here taking civics lessons from a hooker, Laurie!

SAM: Josh—

LAURIE: Well, I'll give you a name, hop in the shower, and you can leave the money on the nightstand, how 'bout that.

SAM: He didn't mean—

LAURIE: Yes, he did.

JOSH: (pause) No . . . I didn't . . . as a matter of fact. I'm sorry. (beat) That was . . . very rude. I'm sorry.

SAM: (beat) Laurie, we wouldn't have asked except this person means a lot to us.

LAURIE: You're the good guys. You should act like it.

The hate crimes debate rages on between Leo and C.J., but Leo has a more immediate problem: Sam and Josh. He had them tailed, and resents their degrading methods of problem solving.

JOSH: (pause) We meant well, Leo.
LEO: Is that supposed to mean something to me?
JOSH: No.
LEO: It does.

Danny hops on board the hate crimes debate and he too is on the opposite side as C.J. No murder is better or worse than another, and punishing people for their beliefs is the beginning of the end. C.J. offers him a chance to convince her of his viewpoint, perhaps over dinner. He's not sure he heard her right—is she asking him out? C.J. says, "I didn't ask *you* out, you asked *me* out about forty-nine times, and I'm saying yes to one of them." But she warns him it's just dinner, not a fling.

Josh didn't heed Donna's Christmas wish list, but he bought her an antique book on skiing. He wrote an inscription that moves her to the edge of tears. Toby is summoned before the President. He reprimands Toby for arranging an honor guard for Hufnagle in the President's name. Toby doesn't back down—he tells Bartlet it took an hour and twenty minutes for an ambulance to pick up the body. The guy got better treatment in Panmunjom.

TOBY: He went and fought in a war 'cause that's what he was asked to do. Our veterans are treated badly. And that's something history'll never forgive us for.
BARTLET: (pause) Toby, if we start pulling strings like this, don't you think every homeless veteran's gonna come out of the woodwork?
TOBY: I can only hope, sir.

Toby arrives at Arlington National Cemetery, flanked by George Hufnagle and Mrs. Landingham, who asked to join them. At the graveside, the rifle team gives the salute. Six marines fold the flag and hand it to George Hufnagle.

LORD JOHN MARBURY

The National Reconnaissance Office has confirmed naval activity on a Keyhole satellite image, and the Pentagon identifies ships headed to Pakistan. In the Situation Room, Joint Chiefs Chairman Admiral Fitzwallace reports that the Indian army has invaded Pakistani-held Kashmir. In five hours, 300,000 Indian troops have been mobilized, and the CIA failed to notice the movement.

The President reassures his staff that the UN will try to negotiate a cease-fire, but Toby recognizes the clear threat of nuclear escalation. As the President, Leo, Josh, Toby, and Sam discuss strategy and consequence, C.J. asks if she should step in. "No," says Leo; she should tell the press there's a full lid. The five men seem

slightly awkward and embarrassed. Leo waits until C.J.'s walked away and tells the others he'll brief her in the morning.

Josh announces he's been served a subpoena as coolly as he would announce he's been served a terrific steak. He knows the drill by now. When it was reported that Josh ran an internal investigation following Lillienfield's drug charge, Larry Claypool sued for Josh's paperwork under the Freedom of Information Act. He tells Sam he's due for another deposition tomorrow at lunch.

SAM: You should bring a lawyer.
JOSH: I am a lawyer.
SAM just about stifles a laugh.
SAM: No, seriously, you should bring a *real* lawyer.

Zoey comes to visit her father. Charlie is stationed at his desk outside the Oval Office. Making small talk as she waits, Zoey casually asks Charlie if he ever gets a night off, she thought it would be cool to go out. It takes a moment to sink in. "With *me*?" he asks, incredulous that the first daughter is perhaps asking him on a date. Zoey sidesteps the question, telling him he doesn't have to stand the whole time she's in the room.

Mandy confesses to Sam that she wants to take on Mike Brace as a client. He's a Republican, but Mandy says he's moderate to liberal. She wants Sam to smooth it over with Josh and Toby. She perceives that Sam is more interested in doing the right thing than merely beating the other side. Flattered, Sam admits it's a difficult sell but he'll give it a shot.

At that night's press briefing, a reporter mentions that a source at the Pentagon has confirmed massive troop movements on the Kashmir border. C.J. brushes it off, telling the reporter that he needs a new source, someone who doesn't play practical jokes.

The following morning Leo brings C.J. up to date. She's aghast at being left out of the loop, and humiliated that she ridiculed a reporter who had solid intelligence. Leo keeps his sympathy to a minimum—she's going to have to expect not to be uninformed sometimes.

Josh won't be bullied and he's arrived at his deposition alone. Claypool demands records of Josh's "investigation" into White House drug use. Without offering any paperwork, Josh explains he would hesitate to call it an investigation, it wasn't that serious. After a moment, Claypool twists Josh's words, asking him if he considers illegal drug use serious. Josh says he does, of course, he meant his investigation wasn't serious. After Lillienfield's absurd accusation, Josh took it upon himself to look into the situation, but didn't keep any records. He gives Claypool the bottom line: his lawsuit is

moronic, he should stop looking for headlines and money.

C.J. knows she has to deal with the India-Pakistan issue in the press room, but she is furious. Larry and Ed try to ease her load by giving her a pointless briefing on life expectancy and rainfall in India and Pakistan.

A deputy defense secretary gives an alarming report on India's nuclear forces, which are simultaneously powerful and unreliable. The President announces he wants to bring in Lord John Marbury, former British ambassador to India, for his expert advice on this military mess. Before Marbury's name is out of Bartlet's mouth, Leo protests that the man is certifiable. "You're really gonna let him loose in the White House where there's liquor and women?" Bartlet says they can hide the women but the man deserves a drink.

At the risk of being patronizing, Toby wants to sit C.J. down and explain to her why she was left in the dark about Kashmir. C.J.'s engaged in one of her crusades to fix her staff's spelling but Toby interrupts, explaining that the story wasn't ready for the press. C.J. doesn't buy it—she was just starting to earn respect and credibility but that's shot because now the press thinks the White House lied to her. Toby can't dance around the issue—there's concern C.J.'s too friendly with the press.

> **C.J.**: Is this about Danny Concannon?
>
> **TOBY**: People see you with Danny—
>
> **C.J.**: This is outrageous.
>
> **TOBY**: It was this one time, C.J., if we erred, it was on the side of—
>
> **C.J.**: You guys sent me in there uninformed so that I'd lie to the press.
>
> **TOBY**: We sent you in there uninformed because we thought there was a chance you couldn't.

While Toby's on a roll with employee relations, he tells Josh to take Sam along to the deposition tomorrow.

As the President is preparing for a politically precarious meeting with the Chinese ambassador, Charlie asks Bartlet how he'd feel about his going on a date with Zoey. Charlie's timing could hardly be worse. The Chinese

Dee Dee Myers

One of the fun things for me is occasionally getting to rewrite the way something happened. C.J. gets to do a little of that. It turns out, of course, that there is something brewing and that C.J. has been kept out of the loop. That happened to me over a situation in Iraq in 1993. C.J. gets to make her point, more effectively than I ever did, that this cannot happen.

Aaron Sorkin

C.J. is the highest-ranking woman in a boys' club. A lot of Dee Dee Myers goes into her. She gets the brunt of it when she was left out of the loop on India and Pakistan. One of the really nice things about her is that she takes the anger and she puts it on a shelf for later. "What do you need me to do now?" She stays in the game.

ambassador implies that his country might intervene to stop India, and Bartlet finds no ally in the Pakistani ambassador, either. Diplomacy doesn't seem to offer any solution to the crisis.

Josh has no room for sensitivity in his work life, and when he hears of Mandy courting Mike Brace, he says he's gonna kill her. Leo needs a lesson in sensitivity too—he's getting a kick out of Bartlet's discomfort about Zoey and Charlie. Bartlet says he should have put Zoey in a dungeon when she came of dating age. Leo hesitates, and asks if Bartlet has a racial problem.

BARTLET: I'm Spencer Tracy at the *end* of *Guess Who's Coming for Dinner*.
LEO: Okay.
BARTLET: Racial problem.
LEO: I'm just sayin'—
BARTLET: My problem isn't she's white, he's black. It's she's a girl, he's not.
　　　　To say nothing of he's older than she is.
LEO: She's 19, he's 21.
BARTLET: A guy learns a lot in those two years.

Josh has taken Sam with him to his deposition. Claypool makes his move. He asks if there are any alcoholics working in the White House. Josh imagines there are and Claypool asks who they are. Does Josh think the public has a right to know? Then he asks if Leo McGarry is an alcoholic. Josh won't answer. Claypool asks if Leo has received treatment for alcoholism. Or for Valium addiction. Josh won't answer and Sam says he's not obligated to. The questions are irrelevant to Claypool's cause of action, which was about Josh's investigation of illegal drug use in the White House.

Claypool asks Josh if he looked at the Secret Service file. Josh says yes. So Josh would know Leo McGarry spent twenty-eight days at an alcohol and substance abuse facility called Sierra-Tucson. Claypool has the file. Josh asks him where the hell he got it. And Claypool says he'll ask a judge if his questioning is relevant. Sam needs to get the two of them out of there, but Claypool goads them for standing up for such an "egregiously unqualified" man. Josh grabs Claypool by the lapels and shoves him against a wall. Sam pulls him off and forces him out of the room.

SAM: (to CLAYPOOL) You're a cheap hack. And if you come after Leo I'm gonna bust you like a piñata.

Lord John Marbury (Roger Rees) has arrived in the Oval Office. His help is needed, as the

Indian ambassador has just told the President that his country will be a nuclear power and won't be dictated to. In search of a light for his cigarette and another drink, Marbury says he thought Leo was the butler. They've only met ten or twelve times. This is the man of the hour? Leo won't let him light up. Later, Lord Marbury lectures his hosts on the failure of their non-proliferation initiatives and intelligence gathering. He says India and Pakistan both have the bomb and they're not afraid to use it.

Fulfilling his final duties as the office peacekeeper, Toby apologizes to C.J., in his own way, for freezing her out. Mandy approaches Sam about Mike Brace, and Sam firmly tells her it's a bad idea. Mandy's job as a political consultant isn't to end the fight, it's to win. With Lillienfield's case on the forefront, Sam says she can work for them or for us, but she can't do both.

The fight for Leo's political life has tumultuously begun and C.J., Toby, Josh, and Sam are behind him all the way. Josh tells Leo that Claypool has obtained his records from rehab, and Claypool's next step will be to call a reporter. Leo has the most important bases covered—his family and the President know. He's ready. Josh is speaking for all of them: "We're here for whatever you need and we wanted to come in and tell you that."

The President thinks of Charlie like a son and explains to his aide with sincerity that his hesitation about his going out with Zoey has nothing to do with the fact that Charlie's black; it's that he's a guy. They can go out, sure. "Just remember these two things: She's nineteen years old and the 182nd

Airborne works for *me*." He warns Charlie that a lot of people are going to be unhappy seeing him with the President's daughter, but he should keep his head up.

Just as Lord Marbury is returning to brief the President on India-Pakistan, Leo tells Bartlet the drug story will break, probably tomorrow. Bartlet says this isn't the first battle they've gone through together. Marbury interrupts to report that there'll be a two-week cease-fire brokered by the UN. They're facing a religious war whose consequences would be disastrous. Marbury offers to stay and help. He remembers a quote from Revelations that the President has been trying to recall: "And I looked, and I beheld a pale horse; and the name that sat on him was death, and Hell followed with him." They have two weeks to stop a war.

Aaron Sorkin

The thing about job titles in the White House is that they really don't mean much. In the current White House there are three women and it would be difficult to say where one person's job left off and the other began. They are all basically director of communications. Josh is the deputy chief of staff, Toby is the communications director, Sam's deputy communications director, C.J.'s press secretary. Their jobs are going to overlap. Mostly, they are senior counselors to the President. These are the people the President likes to talk to. Ed and Larry are two people these people like to talk to. The reason why you want Eds and Larrys out there is because you don't want it to seem like the only people working at the White House are the stars of our show. You want to constantly remind the audience it's a much bigger world and our camera is just focused on this right now.

HE SHALL, FROM
TIME TO TIME . . .

On the Monday night before the State of the Union, the staff is scattered around the Press Room, listening to the President rehearse his speech. As he regurgitates a slew of statistics, Josh and C.J. remark that Bartlet is pale and sweating, he doesn't look so good. The speech isn't looking so good either; the staff is still nitpicking the final details and wording. The TelePrompTer text is full of typos, and Josh argues to include "The era of big government is over." It's what the American people want to hear. Toby wonders when the administration decided to offend poor people. Bartlet can't endure any more bickering and goes into the Oval Office for a moment's rest. The sound of breaking glass pierces through the prattle in the press room and the staff rushes to find Bartlet lying facedown on the floor.

Within moments, Bartlet's propped up, and a small crowd has gathered around him. The doctor reports the President has a temperature. And while he's fairly certain it's the flu, he wants to take Bartlet to Bethesda for additional tests. Amidst the chaos, Bartlet is handed a note and without further drama or explanation, he and Leo proceed to the Situation Room. As he leaves, Leo tells Josh to convince the witnesses that they never saw this happen.

In the Situation Room, Fitzwallace reports clashes along the cease-fire line between India and Pakistan. Four days ahead of the cease-fire expiration, India is moving its forces up and Pakistan has given field commanders control of some of its nuclear weapons.

C.J. waltzes into her office to find Mandy and Danny flirting innocently on her couch. Exasperated, she asks for the privacy of her office and Danny leaves. Keenly conscious of C.J.'s wariness, Mandy merely warns her that Leo's story will break tomorrow, it's already showing up on the Internet. C.J. gives Leo the heads-up. She suggests they preempt the story with a press conference in the morning.

The first lady cancels a trip to take care of the President, although when she threatens to kill Bartlet right then and there, it doesn't seem like her heart is in the gesture. The physician quickly fills her in on the President's state and she suggests medications. Abbey's a no-holds-barred type of woman, and she tells her husband she's annoyed he went into the Situation Room before he called her. Bartlet tries to explain the urgency of the Situation Room crisis but it becomes clear Abbey has dealt with this before and is in no mood to be handled.

Josh has the depressing task of choosing someone in the line of Presidential succession to be absent from the Capitol Building during the State of the Union in case it's attacked during the speech and there's no one to run the country. Although Donna pleads a strong case for herself, he selects Roger Tribby, the secretary of agriculture. Leo feels ready to face the press about his trials with alcoholism and drug abuse. Sam has drafted a Presidential statement of support, but Leo is adamant that Sam bury it. If he goes down, he's not taking anyone with him.

The President refuses to let the flu shut him down—he is conducting business from his sickbed. Marbury keeps him up to date on West Wing business. In the Briefing Room, Leo tells the world that in June of 1993 he admitted himself to the Sierra-Tucson rehabilitation facility to treat addiction to alcohol and Valium. "I am a recovering alcoholic and drug addict," he says. "I deeply regret the pain and trouble this has caused for the people in my life."

Unbeknownst to Leo, Sam has shown his statement of support to the President. He knows

Leo will threaten to kill him, but he doesn't care. When Leo finds out that the statement is circulating, he's angry, but Sam is defiant. "I disobeyed you. I apologize. But that's the way it is."

The first lady summons Leo. She seems in good spirits, and casually asks Leo whether they might postpone the State of the Union a day or so. Leo's not fooled by Abbey's apparent vivacity: Why would they postpone the speech if the President just has a temperature?

> **LEO:** This is me. (pause) This has happened before. (beat) I see you trying to cover the panic. I see you prescribing medication, I think you're giving him shots. (pause) He wanted to run for President. What does he have he can't tell people?
>
> **ABBEY:** He has the flu, Leo.
>
> **LEO:** You didn't come back for the flu, Abbey.
>
> **ABBEY:** He fainted. He was running a fever.
>
> **LEO:** Abbey—
>
> **ABBEY:** He's got multiple sclerosis, Leo.
>
> LEO stares at her in disbelief.
>
> **LEO:** (pause) Abbey—
>
> **ABBEY:** A fever can be life-threatening.

Devika Parikh (Bonnie)
The West Wing is on my résumé. It's like having Harvard on there. I heard a casting director say "I look for actors that have *ER* on their résumé." This was before *The West Wing. The West Wing* is probably the same way. "Oh, she's worked with these award-winning directors and Aaron Sorkin and these writers and the producers and Tommy Schlamme. She's got to know what she's doing."

Stunned, Leo goes to Bartlet's bedside. The President tells Leo he was diagnosed with relapsing-remitting MS seven years ago. He recovers after attacks, and his life expectancy is normal. Abbey injects him with Betaseron, which reduces the frequency of attacks, which can be induced by fever and stress. This news is earth-shattering, and Leo's world has been shaken to its foundation. Without thinking, Leo calls him "Jed," instead of Mr. President. He asks why Bartlet didn't tell him; he could have been a friend. Bartlet says he wanted to be President, and assures Leo he *has* been a friend. He confesses his biggest concern: he wonders if putting Hoynes on the ticket was a mistake.

Toby has previously told his staff he'll be hunched over the draft of the speech the next two days, revising and reworking until he reaches perfection. He apologizes in advance if his mood "darkens a little."

> **BONNIE:** It's not like you're Red Buttons the other three hundred and sixty-three, Toby, I think we can handle it.

Toby's knee-deep in speech revisions with Democratic Party officials, who think there's too much emphasis on the role of the federal government

in the speech. One complains about the idea of increasing spending on the National Endowment for the Arts by 50 percent. Toby points out that the NEA is less than 1/100 of 1 percent of the budget: thirty-nine cents per taxpayer. "Well," the official responds, "Arthur Murray didn't need the NEA to write *Death of a Salesman*." "Indeed not," says Toby. "Arthur Murray was pretty keen on teaching ballroom dancing. Arthur Miller, on the other hand, *did* need the NEA," Toby says smugly. "Only back then it wasn't called the NEA, it was called the WPA . . ." As he hammers his point, something clicks in Toby's mind and he walks out of his meeting.

Lord Marbury gives his expert opinion on how to combat India with a handy little thing called wheeling and dealing—buy them off with the infrastructure for a computer industry. It's not the crux of morality but it's the price you pay "for being rich, free, and alive, all at the same time." The President will make the deal, but only starting in three months to avoid looking like a *quid pro quo*. Leo's the enforcer—he wants to wield the stick. He says if they don't see evidence of Indian forces withdrawing in twenty-four hours they'll seize Indian assets, deport their students, and the G-7 will call in its loans.

Toby's mysterious brainstorm brings him and Josh to the presidential sickbed. Toby is still on a rampage to axe the "era of big government" line from the State of Union address. There may have been a point in time when citizens wanted to hear the easy answer, when they were content with the expected.

TOBY: But we're here now. And tomorrow night, we do an immense thing. And we have to say what we feel. That government, no matter what its failures in the past, can be a place

where people come together and where no one gets left behind. *No one gets left behind.* (beat) An instrument of good. (beat) I have no trouble understanding why the line tested well, Josh. But I don't think that means we should *say* it. I think that means we should *change* it.

It's a vital moment, a change in policy, a total shift of emphasis. The President agrees with Toby and so does Josh. They have one day to flawlessly work a new concept into the text. This is what this administration lives for.

Twenty-four hours fly by. At a cocktail party before the main event, Josh accuses C.J. of being jealous because Mandy flirted with Danny. C.J. stubbornly denies it.

SAM: You know, C.J., it can be pretty confusing sometimes. I'm at this place with Mallory where I don't know if she likes me or she doesn't like me or she's indifferent altogether. Sometimes I wish the woman would just take the bull by the horns and get past it so you can move on.

MALLORY comes over and stands in front of SAM with a piece of paper.

MALLORY: Did you write this statement defending my father?

SAM: Yes.

MALLORY grabs SAM'S head and kisses him on the mouth. She pulls back and then does it again. Then she walks away.

SAM: Well, now I'm actually more confused.

C.J. beckons Danny to her office. She's inspired.

C.J.: I thought what I'd do is kiss you. You know, on the mouth. And that way I'd just get *past* it. (beat) I'd get *past* it and then I'd be able to give my work the kind of concentration it really deserves.

DANNY: Okay.

C.J.: How's right here?

DANNY: That's fine.

The President is mentally and physically prepared to deliver the State of the Union. Before he leaves for the Capitol, he shows Lord Marbury pictures indicating Indian forces are retreating from

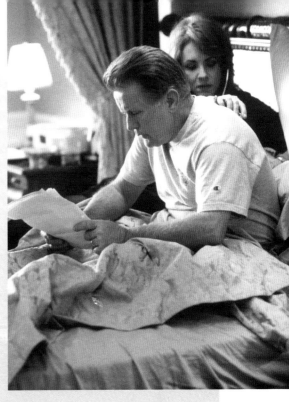

AARON SORKIN

I think the thing that probably frustrates television journalists who write about this show the most—and possibly some of the people who work on the show, as well—is when they'll ask the question, "What's going to happen next year? What's going to happen next week?" I honestly have no idea. There's no Bible for the show. I only want to decide that if I'm writing an episode in which it's going to become important. So the MS thing happened this way.

Stockard Channing had wanted to do more episodes and, of course, we wanted Stockard to do more episodes. At the very same time, I was thinking about the next episode and thinking, Where don't we get to see the President? We don't get to see him when he's sick in bed with the flu. There's a part of his character that's not quite of this world, it's of a different era.

And then I had this lunch with Stockard. I thought, What if she's a doctor? If she's a doctor, I want there to be a story. I want there to be a reason to make that decision. So, it's not the flu. It's something worse than the flu, but it looks like the flu to everybody else and Abbey has had to come back.

And all of the sudden, simply for the sake of that episode, I made a decision that was going to affect the series for the life of the series. I did it and there was no turning back once I did it. I said, "Okay, now this is part of the universe of our story and we're going to be telling stories about this." That's frequently how decisions are made.

Pakistani borders. Marbury's work is done. With genuine regard, Marbury wishes Leo good luck.

Bartlet settles Roger Tribby in the Oval Office. As a gesture of luck, Tribby presents the President with a copy of the Constitution in Latin. The President recites the appropriate part of Article II, Section 3 of the Constitution, "He shall from time to time give to the Congress information of the state of the Union, and recommend to their consideration such measures as he shall judge necessary and expedient . . ." Knowing he's speaking with his would-be successor, Bartlet asks Tribby if he knows what to do if anything happened. He quickly runs through the emergency acts, and then:

BARTLET: You got a best friend?

TRIBBY: Yes, sir.

BARTLET: Is he smarter than you?

TRIBBY: Yes, sir.

BARTLET: Would you trust him with your life?

TRIBBY: Yes, sir.

BARTLET: That's your chief of staff.

Leo has overheard his old friend say that. Together they leave to give the State of the Union.

TAKE OUT
THE TRASH DAY

C.J. is briefing the press about a Rose Garden ceremony where the President is going to sign hate crimes legislation into law. Always a fountain of quirky information, C.J. mentions that he will use fifteen pens. Danny points out that Bartlet's name has only thirteen letters, and wonder how he's going to use fifteen pens. C.J.'s saved by her briefing notes—he will literally dot the *i* and cross the *t*'s. C.J. continues that Jonathan and Jennifer Lydell, parents of Lowell Lydell, whose death sparked the debate on hate crimes, are attending the signing and will be available to answer questions. Gossip flies through the press corps, however, that the Lydells are not big Bartlet fans.

After the briefing, Mandy offers her expert PR advice and admonishes C.J. for guaranteeing the Lydells for the bill signing. Mandy's not sure she wants anti-Bartlet propaganda flying around the Rose Garden. Josh asks C.J. to read a report on sex education in public schools. It says that standard "abstinence only" theories aren't proving effective in today's schools, and recommends a new curriculum entitled "Abstinence Plus," or what Sam calls "everything but." Congress has offered to fund the 100,000 teachers the White House wants on the condition that sex education classes continue to teach abstinence only. For C.J., it's just something else that'll keep her in the office past midnight.

Danny wanders in to see C.J. He insists they go out on a date—she can't just keep grabbing him and kissing him in her moments of passion. Danny actually has come with a purpose: he's hearing about an advance man for Hoynes who took a navy helicopter to Pebble Beach to play a round of golf. He won't reveal a source but C.J. grabs him and kisses him anyway.

Donna's caught wind of some political jargon, and she's at a loss for what "Take Out the Trash Day" could possibly be. Josh explains that the administration gives all the bad stories they want to bury to the press at once on a Friday. Strategically, if a paper chooses to report all of them, each story will get less attention than if they were announced separately. And the conventional wisdom is that fewer people read papers on Saturday.

As with any other day in the White House, events of varying degrees of seriousness crop up

Two scenes fleshed out this story in another version of the script. In the first, Bartlet demands that Zoey drop the class. He can't have the first daughter taking notes in a class where the professor said Head Start was overfunded. The press will make the implication he's saying there's no point trying to educate black children. Zoey argues that the professor's not a racist.

BARTLET: It's a gut course, you don't need it, I've got problems with the Black Caucus already, drop the class.
ZOEY: It's three credits, I've gotta make that up somehow.
BARTLET: Take Latin.

Charlie is equally upset with Zoey for not walking out of the class in protest. Charlie says he was a Head Start student but Zoey says he's a bad example because he has an IQ of 823. Does she have to disown everyone she disagrees with? Charlie apologizes for getting mad.

and demand attention. Sam reports there's a story in the *Georgetown Hoya* about a sociology professor espousing what sound like racist viewpoints in school. It's their problem because Zoey's in the class.

A group of assistants are having a quiet huddle, but Mrs. Landingham reminds them that they are federal employees and this is no place for gossip. Donna tracks down Sam and Josh, because she has no intention of extinguishing this gossip: the assistants know who leaked the story about Chad Magrudian, the vice president's advance man: a woman named Karen Larsen, who was rumored to have a slight crush on Hoynes.

When it doesn't seem like the events of the day can sink much lower, Bartlet learns he's in trouble with the banana lobby. The Europeans favor bananas from their former Latin American colonies, and U.S. companies lose out. Switching gears, Bartlet asks Toby to concentrate on freeing up five appointments to the Corporation for Public Broadcasting that the House is sitting on. After a moment, the President admits he doesn't think it has anything to do with the bananas.

Kathryn Joosten

There was a scene where the secretaries were all standing around gossiping and I stopped in and said, "What are you girls doing?" Then one of my lines was "We work for very important men here." And I said, "Time out! There are women in this place. So I would like to change that line to, 'We work for important people.' " It went up the chain, and it came back down, "Okay."

TOBY: I was raised on *Sesame Street*, I was raised on Julia Child, I was raised on *Brideshead Revisited*. Their legacies are safe in my hands.

C.J.'s unsuccessfully stifling a laugh.

TOBY: (to C.J.) You got a problem?

C.J.: You watched cooking shows?

TOBY: I watched Miss Julia Child.

Much to his disappointment, C.J. tells Danny there won't be any more kissing. Distracted by other issues swirling around the West Wing, C.J. asks Danny if it's possible a father could be embarrassed that his son was gay even after the son was murdered. C.J. can't conceive of the Lydells' reluctance to support a bill which would impose stricter penalties on the perpetrators of hate crimes. Exhausted, C.J. promises they'll have information on Hoynes's advance man on Friday. It's going out with the trash.

Josh and Sam arrange to meet Congressman Bruno from an Appropriations subcommittee, who demands to know why Josh withheld information gathered during the drug "investigation." He threatens to hold hearings about the possible White House cover-up of Leo McGarry's drug and alcohol problems. Bartlet warned Josh and Sam to avoid a hearing at all costs, and Bruno seems like a reasonable guy, right up to the point when he asks, in a casually non-confrontational way, "What happened?"

At the same time, Washington elder statesman Simon Blye (Dakin Matthews) has come to see Leo about the imminent crisis of Leo's drug charges. Leo assures Bartlet that Blye is an old friend but the President doesn't trust him. Blye gives Leo the bottom line: there's no chance of Josh and Sam avoiding a hearing. Furthermore, the administration needs to consider that the President has a budget to pass, he has to get Mendoza confirmed and a Democratic Congress elected in nine months. Leo asks if he's come to ask him to resign, because he's already offered and the President turned him down. Blye sneers that Bartlet is blinded by friendship and is putting his own Presidency at risk. Leo realizes Blye is making his own capital out of Leo. He has an op-ed published in the morning's *Post* and he'll be doing the rounds of morning talk shows on Sunday. Bartlet was right, and Leo throws Blye out.

Blye was mistaken about the unavoidability of the hearings, because Bruno is armed with a deal for the White House. If they put the sex education report in a drawer until after the midterm

elections, he'll guarantee that there will be no hearings. Bruno admits no one wants to debate the report; no one wants to be the one to oppose or support a sex education bill. Sam doesn't think the President will go for it and Josh jumps to Leo's defense, claiming their administration has nothing to hide. Bruno has to spell it out: no one wants a hearing on drug use in the White House. He's throwing them a rope.

> **BRUNO**: This is what happens when you put teenagers in the White House. You guys screwed this up from the beginning. You shoulda been there *first* on McGarry, you shoulda had the White House Counsel's Office run the internal investigation, you came remarkably close to perjury in the Claypool deposition. . . . I'd like to hold hearings into the two of you being *stupid*. (beat) But I don't have that kinda time. There's the phone. I'm sure the President's waiting for your call.

When C.J. and Mandy meet with the Lydells, they find they've been reading it all wrong. Mr. Lydell (Ray Baker) is not embarrassed by his son's sexuality, he's furious about Bartlet's politics.

> **MR. LYDELL**: I don't understand how this President, who I voted for, I don't understand how he can take such a completely weak-ass position on gay rights. . . . Gays in the military, same sex marriages, gay adoption, where the hell is he?! (beat) I want to know what quality necessary to being a parent the President feels my son lacked. I want to know from this President—who has not served one day in uniform, I had two tours in Vietnam—I want to know what quality necessary to being a soldier this President feels my son lacked. Lady, I'm not embarrassed that my son was gay, my government is. (beat) I want my vote back.

Although C.J.'s first instinct is to let the Lydells speak their minds about complaints which are quite reasonable and poignant, Mandy insists they'll have to go home.

Sam, smoldering with rage, unabashedly reproaches Karen Larsen (Liza Weil). He tells her he doesn't care about her giving up the advance man. But he thinks it was Karen who released Leo's personnel file to Lillienfield and Claypool. She starts to say Mr. Claypool's a family friend but Sam cuts her off. She has fifteen minutes to clear out of her office.

As Bartlet asked, Toby is defending PBS before a group of congressional aides. They say it's TV for rich people. With some personal integrity at stake, Toby argues that PBS viewership is reflective of the nation. He doesn't care about their complaints; they will, by God, protect Julia Child.

The President informs C.J. they're sitting on the sex education report until further notice. C.J. believes it contains timely and consequential information about safe sex for teenagers, but they've made the deal and she understands. When C.J. asks what to tell the press, Bartlet says tell them only that we're looking at it—throw it out with the trash.

The press briefing room awaits, but C.J. can't shake the image of the Lydells. She wants to confide her inner chaos to Danny, but he stops her before she can leak him a story. In twenty minutes' time she'll remember she's the press secretary and she won't like Danny, the reporter, anymore. He's not too concerned—if there's a story, he'll find it. C.J.'s not too sure—they've gotten very good at burying the trash.

Leo stops Karen Larsen on her way out of the White House for the final time. Leo asks what went through her mind when she flipped through his file. Evading the question, she admits her father drank a lot. Leo says his did too. One night his father came home drunk and he and Leo's mother argued. Leo's father went to the garage and shot himself.

KAREN: Is that why you drank and took drugs?

LEO: I drank and took drugs 'cause I'm a drug addict and an alcoholic.

KAREN: (pause) How long did it take you to get cured?

LEO: I'm not cured. You don't get cured. I haven't had a drink or a pill in six and a half years. Which isn't to say I won't have one tomorrow.

KAREN: (pause) What would happen if you did?

LEO: I don't know. But probably a nightmare the likes of which *both* our fathers experienced. And me too.

Clearly, Karen believed when she handed over the file that she was saving the White House from utter destruction at the hands of an alcoholic. But, Leo's not like she thought, not like her father, perhaps. The wheels in her mind are turning. She murmurs that Leo has such an important job. Important decisions. People's lives. Leo says he's not sure what she did "wasn't a little bit brave" and offers her a second chance at her job.

At her briefing, C.J. says there are just a couple of quick things she needs to go over. In rapid succession, she reports that Chad Magrudian has resigned. The President's appointees to the Corporation for Public Broadcasting will be confirmed, and the Lydells have family business in St. Paul to attend to that will keep them away from the signing of the hate crimes bill. She's taking out the trash.

TAKE THIS
SABBATH DAY

On a Friday night, a Supreme Court justice is perfunctorily reciting a verdict in a fairly empty gallery to three dejected lawyers. The application for a stay of execution has been denied. The petitioner will be executed at the federal facility in Terre Haute, Indiana, on Monday morning at 12:01 A.M. The lawyers, exhausted and numbed, want to call the White House for support, but it's a federal case, so the President is the last resort. Bobby Zane (Noah Emmerich), one of the lawyers, speaks up: he knew Sam Seaborn in high school. He'll call him.

As the sun sets over the White House, Sam is packing up for a weekend getaway of yacht racing. To his delight, Ginger has packed his bright yellow foul-weather gear. Unwilling to be outdone, Josh announces he's going to a bachelor party. Donna clucks her tongue—she's worried that Josh will drink too much and he'll harass the strippers.

JOSH: There aren't gonna be strippers. Men don't like that anymore.

DONNA: Men don't like naked women anymore?

JOSH: No, we still like naked women a lot, it's just looking at them with a room full of your best friends that makes you feel a little—

DONNA: Sleazy?

JOSH: —uncomfortable.

Before Sam can free himself of the West Wing he has to persuade Josh to take a meeting the next morning with the campaign manager of a candidate named O'Dwyer, a guy called Joey Lucas. They've never heard of him. After much haranguing, Josh agrees to see Lucas. Sam procrastinates just long enough to be there when the phone rings. He clearly doesn't want to answer it and defiantly takes a step out of the office. Then a step back in. He stands there, then heads out the door. The phone's still ringing when Sam walks back in, drops his bag, and picks up the receiver.

There are no pleasantries exchanged between the high school acquaintances. Zane tells Sam his client killed two drug kingpins, and he won't let the President run from this one. The President has the authority to grant a pardon, but Sam explains that Bartlet is a firm believer in the separation of powers and the judicial branch has spoken. Regardless of any moral concerns, Bartlet's on a plane coming back from Europe and is not due back until seven in the morning. Zane is insistent, a man's life is at stake, and Sam promises he'll talk to Toby when he returns from temple.

Sam eyes his yellow rain gear with longing and goes in search of Leo with a sigh. Leo tells him the administration has been following the case of Simon Cruz, although they thought it would be sent back to the Sixth Circuit. The President's not going to want this ball in his court. Having unloaded the case from his shoulders, Sam tells Leo he's going sailing for the weekend. Leo's hooked now—he's curious why they're waiting until Monday to execute Cruz. Sam explains to him that people are not executed between sundown on Friday and sundown on Sunday. Not on the Sabbath. Sam returns to his office to pick up his gear. Again, he walks out, and is drawn back. He flicks on a light, throws his sail bag in a corner, and grabs a law book.

The following morning, fresh from his visit to Scandinavia, Bartlet is torturing C.J. with his encyclopedic knowledge of the natural world, fjords in particular. C.J. says she'd like to drop-kick the President into a fjord.

Donna comes to work to find Josh asleep in his office, his head resting on his balled-up suit jacket. The party died down a couple of hours ago, and Josh didn't go home because he couldn't find

his keys or remember where he lived. He moans that there might have been strippers before closing his eyes again. He's a real mess. Donna reminds him he has a meeting, and he swears he knows that—but what's it about again? Donna gives him a cup of old coffee and Sam's foul-weather gear to wear while she gets his suit cleaned.

At temple, Toby is listening to a sermon about violence. "Vengeance is not Jewish," says Rabbi Glassman (David Proval). Embarrassingly, Toby's beeper goes off, and he's acutely conscious of the loud clacking of his shoes as he scouts for a quiet place to answer his page. He testily calls Sam, clearly aggravated at the interruption of his religious service. Undaunted, Sam asks if his rabbi is giving a sermon on capital punishment. Toby knows something is wrong, and Sam tells him the appeal was denied. Toby says he'll be right in. To complete his performance, Toby knocks over a stack of folding metal chairs as he goes back to his seat to retrieve his coat.

Josh, horribly hung over and wearing Sam's garish yellow sailing gear, is fast asleep in his office again. The door is flung open, crashing into the wall. Josh sits up with a start and is confronted with a young woman signing with her hands and a man rapidly translating for her. "Are you the unmitigated jackass who's got the DNC choking off funding for O'Dwyer's campaign in the California Forty-sixth?" Josh doesn't know what's hit him. The woman signs; the man announces, "I'm Joey Lucas." Josh says to the translator Kenny (Bill O'Brien), "You're Joey Lucas?" "*I'm* Joey Lucas," says the woman tena-

Richard Schiff
When we did the death penalty, I was surprised that, at the beginning, Toby really didn't have a strong opinion. I lobbied—to use that word pointedly—I lobbied Aaron Sorkin to have Toby be staunchly in favor of the death penalty because it's an oddity, something that's very personal. You never know how people are going to feel about the most important things. I think that would be a subject that Toby would be fiercely on one side or the other.

ciously. Josh, dumbfounded, says he was expecting a man. As he stumbles out of his office to change into his suit, Josh tells Donna that Joey Lucas (Marlee Matlin) clearly isn't a guy—she's a woman and she's deaf.

Toby charges into the West Wing demanding to know how his rabbi penned up such a timely sermon. Sam thinks Bobby Zane got to him. Toby has two main concerns at this juncture: why did Sam tell a lawyer where he goes to temple and what the hell is Josh wearing? The three men discuss the politics of the death penalty. Sam, newly knowledgeable on the ins and outs of execution, says the last federal execution was 1963. More important, Josh intervenes, the last President to commute a death sentence was Abraham Lincoln. Sam is ready to provide Bartlet legal cover if he wants to commute the sentence. Toby knows Bartlet won't do it.

His European trip just a lazy memory, Bartlet gets his first briefing on the case from Leo. Leo says it's a federal case, because the U.S. Attorney tried Cruz under legislation allowing for the death penalty in drug-related crimes. The ball is firmly in his court, but Bartlet admits he's not going to be any good at this, he's going to need help. He asks Charlie to find Father Thomas Cavanaugh, a priest from Hanover, and bring him to the White House. After a moment of silence, Bartlet speaks his mind. He asks Charlie if they caught the guy who killed his mother, would Charlie want to see him executed?

> **CHARLIE:** I wouldn't want to see him executed, Mr. President. I'd want to do it myself.

It's not the time for games, and Josh tells Joey Lucas that they're cutting her candidate's funding because there's a chance he might win. The incumbent is an entrenched reactionary who is useful right where he is, sounding off on immigration and gun control and providing material for Democratic fund-raisers. Joey's not satisfied with blunt honesty, and says she won't leave unless she sees the President. Just as Josh is explaining there's no chance of that, Bartlet appears at the door. He's been wandering the halls, thinking, and offers Joey a tour of the White House.

Joey tells the President she's of Dutch ancestry,

Quaker, and she attended UCLA and Stanford. Bartlet's beyond small talk, and picks her brain about the impending execution. Joey says he should stay the execution. "The state shouldn't kill people." Bartlet asks if she studied St. Augustine and Thomas Aquinas at Stanford, because they were two pretty smart guys, and believed the Bible allowed a life for a life. Joey adds that Kant said that capital punishment is a categorical imperative, but these writings are from another century.

> **BARTLET**: I've got a Harris poll says seventy-one percent of the people in this country support capital punishment.
>
> **JOEY**: That's a political problem.
>
> **BARTLET**: I'm a politician.

Bartlet is ready for this impromptu meeting to draw to a close, but Joey takes a chance and brings up O'Dwyer. Bartlet says he's an empty shirt. "Get yourself a live one and I'll get interested." Clearly, her White House excursion is over, and as she leaves, she signs a couple of things to Josh that her translator doesn't need to spell out.

Sunday dawns with a cold sun, and Toby returns to his temple where a female cantor is practicing a haunting funeral song. Toby's rabbi explains that his sermon was a catalyst in getting Toby to ponder his feelings on the death penalty. Toby is not looking for a debate, but points out the Torah preaches an eye for an eye. Yes, but it also says that homosexuality is punishable by death and that polygamy and slavery are acceptable. "Ancient teachings can be just plain wrong by any modern standard," he says. Toby thinks the rabbi laid on the cantor just for his benefit. He did. "She's *our* communications director."

C.J. has the unfortunate job of alerting the President when Cruz is dead. She maintains she has no position on capital punishment and doesn't care about the life or death of Cruz. But she's haunt-ed by the visuals of death by lethal injection—the twitching, the straining against the restraints, the head snapping back, the convulsions. She can deal with the death of a murderer, but is unnerved that she knows Cruz's mother's first name.

Toby can't offer much advice or solace to Bartlet, but volunteers that regardless of the Torah, rabbis always made sure there were so many legal restrictions, it was impossible for the state to kill someone. Bartlet wishes he could simplify the issue that easily, but if he pardons Cruz just because he doesn't like the death penalty, the next president will have "Eighth Amendment problems up the ass." It would be cruel and unusual to execute some people and not others depending on the mood of the Oval Office. Leo says if that's the only thing stopping him from saving this man's life, he should guiltlessly give the next guy the problem. But the President has made his mind up.

Sam is patiently waiting to put forth his case. Leo tells him Bartlet's done. Sam is not ready to admit defeat and argues that they can sell com-muting the sentence. Leo wants him to let it go—the case was bungled and the White House was severely unprepared. The tension in the room slowly

John Wells
For me, personally, the death penal-ty episode was something that I care very much about and I thought it was deeply affecting. A beautiful piece of filmmaking, wonderfully directed and acted and written.

diffuses until only disappointment is left. "There are times when we are absolutely nowhere," he laments.

Josh slinks to see Joey at her hotel before she returns to California. She wonders if he's come to ask her on a date, but Josh explains that the President wanted him to apologize for his abruptness. While political strategy was definitely at play, Bartlet really does think O'Dwyer's a schmuck. Joey admits she does, too, but she needs the work. Josh continues that Bartlet meant it when he said he'd be interested if she found a live one. Joey asks if he has any suggestions. "Yes," Josh says, "you."

As the sun sets on Cruz's last night of life, Father Cavanaugh (Karl Malden) arrives at the White House. A bit intimidated by his surroundings and the issue at hand, Cavanaugh tells Bartlet he doesn't know whether to call him Jed or Mr. President. Not unfeelingly, Bartlet would prefer the latter: there are times when it's better to think of the office, not the man. Bartlet says he had his staff look for reasons to save Cruz. A technicality, evidence of racism in the court proceedings. Father Cavanaugh compares Bartlet to the kid in right field who doesn't want the ball hit to him. He's just looking for a way out. Bartlet reminds the priest that he is the leader of a democracy and 71 percent of the people support the death penalty.

"Vengeance is mine, saith the Lord," Cavanaugh quotes as he explains that God is the only one who gets to kill people. Cavanaugh mentions that he spoke to some of Bartlet's staff; Toby told him about the rabbi, Josh about the young woman who's a Quaker. Bartlet says he prayed for wis-

dom and none ever came. Cavanaugh tells him a parable about a man in the middle of a flood who turns down various offers of help, choosing to rely on God to save him. He drowns, not realizing God was behind the offers of assistance the whole time.

> **CAVANAUGH:** He sent you a priest, a rabbi, and a Quaker, Mr. President, not to mention his son Jesus Christ. What do you want from him?

C.J. brings Bartlet the dreaded note. Cruz is dead. Now Father Cavanaugh is a priest and the President a sinner like any other man. Cavanaugh calls him Jed, and asks if he wants him to hear his confession now. Bartlet nods yes.

C.J. CREGG
ALLISON JANNEY

C.J. Cregg's introduction on *The West Wing* is inauspicious to say the least. Making the most of her precious free time at the gym, C.J. was trying to talk to an attractive man when she fell off the back of the treadmill after her beeper went off.

Allison Janney

Aaron says the first time that he thought of me for this series was when he saw *Primary Colors* and I had to do that fall down the stairs. That's the first time I came onto his radar.

From there, the only way was up. But it took a while for C.J. to establish herself. C.J. could sympathize with Ainsley Hayes's predicament on coming to the White House. She told Toby it took two years for her to be treated with proper respect. In a place where there may only be fifty women working, as C.J. herself says at one point, the thousand guys there may take one look at you and think you're either dumb or ambitious or both.

Aaron Sorkin takes responsibility for this initially underrealized C.J.

Aaron Sorkin

C.J. was the most underwritten role in the pilot. It took me a few episodes to get traction on the character. It was frustrating because Allison was so obviously stunning in this. You feel a little like Joe Torre does with the Yankees. You have all these players. You pick nine to put on the field, who do you put on the bench? It was that way with Allison. Every director who comes here just lights up when they get to her scenes. They will do twenty takes even though she nailed it on the first, just because they want to see what she's going to do with the other nineteen.

This sentiment is shared by all. Aaron Sorkin himself counts among his personal favorite moments "any scene with C.J."

Rob Lowe

Allison Janney is the best actress I've ever worked with. With all respect to Jodie Foster and Maggie Smith, who are also my favorites. Allison Janney is one for the ages. There is absolutely no fuss about her. She just tees the ball up and hits it out of the park every single time.

ALLISON JANNEY

I was filming *American Beauty* and *Nurse Betty* at the same time. And also doing a film for a friend of mine on the weekends. So I was a little crazy. I wasn't really looking to do a television series at all. I got the script from my agent and read it and I just responded to the snappy writing. I loved the quick banter. I thought, God, if I were to do television, this would be the type of television I would do. And when I found out who was involved, it was such a high pedigree of people. I thought it would be pretty exciting to do something like that. I went in and auditioned. I read a press conference. And I walked out thinking, Well, I bombed that one. I was terrible. I thought, I've got my movies. I'm fine. And then a week later they called me back in and I couldn't believe it.

I was a little daunted by it because I'm not a political person. I vote, but I've never enjoyed talking about politics. I grew up during Watergate and I think it was a very disillusioning time. It was just nothing that I was really interested in. But I've played a lot of parts that I knew nothing about and it doesn't matter. If the person needs to be in control and in charge, I can do that. Just my physical size does that for me. I did read some books. The best was Howard Kurtz's *Spin Cycle*. But I find that research doesn't really help me in my acting at all. It's just interesting to know.

Brad Whitford

Allison Janney is an obscenely talented human being who didn't have a lot of commercial success early on. She acted her brains out onstage for a decade. If you're any good and then you go and do that, you get really, really good.

Martin Sheen

And then, of course, Allison. Look how long she has been around. She talked at the SAG Awards about how she wanted to give it up any number of times for the last twenty years but she stayed at it. She's seamless. We use that term to describe someone whose work is undetectable, the reality of who they are and what they're projecting. You're just in awe of her. She may be the biggest talent in the cast. I mean, really. She may be the biggest talent.

Lyn Elizabeth Paolo

Allison Janney, I mean, what's not to love? She's six feet tall and she's gorgeous. You just put something on her and it drapes beautifully.

As the second season progressed, C.J. became a much stronger presence. By the end, she doesn't just deliver the news to the press, she's confidently shaping it herself. C.J. had to convince her colleagues, especially Leo McGarry, that she wasn't too cozy with the press. When an F-117 went down in the no-fly zone ("What Kind of Day Has It Been"), C.J. lied to them with

consummate professionalism. She wouldn't have to be kept out of the loop as she had over the Kashmir crisis ("Lord John Marbury").

C.J. made a point of picking Danny Concannon to deliver the lie to. The chief of staff's resistance to the idea of his press secretary dating a journalist ensured that Danny never got C.J. to move their relationship past a couple of embraces in the office. In a scene from "The Short List" that didn't make it to broadcast, Leo is explicit about it. He and C.J. are in the President's limo on the way back from the Supreme Court, where Bartlet has met with Justice Crouch. "I don't want you dating Danny Concannon," says Leo. "I see him with you and I know you've got a little thing." C.J. protests that she doesn't, and she won't talk about this with the President in the car. C.J. was always wary, but this confirms her resolute strength: if it's a choice between her job and Danny, there is no choice.

Aaron Sorkin

Unlike a lot of young female characters in films and television today, C.J.'s life isn't about "When is Mr. Right going to come along and save me from this?" She is constructing her world for herself. I'm sure she would love to meet Mr. Right and run off into the sunset with him, but she's not waiting for him to come galloping along. In the last scene she had with Danny, he says, "Look, this isn't a problem for me." And she says, "It's a problem for me." She's doing just fine.

CELESTIAL NAVIGATION

All of the seats are filled with eager students at the third installment of the Majorie DuPont lecture series, waiting to hear gems of wisdom from Josh Lyman's experience in the White House. Backstage, he's on his cell phone, seemingly oblivious to the crowd of fans and admirers in the auditorium. Sam's telling him that within the last half hour, Roberto Mendoza was arrested for drunk driving, resisting arrest, and disorderly conduct. The odd thing is, they know Mendoza doesn't drink.

Leo calls an emergency meeting. Toby is apoplectic, this is a disaster—he has everything riding on getting Mendoza confirmed to the Supreme Court, and now he's being held in jail in Wesley, Connecticut, refusing to take a Breathalyzer. Leo wants

Sam to go to Connecticut. Toby says he's going too. A few miles away, Josh takes the podium to tell the students what it's like to work for the President and how things got out of hand that week.

The White House was enthusiastically gearing up for a Mural Room ceremony to sign a radical new bill on education reform. But, as they do when the air seems too clear, circumstances started to conspire. C.J. had a dental appointment, and intuitively knew that local anesthesia and the White House press corps don't go hand in hand. And HUD Secretary Deborah O'Leary (C.C.H. Pounder) had a fiery and very public argument with Republican Jack Wooden about public housing on C-SPAN. "Are you calling me a racist?" he accused, to which O'Leary replied, "If the shoe fits."

Josh leads the students through Presidential story hour. After the President signed the $700 million education bill with a flourish, he mistakenly offered to take questions. The first was about Secretary O'Leary. Unfortunately, C.J. wasn't there to prevent the first PR disaster of the day, when Bartlet announced that O'Leary went too far and an apology would be appropriate. Josh's tale is interrupted by a call from Sam, who complains that he and Toby are lost on the New England Thruway. It doesn't help that Sam's trying to steer by the stars. Josh reminds them that he's sort of in the middle of something.

Guiding the students back to his story, Josh explains that O'Leary got mad at the President for insinuating she should apologize. She believed her role as the highest-ranking African American in government is to police people like Wooden. Leo set her straight; her role is to serve the President. She has to apologize.

Dee Dee Myers

I'll write a memo that says, "Here's what happened; here's what could happen." Then there's a lot of back and forth. I think "Celestial Navigation" came out of my notion that everybody thinks they can do a briefing better than the press secretary. You choose an idea like that, it just kind of grows.

O'LEARY: Oh, for cryin' out loud, Leo, when are you guys gonna stop running for President?

LEO: When angels dance on pinheads, Debbie.

Josh tells his audience that with O'Leary's apology secured, C.J. had planned to redirect media attention to the education package. But C.J.'s routine visit to the dentist turned into emergency root canal. Or "woot canow" as she put it, with her cheeks stuffed with cotton and gauze. Against C.J.'s muddled objections, Josh decided to take the "bwiefing" himself, which was asking for trouble. Josh was confident, not to say cocky. Even against the guidance of his peers, Josh preened that as a graduate of Harvard and Yale, his powers of debate could meet the Socratic wonder of the White House Press Corps.

Josh's inaugural debut to briefing was a consummate disaster. When a reporter breached the topic of the frequency of Bartlet's cigarette smoking. Josh asked the reporter if he wanted his one question to be "that stupid." C.J. watching the disaster unfold on television, cringed. The reporter retorted it's not a stupid question if the President's going to preach from an anti-tobacco pulpit. Josh said Bartlet quit years ago, but another reporter interrupted, offering that Bartlet just bummed a cigarette from her on Air Force One. Josh changed topics and asked for the next question. Danny, wanting to show Josh just how deep he's waded, asked if the President was worried that lower unemployment would drive up wages and cause inflation. Josh said the President is pleased the jobless rate fell.

DANNY: And I'm sure we all join the President in his joy. But I'm wondering, does the President have a plan to fight the resulting inflation?

JOSH: The President is doing everything in his power to maintain the robust economy that's created millions of new jobs, improved productivity, *and* kept a lid on inflation.

REPORTER #5 (KATIE): But he has no plan to address inflation specifically.

JOSH: Twenty-four Ph.D.s on the Council of Economic Advisors, Katie, they have a plan to fight inflation.

DANNY: Is the reason you won't tell us about it is that it's a secret?

JOSH: Yeah, Danny, we got a secret plan to fight inflation.

Out of Josh's egotistical need to prove himself, the President's secret plan to fight inflation was born. He knows it'll take a while to live down. When he calls Toby and Sam on a break in his lecture, Sam admits they are still lost. Toby thinks the star Sam was guiding by was the Delta Shuttle out of

La Guardia. He moans that he may spend the rest of his life in this car, searching for Connecticut.

After many miles and much stargazing, Toby and Sam find the sterile and unintimidating suburban police station of Wesley. The cops don't believe Toby and Sam are from the White House until one sees a picture of Toby on the front page of a newspaper. As he glances back and forth from the paper to the unamused face in front of him, the blood drains from the cop's face. Sam informs them they arrested a federal judge, the President's nominee for the Supreme Court. The cops are way out of their league.

Josh has to be honest with the students; he dug himself a pretty deep hole with his flippant and ill-considered answers.

> **JOSH**: Tell me what you think I should do right *now*.
> **DONNA**: Go into your office and come up with a secret plan to fight inflation.

He tried to play it off, vowing that he was kidding about the secret plan. With smug satisfaction and muted frustration at the mess he'd made, C.J. told him he "compwetwey impwoded," he was "hostiwe . . . bewidgawint." Toby cut to the chase, asking him if he'd fallen on his head. Josh chuckled nervously, it's not as bad as it looks, but C.J. is adamant: "A seaquit pwan to fwite infrathon??!"

For Toby, the only way that day could get any worse was if something happened with Mendoza. As Josh explains to his captive audience, in the middle of the hazardous confirmation process, Mendoza had decided to break his silence from his vacation in Nova Scotia, commenting that Bartlet was wrong to make O'Leary apologize. To the chagrin of the staff, Mendoza had also recently criticized the American Bar Association, the AFL-CIO, and the New York State Legislature, organizations that helped get Bartlet elected. They'd have to bring Mendoza in to persuade him to keep his own counsel. When summoned, Mendoza said he'd drive to D.C. from Canada, stopping off in Connecticut to do some antiquing.

Attending a labor conference in New Orleans, the President had missed the recent spate of snafus. After giving his boss only three hours' sleep, Charlie had to wake Bartlet to prep him for the new day and new crises. Charlie told the President to dig in. It wasn't a nightmare, Charlie, said he really is the President.

In the Oval Office, Josh confessed to Bartlet about his blunders at the briefing.

JOSH: I was crystal clear. They said, "Do you think if the President has a plan to fight inflation that it's right to keep it a secret?" I said, "Of course not."

BARTLET is staring at JOSH in amazement . . .

BARTLET: Are you telling me that not only did you invent a secret plan to fight inflation . . . *but that you don't support it?!*

Then Toby informed the President of Mendoza's denouncement of Bartlet's attempt to make O'Leary apologize. Throwing his hands in the air, Bartlet told C.J. to untangle the press corps while they wait for Mendoza to arrive. And if anyone asked, Josh said to Bartlet, that cigarette he bummed on Air Force One was for a friend.

Josh's candor with his student audience stops short of telling them that at that moment, Roberto Mendoza is sitting in a jail cell in Connecticut after being arrested on his drive to Washington. A few states away, Toby is confronting Mendoza face-to-face. He knows that Mendoza's hepatitis keeps him from drinking, there's no chance this was a legitimate arrest. But Mendoza doesn't want to be saved by the federal government. He wants to wait until Monday to legitimately clear his name through the system. He was picked up because he looks like his name is Roberto Mendoza and he could be comin' to rob your *house!* Without just cause, a Breathalyzer test is an illegal search and a civil rights violation.

MENDOZA: (pause) I was cuffed and patted down in front of my nine-year-old boy. And he and his mother watched while they put me in a squad car and took me away.

TOBY: He's also seen you wearing a robe with a gavel in your hand.

MENDOZA: He doesn't understand that, he doesn't know what that is. He understands the police, he watches TV. *That's* what he's gonna remember. That they handcuffed his father. So America just got one more pissed-off guy with dark skin.

Toby understands Mendoza's desire for justice and his feeling of humiliation, but he says he can't get Mendoza confirmed if this story gets out to the press. "There's nothing about this that doesn't stink. And nothing about this that wouldn't be better if you were a Supreme Court justice," Toby says. He extracts an apology from the cops who arrested the judge. Mendoza leaves with Toby under the condition that the cops will apologize to his son too.

Toby calls Josh to tell him the emergency is over. Josh is still on the platform, and smiles and promises that's the last time his phone will ring. He can't tell the students what the calls have been about just yet, but he'd be happy to take some questions about daily life in the White House.

20 HOURS IN L.A.

The presidency isn't just fun and games, and Bartlet is well aware of this as he stares into the predawn sky outside his limo window. The President is taking a trip to L.A., leaving Washington at 3:00 A.M. and returning that night after the Hollywood fund-raiser. Leo encourages Bartlet to stay over, but the President insists on coming straight back. There's a slew of important business at hand: most notably, the vote on the ethanol tax credit in the Senate is deadlocked fifty-fifty. But the plane ride isn't without its own excitement; Bartlet's meeting Zoey's new Secret Service agent on board Air Force One.

Already clambering in the confines of the plane, Josh and Toby are clearly unhappy the President is taking a meeting in L.A. with a pollster named Al Kiefer.

Josh is distracted from the bad news when he gets the next round: a bill on gays in the military is going to be introduced that morning. Even if the bill doesn't go anywhere, Ted Marcus, the host of the fund-raiser, will hear about it and that might be a problem.

Ron Butterfield introduces the President to Zoey's new shadow, Special Agent Gina Toscano (Jorja Fox). Bartlet warily asks if she's aware of the letters about Charlie and Zoey. Gina assures him she knows what she's looking for in a crowd. Bartlet insists that Zoey be comfortable as a college student, it's not Gina's job to tell him if Zoey's cutting English lit, or dyeing her hair neon colors. Gina thanks him and starts to exit. Bartlet retracts his earlier statement, he does want to know if she's cutting class, but Gina says, "No deal." Bartlet waves her off and settles back for the long plane ride.

Leo's back in the West Wing minding the farm, much to the annoyance of Margaret, who desperately wanted a free ride to California. The ethanol vote is stuck fast at fifty-fifty and Leo wants it to pass. In a strategic reelection mindset, Leo knows that ethanol accounts for 20 percent of Iowa's corn crop and created 16,000 jobs. They can guarantee they win the vote, but it means having the vice president break the tie.

C.J. rehearses the jam-packed California schedule with the press. There's a meeting with civic leaders in Orange County to discuss a constitutional ban on flag burning, a town hall meeting on school vouchers, and the Hollywood fund-raiser at night. When they arrive at the hotel, Josh picks up his messages and finds Joey Lucas called. She just wanted to let him know she'll be at the fund-raiser. Donna seizes the opportunity to tease her boss about his secret crush on Joey, he should call her back.

DONNA: Gather ye rosebuds while ye may, Josh. You know what that means? It means you should take this time to gather rosebuds, 'cause later on you might not be able to.

But Josh has to deal with Ted Marcus (Bob Balaban) first. He goes to Marcus's mansion to meet the studio chairman, who is clearly a major player. Caterers and florists are consumed by preparations for the party. Filtering out the chaos around him, Marcus gets right to his point: he wants to discuss Cameron's House Resolution 973 banning gays in the military. Josh assures him the bill's a joke, it's not going anywhere. Sensing Josh's impatience, Ted Marcus says he's going to raise $2.5 million dollars for the Democrats and he wants Josh to be a little more attentive. Right then and there Marcus cancels the party and tells the workers to load up the trucks. Josh sees a disaster looming, and reiterates that even if the bill passed, Bartlet would never sign it. Fabtabulous, Marcus says, he will put the event back on if the President declares that publicly. Josh knows that's not going to happen.

MARCUS: Then we have ourselves a problem. (pause) Don't screw around with me, Josh. I've been President a lot longer than he has.

Back in D.C., Leo tells Hoynes that the President would like him to break the tie. Hoynes protests. "You gotta get me off the hook, Leo." He spent eight years in the Senate voting against this tax credit, which has proven itself to accomplish nothing in regard to reducing U.S. dependency on foreign oil. But Hoynes's main problem is that the Republicans'll make him eat that tie-breaking vote for dinner when his time comes.

In Los Angeles, Josh and Toby ponder the Marcus conundrum. Toby points out that if Marcus carried out his threat, it would only lend credibility to Cameron's bill. And the President would look good standing up to Marcus. As a bargaining chip, they want to offer Marcus ten minutes alone with the President at the party. While his staff debates the logistics of the deal, Bartlet listens to complaints about symbolic desecration and the need to protect the flag. He's wondering if there's suddenly an emergency-level epidemic of flag burning that he doesn't know about. No, says Toby, so why even meet with Al Kiefer? Bartlet believes he has nothing to fear from Kiefer, and announces that they are all proceeding to lunch at the restaurant where Zoey planned to eat.

The restaurant is cleared out and sealed for the President. The staff and Al Kiefer (John de Lancie) sit at one table while Bartlet eats alone with his daughter, and the Secret Service stands by as discreetly as possible. Zoey complains her father is cramping her style. With him around, she says, her protection quadruples. Sensing the approach of a conversation he's not ready to have, the President blows her off with a joke. At the other table, Kiefer is saying Bartlet could sew up reelection by leading the charge for a flag-burning amendment. White men, "pool and patio types," think Bartlet's smart and has vision but that he's a wimp in the face of real issues. They voted against Bartlet by twenty points, but they could be his for the taking if he just stepped up against flag burning. The amendment will pass someday, why not take advantage of it? Toby hates this kind of politics.

> **KIEFER:** Toby, you're smiling.
> **TOBY:** I just figured out who you are.
> **KIEFER:** (beat) He's gonna say Satan.
> **TOBY:** No. You're the guy who runs into the 7-Eleven to get Satan a pack of cigarettes.

On the way out of the restaurant, Bartlet seems intrigued by Kiefer's polling analysis. Gina is concentrating on the big crowd behind the police barricades, and can't help but notice a couple of rowdy fifteen-year-olds she's not wild about. She tells Zoey to walk on the other side of her and casually makes sure the young men catch a glimpse of her .44 Magnum. She puts Zoey in her sedan, shuts the door, and slaps the roof.

Marcus's party proceeds without any hitches. It's glamorous, packed with famous Hollywood faces. Toby is cranky and would rather be pretty much anywhere else. A man introduces himself as head of new project development at Paragon. He wants to meet C.J.

> **MARK MILLER**: I was wondering if my money buys me a few words alone with you.
>
> **C.J.**: (to Miller) Sure.
>
> **TOBY**: Throw in some chocolate and a pair of nylons, you'll get a lot more than that . . .
>
> C.J. gets up to follow Miller, giving TOBY a smack in the head as she does.
>
> **TOBY**: I'll be at the bar drinking a lot if anybody wants me.
>
> **C.J.**: Nobody will.

Her Romeo's not all that he's cracked up to be, and C.J. grabs Sam to get away from him after he offers her a development deal. He offered Sam one too. Joey Lucas sidles up to Josh, and she looks like a million bucks. Sparks are flying when Toby calls Josh away. Josh makes Joey promise not to leave.

In Washington, Leo's wishing he was at a glamorous Hollywood gala. Instead, he's in the middle of a very frank discussion with Hoynes. As an aside from the political melange of the tax credit, Leo tells the vice president he knows there's friction between him and Leo's staff. He says they respect him, but they don't trust him, and neither does the President. Leo says he's the one who persuaded Bartlet to put Hoynes on the ticket, so he's got a lot on the line.

> **HOYNES**: Leo . . . one of these days you're gonna have to allow for the possibility that my motives are not always sinister. You and your staff are remarkably smug. And frankly, so is the President. And the fact that you think I give a damn that there's friction between us is certainly proof enough of that. (pause) I need time to think about this.
>
> **LEO**: (pause) John, you will not be able to set foot in the West Wing. You will not be on the ticket in three years.
>
> **HOYNES**: Leo, I think you guys set me up.
>
> **LEO**: You think the President of the United States can just arrange for a fifty-fifty tie in the Senate?
>
> **HOYNES**: I think the President of the United States can do pretty much whatever he wants.

Leo shares this enlightening discussion with Bartlet, who asserts he's running out of reasons not to fire Hoynes. Leo points out that the Constitution may stand in the way of that. Then he tells

Kristin Harms (Producer)
We were presented with a last-minute challenge to get as many notable actors as possible to appear in the episode. As you can imagine, a lot of people were interested, but their schedules didn't coincide. Luckily, we were able to get Jay Leno, David Hasselhoff, and Veronica Webb.

Bartlet that Hoynes is right about the tax credit. Sam, listening in, agrees. He says it's a giveaway to special interests, it subsidizes one fuel over another and distorts the market. Sam says he put three guys in a headlock to vote yes. He could release them, tank the vote, and take Hoynes off the hook. Bartlet agrees: they'll dump the vote.

At the party, C.J. is telling Jay Leno the President appreciates his laying off Leo for the past few months. Leno wonders if the President would be willing to ride his bike into a tree again as a gesture of gratitude. Josh has relocated Joey, and tells her they met a pollster who told them the President would get reelected if he proposed a flag-burning amendment. Joey is on the ball in the polling world, and tells Josh Kiefer asked the wrong question. Eighty percent of people favored the amendment but only 37 percent said it was important to them and only 12 percent said it would swing their vote. Josh is captivated by this intelligent and beautiful woman, but Joey tells him she came with someone, it was good to see him again.

Ted Marcus is having his ten minutes with the President. Bartlet's not having a good day and he's trying to hang in there as Marcus rants about gay rights and impact of the bill. Bartlet tells Marcus he can't publicly announce he'd veto Cameron's bill. He's a human starting gun—if he talks about an issue, it's automatically on the table. Marcus relents—he knows Bartlet's right, he just wanted to hear it for himself. It's clear neither man has enjoyed the party. Marcus says the President looks more tired than he did a couple of months ago, and Bartlet admits he really just wants to get some sleep on the way back.

As they're getting ready to leave the hotel, Donna chastises Josh for giving up on Joey as soon as she said she was with someone. Romance isn't easy, especially for two government officials. Donna reminds Josh that Joey's in the same hotel, he should go and see her before they leave. He doesn't have much to lose, and Josh finds himself ringing the bell of Joey's hotel room. To his surprise, Al Kiefer comes to the door in a bathrobe. Josh is confused, says he must have got the wrong room, but Kiefer asks if he's there for Joey, who immediately comes to the door in her matching bathrobe. Stunned, Josh thanks Joey for her help and they say an awkward good-bye.

Back on Air Force One, the lights are dimmed and everyone's sleeping except for Bartlet, who's sitting by himself on the phone with Hoynes. He says the problem's taken care of. Just as they're about to hang up, he tells Hoynes he admired how he stuck to his guns in Iowa during the campaign. He adhered to his belief on the ethanol tax credit, even though he knew it would be unpopular. Bartlet confesses he's always agreed, but Hoynes was the only one to articulate it. "You had a good day today, John," he says.

The President closes his eyes for a long moment but they open again. He gives up and stares out of the window of Air Force One.

THE WHITE
HOUSE PRO-AM

Surrounded by lights and television cameras, Abbey Bartlet is making an appearance on a live morning television show with fourteen-year-old Jeffrey Morgan, discussing child labor exploitation. Jeffrey started the Children's Crusade when his pen pal in India was bonded to a loan shark to whom his mother was indebted. Sam is watching the show with Lilli Mays (Nadia Dajani), the first lady's chief of staff. She wants press for Mrs. Bartlet's crusade. She knows the President is going to the Hill the next day for budget meetings, and perhaps if they stayed at the White House on the down low instead, Mrs. Bartlet might get the public spotlight. Sam says the symbolism is key: Bartlet is *going* to Congress.

LILLI: Your guy steps out of a motorcade and that's three column inches above the fold, my guy's on page twenty-three.

SAM: Your guy's married to my guy and my guy was elected, which is something you and your people are going to have to get used to.

LILLI: Your guy has a forty-eight percent approval rating, my guy's at sixty-one percent and bite me.

SAM: Ah. Point well argued.

But their argument is moot in the face of larger events: the chairman of the Federal Reserve just died.

BARTLET: The market's going to open two hundred points down.

LEO: If we're lucky.

BARTLET: When was the last time we were lucky?

LEO: Super Tuesday.

Leo's advice to the President is to announce Ron Erlich as the new Fed chairman right away. Even a day's delay could cost the market three hundred points. But Bartlet wants time. "I'm not ready to jump into bed with Ron Erlich yet," he argues. "Making me one of the few people in my family who can say that."

Toby tells Josh, they're holding off on announcing a successor out of respect for the deceased. Josh asks Toby to join him for a meeting with three congressmen about the trade bill. The bill's guaranteed to pass by fifteen votes but Josh wants their votes to broaden the bill's liberal base of support. Toby thinks it's beneath them.

JOSH: We're gonna do good cop/bad cop.

TOBY: (pause) No. We're really not.

JOSH: Why not?

TOBY: 'Cause this isn't an episode of *Hawaii Five-0*. How 'bout if you be the good cop and I be the cop who doesn't go to the meeting.

The death of the Federal Reserve chairman is the top story, and inevitably, Erlich's name creeps into a press briefing. C.J. is trying to say there are a number of candidates when Danny Concannon announces to the room that Mrs. Bartlet has declared a preference for Erlich. Sam trudges to see Lilli Mays again, but she denies being the source for the quote. Imperiously, Sam tells Mays her staff has to work better with his.

As the word starts spreading of Erlich, Bartlet warns Leo and C.J. that it's possible Erlich might not be the guy for the job. With a series of bad Press Room blunders in her recent past, C.J. is anxious to do the right thing. She wonders if she should go and see the first lady to ask her to clarify her position. Bartlet firmly says, "We don't handle my wife." He gets punished when they try that. He suggests they move on, it's not a big deal.

After putting off his discussion for weeks, Bartlet has to tell Zoey the White House has been receiving some unfavorable letters about her dating a black man. Ron Butterfield told him that a newspaper reported she and Charlie will be attending a club opening, which coincides with a white supremacist convention in Virginia. Knowing that he will be accused of meddling in her personal life, Bartlet says Zoey can go, but not Charlie. Judging from the serious concern in her father's voice, Zoey says she'll tell Charlie, and Bartlet advises her to tell him the truth.

Josh is taking the meeting on the trade bill. Toby sits and behaves himself. Josh says that lower tariffs have been negotiated over seven years in Geneva with 130 countries. The bill's finally ready for a vote. Toby points out that with or without their support, it will win. One congressman says they're concerned about cheaper goods and their effect on labor and manufacturing.

TOBY: You're concerned about American labor and manufacturing?
CONGRESSMAN #1: Yes.
TOBY: What kind of car do you drive?
CONGRESSMAN #1: A Toyota.
TOBY: Then shut up.

It's still a mystery who the source of the first lady's quote about Erlich was. Toby suggests that Abbey should mention she supports whomever the President nominates, but C.J. tells him about the President's warning not to handle the first lady.

JOSH: (pause) Did he say he didn't want you to handle the first lady 'cause he didn't want you to, or did he say it like, "Handle the first lady, but I'm not the one who told you to."
C.J.: That's what I don't know.
JOSH: You've gotta learn the signs.
C.J.: I've got most of the signs.
JOSH: You don't have that one.
C.J.: I'm learning that one.

Timothy Busfield

Danny's there to sell papers. That's it. Whether he agrees or disagrees or likes or doesn't like, it doesn't matter. Aaron established this nicely. He's been there for two other administrations and he'll be there for two more administrations or more. It doesn't matter to him who the President is.

Sam sneaks out for some quiet thinking time at the gym, and there, Congresswoman Rebecca Reeseman (Amy Aquino) tells him she's going to introduce a child labor restriction amendment to the trade bill. Abbey Bartlet initiated the movement on TV and she can't be left out. His quiet time comes screeching to a halt as the fifteen-vote margin suddenly looks vulnerable. The bill took seven years to get to a vote and the amendment threatens its easy passage. Without a doubt, Sam will have to ask Mrs. Bartlet to get Reeseman to back off her quest. He has to see Lilli Mays about Erlich regardless.

Over lunch at a diner, Zoey breaks the difficult news to Charlie, explaining they can't go out together on Friday due to an increase in the death threats they've been receiving. Gina chimes in, offering that security would be too difficult where they'd planned to go. Charlie doesn't give a damn about that. When Zoey excuses herself for the bathroom, Charlie walks out.

When Sam goes to see Lilli Mays, he finds Abbey Bartlet waiting for him. He dives right in: the first lady's staff is professional, but prone to amateur mistakes. Just short of wagging his finger in front of her face, he tells Abbey she can't go on TV and have a kid sit opposite her because it would look like she only discovered right then and there that there was a child labor problem. She needs to vet that stuff through Sam's office. Sam concedes to Mrs. Bartlet that she has to talk to Reeseman.

The President has arranged to see Danny Concannon during an evening reception; though warning his staff off his wife, he's not above handling people himself. While he's waiting, Danny lends an ear to Charlie, who's still steamed about his disagreement with Zoey. Danny advises Charlie that the President and the Secret Service don't care that he's black, they only care about

Stockard Channing

In terms of the scenes with Martin, we're two actors who make up a reality. From the beginning we had a great chemistry. We just said "hello" to each other and it worked. That's an accident. You can't buy that.

You don't fight with someone unless you care about them, especially in a marriage. They're not nasty fights. They're very responsible, energetic disagreements. She was furious because she was being manipulated by him. I believe she does not have a lot of use for the politics of the West Wing. She knows that's part of her job to be.

Zoey's safety. He tells Charlie to let it go. Zoey gets two thousand marriage proposals and two thousand death threats, look at all she has to put up with to be a young woman in the public eye. Perhaps Charlie should make sure he is the one guy in her life who's totally hassle-free.

Playfully, the President tries to pry from Danny his source on his Erlich story. "Danny, I miss our little late-night talks," he coos. There's no way Danny's ever going to give the information up, but the President will do anything to avoid having to face down his wife.

Reluctantly, Abbey Bartlet finds a quiet spot at the reception to talk to Rebecca Reeseman, explaining that her amendment will kill the trade bill in the Senate and this bill needs to pass comfortably. Reeseman says she felt the train was leaving the station without her. She's got her eye on a Senate seat and Abbey's sure the President will do what he can to help. Reeseman confesses she's worried too many people know about the proposal, can she trust Bartlet's staff not to talk about it? Yes, says Abbey, without a pause. She has delivered.

His bill is secured, but Bartlet's going to have to pay for it. Abbey is furious that Sam felt he had the right to visit and order around her chief of staff twice. Bartlet admits C.J. got the signal right, he did want her to send someone. The wire piece about Erlich was a problem, the kid on TV was a mistake, and Reeseman's amendment could have killed the bill. He says he staffed it out to C.J.

ABBEY: You don't staff me out. You don't give C.J. signals, you don't send Sam, and you don't bring Danny Concannon up here. Don't handle me, Jed.

BARTLET: Then don't *play* me, Abbey. Don't *work* me.

Bartlet knows Abbey planted the story about Erlich and now, if he names Erlich to the Federal Reserve Chair, it looks like Bartlet is taking instructions from his wife. Abbey counters that he was going to name Erlich anyway, but merely waited a day because Erlich was her boyfriend thirty years ago for a month. Bartlet doesn't disagree—but he tells her she can't send him messages through the press or stake out agendas on morning shows. Abbey declares she's not going to stop kicking his ass on child labor. If it was one of his girls in a factory, he'd send in the marines. The anger dissipates and their voices grow lower. The first couple have had their first Oval Office fight.

Charlie arrives at Zoey's dorm armed with flowers, a video, and popcorn. He's come to apologize for leaving her in the restaurant and for anything else she can think of. Zoey pulls Charlie into her room and the door closes behind them. "Bookbag is in for the night."

SIX MEETINGS
BEFORE LUNCH

Roberto Mendoza's confirmation vote is before the Senate. A small crowd has begun to gather around televisions in the Mural Room. It's the final moments of a game that's already won, so rather than nervousness, there's a growing sense of giddy anticipation. It's early in the roll call and Toby says no champagne until the fifty-first "yea." He doesn't want to screw it up by tempting fate.

As if on cue, Leo hears that an administration nominee to a Justice post favors reparations to African Americans for slavery. Whatever the merits, this is bound to jeopardize the appointment. Amidst the drama, Mallory finds Sam to tell him she despises him for a position paper he wrote concerning school vouchers. As she accosts him, the fifty-first senator votes for Mendoza, and the champagne corks fly into the air.

Allison Janney

My trailer's been known as the party trailer. It's decorated with lots of red and it looks like a den of iniquity. I like music. I like to dance. Some nights in the first season we couldn't get our scheduling together. So most of the time we were hanging out in our trailers for so many hours it was unbelievable. And we were bored out of our minds. I brought my CDs and there was a compilation with a song on it, "The Jackal." I memorized all the lines to perform it for Richard, because I wanted to make him laugh. He became a part of it, the air drummer, the air saxophone player, the air everything. And he would make me laugh harder than I've ever laughed, seeing him do these little moves of being this cool jazz guy.

One night we brought Aaron and Lew Wells and a bunch of people into my trailer and we did it for them. Aaron laughed so hard and the next thing I knew it was in the script. I was amazed that he was able to bring that into this show. They had to reshoot it because the first time, it was more like Allison Janney would do it, not like C.J. It was wild. I was just going crazy. And they said, "You can't be so good at it. C.J. wouldn't be as good at it as you are."

At 11:30 P.M., the party's clearing out but the night's not over yet. Leo is telling Josh that Jeff Breckinridge, the nominee for assistant attorney general for civil rights, wrote a jacket blurb for a book supporting reparations. Leo wants Josh to deal with it, and Josh is moaning about it. They hear chanting coming from the Press Room: C.J.'s going to lip sync a jazzy number called "The Jackal." They can't miss this performance, and they head into the room where the lights have been dimmed. There's cigar smoke in the air, much of it from Toby's Cuban. At this moment, Toby might be mistaken for the house piano player at a jazz dive. He's relaxed for the first time in months.

Meanwhile, in Sam's office, Mallory and Sam are engaged in hot debate. As an elementary school teacher, she can't believe Sam's in favor of school vouchers. On a personal level, she thought they had something going on, but this turn of events frankly repulses her. Sam argues they haven't even been on a date. He's spent three months putting Mendoza on the bench and now he's done for the day. There *is* something going on between them but she's not been doing a good job, so he's taking over, they should get dinner. Mallory's not buying his egotistical masculine attitude and she leaves. As Sam watches C.J. do "The Jackal," Leo confesses he gave the paper to Mallory to have some fun with him.

Danny arrives at C.J.'s office a few minutes too late for "The Jackal." He's come to give C.J. a heads-up. He heard on his police scanner that David Arbor, son of a big Democratic fund-raiser, was arrested outside a frat party that Zoey attended. He'll be charged with felony possession and distribution. News aside, he asks her to do "The Jackal" for him right there.

Meanwhile, C.J. thinks she can defuse the Arbor story easily enough. Mandy tries to interest Josh in getting a replacement for Lum-Lum, a giant panda who just died at the National Zoo. With a small smile playing on his lips, Josh advises her to talk to Toby, the resident animal lover.

Zoey's having coffee at a college cafeteria with some friends. When they're finished, Gina wants to leave through the back entrance, because reporters are sniffing around. As they're walking through the kitchen they're ambushed by Drumm, a reporter for the *Charleston Citizen*. Barking questions, he's gotten a little too close a little too fast, and Gina knocks him back and pins him against a door. He shouts a question about the President's daughter partying with drug dealers. Zoey knows she should walk away, but she's goaded and has stayed silent for too long. She says she didn't know Arbor was going to be there. Drumm's been a jerk, but he's got his story.

When Jeff Breckinridge (Carl Lumbly) comes to meet with Josh, Josh recognizes him as a former summer intern at his father's firm. Breckinridge says Noah Lyman is a wonderful man and asks about him. Josh regrets to tell him that his father died the night of the Illinois primary. Jeff offers his condolences but Josh just wants to get to business. Jeff remarks that Republicans on the Judiciary Committee have a problem with him, and Josh points out his rather controversial book endorsement. Jeff says his family was seized and enslaved. He wants reparations to the tune of $1.7 trillion.

Charlie gives C.J. a heads-up about Drumm's performance in the school cafeteria. C.J. knows Drumm's a Bartlet baiter and his paper's a rag. Charlie adds that David Arbor's not a dealer, he's a user. Zoey has been trying to help him, and she was at the party because she was bringing him back his car keys she'd confiscated the week before.

In the wake of the Mendoza confirmation, Toby is smiling and happy. It's scaring people.

MARGARET: You usually wouldn't say "Hello there, Margaret."

TOBY: What would I usually say?

MARGARET: You'd usually growl something inaudible.

To his chagrin, Mallory scheduled an actual appointment with Sam's office and has dragged him into an hour-long debate on school vouchers. Breckinridge and Josh are still locked in a debate

too. Jeff says reparations aren't new. Sherman gave land to freed slaves in 1865: the famous forty acres and a mule. Josh says that 600,000 white men died in the Civil War over slavery. "Is that why they died?" presses Breckinridge.

Digging for the story that will no doubt hit the presses, C.J. asks Danny if he's heard anything about Drumm. Danny says he knows Drumm asked about the party, and Zoey responded that she didn't know Arbor was going to be there. C.J. looks up in surprise; defusing this story might not be as easy as she anticipated.

Toby is still being uncharacteristically amicable. He says, "Bonnie, you are dedicated and you are beautiful. Ginger, you're . . . other nice things." He sees Mandy.

TOBY: I'm not kidding, Mandy. I feel like I've lost a hundred and eighty pounds. I'm smiling. I'm laughing. I'm enjoying the people I work with. I gotta snap outta this. What's on your mind?

MANDY: I want you to help me get the Chinese to give us a new panda bear to replace Lum-Lum.

TOBY: (pause) Well, that did the trick.

Determined to get to the bottom of the story, C.J. calls Zoey in. C.J. looks the first daughter squarely in the eye and asks her why she lied when she told Drumm she wasn't expecting to see Arbor at the party. Zoey protests that she didn't lie. C.J. suggests she stop lying altogether. If Zoey didn't know Arbor was going to be at the party, why did she have his car keys with her?

Butterfield is discussing some new hate groups at a Secret Service briefing. The latest letters they've received have been signed off "14 Words," which Gina spells out as "We must secure the existence of white people and a future for white children." There's been two death threats, one for Charlie, one for Zoey. The style and phrasing leads Gina to think they're looking for a couple of fifteen-year-old boys.

Gina won't disclose to C.J. what happened at the party. If Zoey feels she has to do things behind Gina's back, Gina can't do her job. Without seeing an easy or tactful route out of the story, C.J. approaches Sam for advice. Sam tells C.J. she can't back down, she has to "get in the President's face" and be there for him when he rages about a reporter approaching his daughter on campus. In return, Sam asks for C.J.'s advice about Mallory. C.J. says they should continue their fight over lunch. Huffily, she says that's better advice than "get in the President's face."

Seeing no other way to regain peace, Sam and Mallory take their argument to Leo. Eventually Leo tells Mallory Sam's not really in favor of school vouchers. He wrote the position paper as opposition prep to detail the arguments of the other side. Quite the impassioned issue man of the West Wing, Sam knows how important education is.

SAM: Education is the silver bullet. Education is everything. We don't need little changes. We need gigantic, revolutionary changes. Schools should be palaces. Competition for the best teachers should be *fierce*. They should be getting six-figure salaries. School should be incredibly expensive for government and absolutely free of charge for its citizens, just like national defense. That is my position. I just haven't figured out how to do it yet.

C.J. has to bite the bullet and talk to Bartlet about Zoey. She respectfully requests he not

Thomas Schlamme (Executive Producer/ Director)

First, I love actors. Between actors and directors it's often "the farmer and the rancher must be friends," you know, from *Oklahoma*. "We've got the same terrain, but we're fighting." That's not my feeling. I think actors get it pretty quickly that I am completely in awe of where they go. Especially people who are really actors. I think they feel that and that it's genuine. It's not, "Okay, I need to tell you I love you."

Actors irritate me, they're neurotic sometimes, they're selfish, they're indulgent, they're all the things, but sometimes I just love sitting at the monitor and watching Allison and Richard and John—I could list them all—act. I like watching a great athlete play ball and I like watching great actors act. I just hope that I can help them shape what it is that they are doing.

blow his stack, then tells him Zoey lied to a reporter. Bartlet's enraged, not about the lie, but because a reporter approached her on campus. He wants a confrontation. C.J. duly gets in his face. For the first time, C.J.'s standing up to the President. She says this is not about Bartlet's daughter, it's about the first daughter and that's C.J.'s job. The President, C.J., Charlie, and Zoey are the only ones who know. She tells him, "You go down there and it's a *big* story." C.J. doesn't back down, and convinces the President not to go off on the press.

Breckinridge and Josh are just hitting the crux of their discussion. Jeff says they gave $1.2 billion to Japanese Americans as recompense for internment camps. Josh points out that they were still alive to give money to. And the U.S. doesn't have $1.7 trillion in its pockets. Breckinridge says he'll take tax deductions and scholarships. Josh suggests affirmative action, empowerment zones, and civil rights.

> JOSH: You know, Jeff, I'd love to give you the money, I really would. But I'm a little short of cash right now. It seems the SS officer forgot to give my grandfather his wallet back when he let him out of Birkenau.
>
> JEFF: Well, your beef is with the Germans.
>
> JOSH: You're damn right it is. (pause) What the hell are we talking about?
>
> JEFF: (pause) We have laws in this country. You break 'em, you pay your fine. You break God's laws, that's a different story. You can't kidnap a civilization and sell 'em into slavery. No amount of money'll make up for it, and all you have to do is look, two hundred years later, at race relations in this country.

Jeff asks Josh for a dollar, and asks Josh to look at the back. He says the seal, the pyramid, is unfinished, and it's meant to be. We're meant to keep doing better and discussing and debating. That's why he lent his name to the book. He wants to be assistant attorney general and do an outstanding job for all the people, to raise the level of discussion, and not search for treatments, but for cures. Does Josh have any problem with Jeff saying that to the committee? He doesn't. Breckinridge offers to buy Josh lunch. Josh sighs, and says they're going to have a lot of meetings like this before the confirmation, he'll get the first one.

LET BARTLET
BE BARTLET

The President is due to address the United Organization of Trout Fishermen outside the White House. It's raining, so the remarks are moved inside to the OEOB. Toby reminds Sam to be sure he changes the opening line of the speech, which refers to a "magnificent vista." Bartlet's distracted and the tiniest bit annoyed—his staff is a no-show at the OEOB, claiming they didn't know it was raining. "Nothin' like surrounding yourself with the best and the brightest." Bartlet perks up when he hears that two FEC commissioners resigned. Leo assures him the Senate leadership will fill the seats, but Bartlet wonders why they can't suggest their own guys. He wants to dangle his feet in the water and tells Josh to

find candidates who back aggressive campaign finance reform. After missing the rain cue, Sam forgets to change the remarks, so the President, firmly indoors, begins his speech, "As I look out over this magnificent vista—"

Josh recites the Federal Election Commission protocol for Donna. There are six commissioners who serve rotating six-year terms. Two seats are up every two years. The party leadership on both sides always advises the President whom to appoint.

The press and staff alike are speculating about "a mysterious piece of paper" that's floating around. C.J. intuitively asks Mandy, who knows what it is because she wrote it. It's a memo she prepared for her former boss, Lloyd Russell, on the weaknesses and vulnerabilities of the Bartlet administration and how to beat him for renomination. Mandy's embarrassed but C.J.'s just flat-out pissed.

Leo's e-mail is going haywire. Margaret begins to explain about a message she forwarded regarding the calorie count in raisin muffins that has since clogged the entire computer system. Leo would rather not hear about it in detail. Josh reports he has a couple of good FEC candidates, John Bacon and Patty Calhoun. The leadership will hate them both. Leo tells Josh to sound out the leadership's front men, not the leaders themselves.

In the Roosevelt Room, Sam and Toby are toiling over a lost cause of their own. Toby explains to two congressmen and two young military officers that the Bartlet administration is hamstrung by the policy they inherited on gays and lesbians in the military. They want more input before Sam makes recommendations to the President. An officer asks Sam what consequence his recommendations will have, and Sam admits very little. But if the commander in chief orders that gays can serve openly, then anyone who disobeys can stand court-martial. The officer replies that the chief can order what he wants, but the uniform code makes sodomy a crime, and it takes an act of Congress to change that.

In a room tucked away in the Capitol, Josh is talking to congressional aides about the soft money loophole, which renders the 1974 Campaign Reform Act toothless. Josh argues that soft money is corrupt, an aide contends that it's free speech. Josh says ads and bumper stickers are free speech; money isn't speech. The aides brush Josh off—they have their FEC candidates.

JOSH: The President makes appointments to the Federal Election Commission.

ONORATO: And the Senate confirms them. And I'm speaking for the majority leader. Embarrass us this way, and we will give the same back to you tenfold. Every piece of legislation the White House wants off the table will make a sudden appearance.

BLAKELY: Steve's talkin' about all our greatest hits, Josh. Five forty-one, school prayer, the Family Support Act, the Entertainment Decency Act—

GRAHAM: English as the national language.

ONORATO: English as the national language will be first up, that's gonna be our leadoff hitter.

JOSH: Wouldn't it be easier just to not confirm the nominees?

ONORATO: We're gonna do that, too.

Josh takes this as a challenge. Four hours ago, this was a fool's errand: he was sending up a test balloon. Now they've managed to get him on board.

Sam and Toby are still at it with the congressmen. " 'Don't Ask, Don't Tell' works," says a representative, but Sam disagrees. He says 1,145 people were discharged for being gay in 1998, a 92 percent increase since the policy was initiated. C.J. pulls Sam and Toby out of the meeting. She's read Mandy's memo, and it's devastating for the administration. She quotes: "The reality of the Bartlet White House is a flood of mistakes." It goes on to discuss the indecision and the lack of a coherent strategy. But the worst is reserved for the President and Leo.

Toby takes the responsibility of passing the news on to Leo. As Toby waits for Leo, Margaret tells him that since she sent out her muffin mass e-mail, the pipeline's been flooded and e-mails are bouncing around all over. Admiral Fitzwallace exits Leo's office and Toby warns him there's a security breach with the White House computers, but Fitzwallace knows they aren't secure. Toby informs Leo about the existence of the memo, which says the President's instinct is to be aggressive, but Leo moves him to the safe ground. Leo shrugs it off—he says don't worry about it, and tells Toby he doesn't want to see a copy.

As the political consultant, Mandy's still trying to do her job, but Josh doesn't want her advice just now. Hasn't she ever heard of a burn bag? Mandy says someone got the memo off her hard drive. Morale in the West Wing is dangerously low. Josh asks Donna if everyone is feeling this way. They are.

Tempers are running precariously high in the Roosevelt Room when

Lyn Elizabeth Paolo

There's a lot of attention to detail [in costume design]. I worked on a World War II movie and the prop man put a ribbon on somebody. I'd finished a Vietnam movie and I said, "Isn't that a Vietnam ribbon?" He said, "Oh, well, no one will know." I said, "No one except all the guys who were in Vietnam and all the guys that were in World War II, so let's do it right, if we're going to do it." I think there's a responsibility on our part to make the show look real. Why do it incorrectly? Mistakes happen, but, one would hope, not on my show.

Fitzwallace enters. He knows what they've been discussing, and he asks the officers what they think. One says the military has no prejudice toward homosexuals, but gays threaten discipline and cohesion in the armed forces. Fitzwallace agrees. But that's what they said about blacks in the military fifty years ago, and they *did* disrupt the unit, but now he's the chairman of the Joint Chiefs of Staff. "Beat *that* with a stick," he says. Outside the room, Fitzwallace cautions Sam that he's not going to get anywhere. Sam knows but says the President just wanted some exploratory meetings.

C.J. asks Danny if he's heard the rumor about the "piece of paper." In fact, he has a copy of it and he's going to write about it because it's news. It may not be good news for C.J., but it's news all the same. What's more, he says, Mandy's right.

> **DANNY:** You guys are stuck in the mud around here, and none of it is the fault of the press. I know you're frustrated, but that ain't nothin' compared to the frustration of the people who voted for you.

Sam's meeting on gays and lesbians in the military drags on. The two sides zing points back and forth but they're not getting anywhere. Finally, the congressman says if the President wholeheartedly wanted to change the law he'd get a resolution in the House with high-profile co-sponsors. He wouldn't have Sam take meetings like this. This is just a waste of time.

Now the whole White House has a crisis of confidence. Toby tells Leo there's a CNN/USA *Today* poll with a job approval rating of 42 percent, a decrease of five points in a week. Bartlet's unfavorables are higher than the favorables for the first time in his term, and 52 percent are likely to vote for a Republican congressional candidate in November. Toby says they've had one victory in a year—Mendoza.

> **TOBY:** One victory in a year stinks in the life of an administration but it's not the ones we lose that bother me, Leo, it's the ones we don't suit up for.

Because the memo's going to appear in the paper, C.J. confesses to Leo that she gave Bartlet a copy to read. Josh lays out what the leadership has threatened to do if the Senate is asked to confirm Bacon and Calhoun. First up: English as the national language. Josh wants to pick a fight, but Leo says they should relent and take the leadership's nominations.

Leo goes in to the President. Leo *is* bothered by the memo. But he says it's wrong, he doesn't drive the President to the safe ground, it's the other way around.

LEO: Everything you do says, "Leo, for God's sake, I don't want to be a one-term President."

BARTLET: Did I not say put our guys in the FEC?

LEO: No, sir, you did not say that. You said let's dangle our feet—

BARTLET: Leo—

LEO: —in the water of whatever the hell we dangle our feet in when we want to make it look like we're trying without pissing too many people off.

Leo tells Bartlet he's always dangling his feet. Sam can't get real on "Don't Ask, Don't Tell" because everyone across the table from him knows the President isn't committed. Leo's charged

Richard Schiff

People are very generous about what they give off-camera here and that's imperative if I'm going to stick around. I'm not going to say, "Okay, you want to go home, just put the grip stand over there. I'll be fine." I can't do that. Tommy is a purveyor of that atmosphere. He encourages it. When I won an award and I got up there and spoke about him it came out, luckily, the right way at that time. "He allows us, encourages us and enjoins us in the pursuit of excellence." That was heartfelt that night. As much credit as goes to Aaron, it's really a fifty-fifty partnership as far as we can tell, because without Tommy we'd derail and we'd go off the cliff. He's the one that provides the energy and the passion and the under-standing to allow the work to hap-pen so that it reaches the levels that it does.

up. He says he can get aggressive, he can orchestrate it right now. Leo says the people who work for Bartlet would walk into fire for him. Like Charlie, who's getting death threats and goes on with his job. Everyone's waiting for Bartlet, Leo says. Leo is getting into Bartlet's head. Bartlet says, "I want to speak."

BARTLET: This is more important than reelection.

LEO: Say it again.

BARTLET: This is more important than reelection. I want to speak now.

LEO: Now we're in business.

Leo's going to take everyone off the leash. The President asks if he has a strategy. Leo grabs a pad and scribbles something on it with a marker. He throws the pad down on the desk. It says, "Let Bartlet be Bartlet." Leo goes back into his office and tells the staff what's up. "If we're going to walk into walls," he says, "I want us running into 'em full speed." First off, they can tell the Hill the President's named his nominees to the FEC.

LEO: We're gonna lose a lot of these battles, and we might even lose the White House, but we're not gonna be threatened by issues; we're gonna put them front and center. We're gonna raise the level of public debate in this country, and let that be our legacy. That sound all right to you?

The staff takes this pledge in. Josh announces, "I serve at the pleasure of the President of the United States." C.J., Sam, and Toby join in Josh's vow. "Good," says Leo, "then let's get in the game."

SAM SEABORN
ROB LOWE

In the script for "In the Shadow of Two Gunmen, Part I," Leo McGarry tells the bemused candidate Bartlet he's just fired the entire campaign staff. Leo plows ahead, ticking off the new roster. He says Josh Lyman is going back to New York to pick up Sam Seaborn. Sam will be Toby's deputy, writing speeches, and also Bartlet's "issues director."

Even in the multitasked environment of the Bartlet administration, the portfolio of issues director covers a multitude of sins. More than any other staffer, perhaps, Sam is concerned with being on the right side on a particular issue rather than just the winning side. While Toby has that element, and C.J. has her moments, Sam Seaborn is the staffer most driven by his convictions.

Even if Josh Lyman hadn't come to rescue him, Sam's heart clearly wasn't in big-time corporate law. Despite his manifest success in a major New York legal firm, Sam can be, by the hard-nosed and embittered standards of political Washington, somewhat naïve.

Aaron Sorkin

While as politically savvy as anybody, there's a rookie quality about Sam, a freshman quality about him. One of my favorite scenes was when Sam has a face-off with C.J. because he didn't tell her about his fling with a local call girl. He absolutely stands by this woman, stands by his friendship with her, and stands by the idea of being good rather than looking good. When, later in the year, it's told to him that he has possibly been slightly duped by a congressional aide, Josh even likens it to the moment when Michael Corleone says, "I'll kill the cop." I like that quality in him as well.

It might be easy to overlook the fact that Sam will be as partisan as the next person when it's necessary. Mandy Hampton found that out when she tried to use Sam as her advocate when she wanted to work for Republican Mike Brace. Politely and diligently, Sam did what he was asked, but ended up telling Mandy where her real loyalty had to reside. Rob Lowe enjoys these dualities that coexist in his character.

Rob Lowe

What is interesting about all White House staffs is that there are no hard and fast rules. For example, Reagan had no chief of staff. John Kennedy had no chief of staff. It's really about the personnel and what they bring to it. Even though Sam's title is deputy communications director, he has turned into the "go to" counsel, the "go to" lawyer in the inner circle. Mind you, the inner circle are all lawyers but Sam's the one they go to when they want to be sure they have it right. He is a great writer, although he thinks Toby's better.

Aaron Sorkin

Sam is optimistic. He is incredibly energetic. Smart, in the strangest ways, as well as smart in the regular ways. Prone to step in it from time to time. It isn't that so much as things happen to him. He is a lawyer—several of them come from very lucrative private sector jobs to not very lucrative public jobs. He's a fantastic lawyer and a wonderful writer. Sam obviously provides romance of a leading man quality. And a great sense of humor.

Rob Lowe

Sam also has the ability to be the enforcer, which is nice. There have been a couple of moments where, I think, Sam has a lot of Bobby Kennedy in him. Bobby had all that great bone structure, but you didn't want to be locked in a dark room with him if he disagreed with you. Sam threw Claypool against the wall and said, "If you come after Leo, I'll bust you like a piñata." And he said to the FBI agent, "Please tell me you didn't just threaten Toby Ziegler." Like Sam said to the Hollywood producer, "If you ever call the President a coward again, it won't be C. J. Cregg you have to deal with, it's gonna be me." I love the juxtaposition of loyalist attack dog with the exuberant puppy.

Bradley Whitford

The great thing about this show for Rob is that Rob has never had a part that's as smart or as funny as he is. He can fire on all cylinders.

ROB LOWE

When you're in a hit movie, nothing can approach a big opening weekend. But on television, if you give a performance you're proud of and you wake up the next day and they tell you that nineteen million Americans watched it, and you realize that more people saw work you wanted them to see than will have ever seen *Titanic* in a movie theater, that's a good day. That's a very good day.

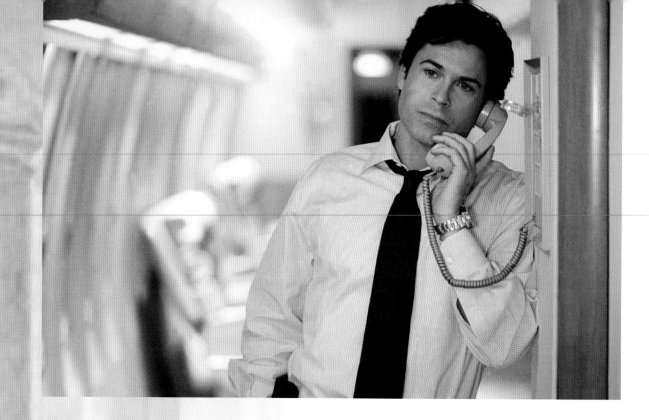

More than once, Sam has turned his hounds on his boss to whom he has, by now, shown all sides of his character.

Rob Lowe

Sam and Toby are alike. When Sam and Toby were described as Batman and Robin, they were arguing over who was Batman and who was Robin. Really what they are is the big brother and the little brother. The big brother likes to cuff his little brother around a lot, but little brother's a genius. Sometimes, you have to back off and let him have his room. In "The Drop-In," Sam got in Toby's face, big-time. That's a moment brothers have, and fathers and sons have. All of the sudden the younger one goes, "Hey, you know what? I know what this relationship is, but I have a boundary and if you cross it, I'll break your head."

Aaron Sorkin

Sam looks up to Toby like a big brother.

Richard Schiff

Sam is someone who Toby has a lot of respect for but has absolutely no need to show any of it. When Sam was in trouble with the prostitute, I came to his defense. There was a time on "The Portland Trip" when he was having a writer's problem and Toby was very sympathetic toward him. When Aaron called us the Batman and Robin of speechwriting, Sam was somewhat offended that he was Robin. Toby says, "Look at me, am I Robin?" But it's pretty clear how Toby feels about Sam.

MANDATORY MINIMUMS

The President is addressing a ballroom crowd of a thousand, sarcastically asserting that mandatory sentencing is the only way to assure that justice is dispensed. The staff watches from monitors, and the press corps taps away on laptops while C.J. roams the room, doing her spin. She tells them to pay attention, the President's throwing his cap over the wall. Bartlet tells the story of the Irish lads whose journey was blocked by a wall too high to be scaled. They threw their caps over and had no choice but to follow. He asks how many times have we done that in this country—come to a wall and thrown our caps over?

In a senator's office, the aide Steve Onorato (Paul Provenza) is watching too, but his boss is having a brandy with his staff and not paying attention to the developments in the ballroom. Onorato senses something's up.

> **ONORATO**: He's gonna announce he's naming two finance reformers to the FEC.
> **SENATOR**: What the hell are you talkin' about, Steve?
> **ONORATO**: Listen.
> **SENATOR**: You said it wasn't gonna happen.
> **ONORATO**: I was wrong.

As pledged, Bartlet is being Bartlet. He unabashedly names Bacon and Calhoun to the FEC. Hearing the news unfold, the senator screams, "Josh Lyman! Get him on the phone! I'm gonna reach down his throat and take out his lungs with an ice-cream scoop!"

Donna brings Josh a cell phone, and he's ready for the call: "Why don't you take your legislative agenda and shove it up your ass," he says, snaps the phone closed, and tosses it back to Donna.

The news spreads like wildfire: The President is bucking tradition by naming his own com-

missioners. C.J. admits to the press the FEC is toothless, but the President upbraided them to symbolically prove a point. C.J.'s assistant Carol (Melissa Fitzgerald) asks Jack, a young reporter, for a follow-up. Jack asks if she's mistaking him for Danny. It's clear Danny's getting frozen out for writing about Mandy's memo.

The staff convenes at a breakfast meeting. Leo brings up drug policy, and Toby says they can make the case to the President for treatment versus enforcement. Going a step further, Sam wants to tackle mandatory minimum sentences for crack versus powder cocaine. Leo insists on undertaking one battle at a time. Leo pauses to take a call, and asks Margaret to write down some names for him to keep on file.

If Congress introduces English as the national language, California, with its large Hispanic population, will be a key state, and Al Kiefer and Joey Lucas are California specialists. In the Oval Office, Kiefer is delivering a doom-laden message to President Bartlet. With an approval rating of 42 percent, if he fights for this treatment for the war on drugs, the midterms are lost and reelection is impossible. Mandy's stepped into the room. Toby glances over at C.J., who hustles over and leads her out.

Josh says drug-control appropriations total $17.6 billion. Two-thirds are spent on enforcement, one-third on treatment, says Sam. They want to reverse the ratio. Kiefer says that the switch will make them look soft on crime.

Joey Lucas has arrived and Josh sets her up with a desk. Josh is all business, despite his special "Joey Lucas" suit, as Donna calls it, worn just for her. In the bullpen, Joey signs something for Kenny to say. "I'm not sleeping with Al Kiefer anymore." Everyone in the bullpen cranes their necks to hear the conversation. Joey remarks, "Nice suit."

Still overly self-conscious about making mistakes in the Press Room, C.J. has realized she misspoke at her briefing. She originally mentioned that the President is under no legal obligation to nominate a Democrat and a Republican to the FEC. The White House counsel argues he is responsible. Returning to campaign finance issues, Josh and Leo want Toby to arrange a meeting with a House Democrat on the Ethics Committee. Waiting, Toby says that sounds like his ex-wife. Mumbling that his meeting will indeed be with his ex-wife, Leo tells Toby to say that the President

AARON SORKIN
I never quite got Mandy right. Moira, who we know is a terrific actress, unfortunately got the worst of that. It had nothing to do with Moira and everything to do with me. I just couldn't get it to work. There was a mutual agreement toward the end of the season, "Why don't we all just shake hands and try again on something else."

Marlee Matlin

Josh and Joey's verbal fireworks are their way of hiding the fact that they really do like each other. But being two smart people who have a job to do, they know better than messing it all up by telling each other. So for now they have fun playing "will they or won't they?" I agree with Aaron—always keep them guessing. Now people don't stop me and ask about my Oscar. Instead they stop me on planes and ask, "Are you getting together with Josh?" Even the first lady asked me about Joey and Josh.

will not ask Democrats to unilaterally drop soft money. Leo asks Margaret to reach back into her memory and arrange a meeting with the list of names he'd given her.

Steve Onorato surprises Sam in his office. Sam thinks Onorato wants Josh, but Onorato has other plans. Meanwhile, Toby's having a picnic with Congresswoman Andrea "Andy" Wyatt (Kathleen York), on a patch of grass astride the Tidal Basin. As far as drug policy is concerned, she wants action on mandatory minimums. Ethically, she doesn't have a problem with what Leo's got cooking, but she wants to be there.

Steve Onorato is telling Sam that the Senate will have to confirm Bartlet's FEC nominees. However, he knows the White House is gearing up for a major drug policy initiative, and that Sam's been the point man for it. Onorato says if they dump the nominations and the campaign finance reform that rides on their coattails, there might be room to work on drug policy.

Leo reprimands C.J. for her stupid, amateur FEC mistake. A moment after that, Danny tells her it's bush league to deny him access. C.J.'s less than sympathetic after the attack. "You're on the outside lookin' in for a while, so get used to it."

C.J. has set up Leo's mystery "special event," and seven senior congressional aides are sitting in the Press Room but don't know why. Leo explains that a debate is about to begin on the best

way to fight the drug problem. The White House believes that more money should be put into drug treatment. Their bosses want to spend more on prisons. Leo shoots the starting gun.

> **LEO**: Dick, in July of '96, your boss's son was arrested for carrying twenty-five grams of cocaine. That's a crime that usually carries what, Toby?
>
> And they all turn to see TOBY standing at the back at the side. Near him is ANDY.
>
> **TOBY**: Eight to fifteen years.
>
> **LEO**: And what did the congressman's son get?
>
> **TOBY**: Six months' house arrest.

Leo's hammering his point. "The President wants a lively debate. He wants to hear opposition. But he's not going to stomach hypocrisy." Leo says if they start bleating that Bartlet's soft on crime, he's got seven great stories for the press. An aide accuses Leo of bluffing. Leo motions to Carol, who opens a door to reveal that the press is right there. Leo assures them, "We play the full nine innings at this level."

Andy admits that "it was a little fun." In the interests of full disclosure, she tells Toby she was recently on a date and her date bumped a car. A cop was going to Breathalyze him but didn't when he recognized the congresswoman. Whether of political or personal curiosity, Toby asks who she was out with. The general counsel for the Baltimore Orioles. Andy wonders if Toby's upset about the date or the fact that the guy works for the Orioles. Toby's not sure but she should keep away from the Yankees' divisional rivals, or the American League altogether.

Toby calls Sam to Josh's office and asks Sam to repeat what he just said. Sam recites that Steve Onorato came by and said if they dropped the FEC, he could warm things up on drugs. Josh and Toby chuckle at an inside joke that Sam's clearly not a part of.

> JOSH starts LAUGHING, then claps SAM on the shoulder—
>
> **JOSH**: You made the big time, Sam.
>
> **SAM**: What's goin' on?
>
> **JOSH**: He knows about Laurie.
>
> **SAM**: What do you mean?
>
> **TOBY**: He knows you're friends with a call girl.
>
> **SAM**: (beat) What does—
>
> **JOSH**: He wants to move you out to the front of the field so he can drop Laurie on you.
>
> **SAM**: Are you serious?
>
> **JOSH**: Yeah.

Sam's steamed. He feels like he's been made a fool of. He says he wants to call the senator and tell him to shove it.

JOSH: You know what this is like? This is like *The Godfather*, where Pacino's telling James Caan he's gonna kill the cop. It's a lot like that scene, only not really.

Josh finally goes to talk to Joey. On Charlie's advice, he's found a memento of the White House to give her—a coffee mug. He asks Kenny for a private moment with Joey. He tells her he wore a special suit today. "For me?" she asks. Josh nods and shyly says he's got to go.

Up in the residence, Leo is telling Bartlet he's self-conscious talking about drugs two months after announcing that he's a recovering addict. Bartlet sympathizes, but argues that there's no one better qualified to talk about treatment. C.J. comes in to apologize for her FEC gaffe. Within moments, Sam, Toby, and Josh arrive at the presidential bedside. Sam asks if the President is any closer to a decision on drugs. He says he's a day closer. There'll be more meetings tomorrow, and in the meantime everyone's got to calm down. There'll be mistakes. "Minimize them. Fix them. Move on."

BARTLET: Listen to me. I've never lost an election in my life. We do this right and people are gonna respond. You all had a good day.

He says they have to let Mandy out of the doghouse. She was doing her job, and Danny was, too. Toby lingers a little and says he saw Congresswoman Wyatt. He mentions mandatory minimums and says that Andy's right. Mandatory minimums for crack—the majority of which is used by blacks—are much higher than for powder, which is used predominantly by whites.

TOBY: That should be part of the discussion.
BARTLET: It will be.
TOBY: Good.

As the staff files out, Leo's left alone with the President. Bartlet says he's sleeping better and he's dreaming about a great discussion with experts and ideas, with energy and honesty. He says he wakes up and he thinks . . . "I can sell that." They say good night and Leo leaves him to sleep.

LIES, DAMN LIES, AND STATISTICS

In a high-end telemarketing room, thirty pollsters are at their consoles with their headsets on. The room is silent, tension hangs in the air. They're primed and ready to start the calls, but the staff is still debating the questions. Toby thinks one of them is "asymmetrical," but C.J. doesn't agree.

TOBY: Since when are you an expert on language?

C.J.: In polling models?

TOBY: Yeah.

C.J.: Nineteen ninety-three. Since when are you an uptight pain in the ass?

TOBY: Since long before that.

Leo asks for predictions on the poll results. Everyone agrees they'll hold at 42 percent approval, give or take, but C.J. forecasts, "We're gonna go up five points."

The polling details will take forty-eight hours. Sam explains that thirty callers need that time to make the 6,000 calls it takes to garner 1,500 responses. Quietly, Toby tells Sam he can't go see Laurie graduate from GW Law School tomorrow. Onorato knows about Sam's controversial friendship, and while Sam wonders what business it is of anyone's, he agrees not to go.

Leo has brought in Barry Haskel (Austin Pendleton) of the FEC and is putting on quite a show. As he walks a very nervous Haskel down the hallway, a dress marine appears to present arms. Amidst the entertainment in the corridors, Leo says he knows Barry favors banning soft money and reads him quotes he had made anonymously on the subject: "You've been outed." Haskel says he has always been outnumbered five to one on the FEC, so he never saw the sense in going public. Furthermore, Barry says his wife warned that the White House would try to dazzle him. Nonsense, says Leo, leading him to the Oval Office, where the President, the attorney general, the treasury secretary, and the CIA director just happened to be having a drink.

Laurie is in GW's law library the night before graduation. Her friend Janeane is trying to persuade her to call it quits for the evening and go out. Sam calls Laurie to explain to her that he can't be at her graduation in the morning. With a sigh, Laurie tells him she understands.

Toby's got something up his sleeve, and asks Bonnie to arrange a meeting with Ross Kassenbach. Toby wants the President's next two minutes, explaining to Sam that he found the ambassador to the Federated States of Micronesia, which Sam is not even sure is a real country.

RICHARD SCHIFF

Someone asked me, "What are your favorite moments?" My response was, "Any scene with Allison Janney." I think, in a strange way, C.J. is the only one that gets Toby or gets the whole picture. I think she and I have some kind of odd, perverse connection that will never consummate into anything other than what it is. I think we have a knowledge of each other's darkness. I think we communicate on a different level.

ALLISON JANNEY

Richard and I just have a great time together. We always just try to fill scenes out with moments that Aaron may not have intended. We always like to think of ourselves in a French movie. All these little glances and looks at each other. It's just fun to play. He likes to play and I love to play, too. We just enjoy acting with each other.

Bartlet is frustrated that despite their best efforts at getting the message out about drug treatment, Steve Onorato's spinning the story as if they want to legalize drugs. Bartlet thought he was secure at 42 percent. To brighten the mood, Toby mentions Micronesia and, needless to say, Bartlet has the national statistics at hand. Sam details the plan. The ambassador to the Federated States of Micronesia can be promoted to Paraguay, and Paraguay to Bulgaria. Ken Cochran, the Bulgarian ambassador, is having an affair with the prime minister's daughter, so Bartlet has reason to fire him. Bartlet tells Charlie to fetch Cochran and get him to D.C. It seems to Bartlet that Charlie knows Cochran, but he denies it.

With Kenny as the middle man, Joey is telling Josh there's no chance the Republicans will put English as the official language on the table. The two get testy with one another.

JOEY: Don't raise your voice to me.

JOSH: How the hell do you know if I'm raising my voice?

JOEY: *I guessed.*

C.J. is giving a press briefing on mandatory minimums. She says a federal judge is required to give anyone convicted of possessing five grams of crack five years. However, it takes a hundred times as much powder and twenty times as much heroin to receive the same sentence. And the minimums are racist, because 70 percent of powder users are white; 80 percent of crack users are black. Danny asks if the White House is making a crusade out of defending the rights of drug users, but C.J. blows him off.

After the briefing, Danny says C.J. can't stay pissed at him forever. C.J. replies that they're still talking about Mandy's memo they broke against her will. C.J.'s obviously feeling a little tender. She asks Leo why he told the President everyone thought their approval rating would hold level when she asserted they'll go up five points. Leo says he meant in general and she shouldn't read too much into it.

Everyone's still pretty tightly wound at the phone banks. C.J.'s anxious they don't miss the media window and Josh is still arguing with Joey about Republican tactics. C.J. confides to Joey that she's worried about having to tell the President she was wrong. Not about the poll numbers, she says, but about the strategy they've been using. She doesn't know how many more chances she's going to get before her time as press secretary is up.

After her graduation celebration Laurie arrives at her friend Janeane's house, where Sam's waiting on the stoop with a shopping bag next to him. He worked out a surprise with Janeane. He says he bought her a gift. It's a leather briefcase, a nice one. They hold each other and he whispers in her ear, "Way to go, Laurie." As they share the close moment, a car across the street guns its engine and takes off. Sam knows right away he's in trouble, and the next morning he has to face the music.

SAM: I've drafted a letter of resignation.

TOBY: Well, you're not going to give it to him, Sam, 'cause that would deny me the pleasure
   of throwing you out through a plate-glass window.

Leo's furious C.J. didn't tell him about Sam last night. All Sam told her was that there was a suspicious car. It took C.J. three hours to find out there was a picture and another hour to find out it was the *Mirror*. They paid Janeane $50,000 for the setup. C.J. says they'll run it today, and the U.S. press will have it tomorrow.

Sam's seeing the President with Toby. Sam maintains he never paid Laurie for sex. Toby says Sam has always been above reproach in regard to his relationship with Laurie. Bartlet asks Toby if he's sticking up for Sam.

TOBY: I know it's strange, sir, but I'm feeling a certain big-brotherly connection right now. You know, obviously I'd like that to go away as soon as possible, but for the moment I think there's no danger in the White House standing by Sam and aggressively going after the people who set him up.

The President tells Sam to make sure he broke no laws. Sam should tell Laurie the White House regrets the huge inconvenience she's about to experience and say if she passes the bar exam, the attorney general will make sure she's admitted. And congratulations to her on the degree. Sam is thunderstruck by Bartlet's generosity.

The President has parked Ken Cochran (Lawrence Pressman) in the Mural Room. First, Bartlet arranges with a friend of his to put Cochran on the board of directors of a company he runs. Then he goes to the Mural Room and informs Cochran he has to resign. Charlie has been baby-sitting Cochran, whom he clearly does know from his past. Charlie was a waiter at the Gramercy Club, which is obviously an "exclusive" club. Cochran says he resigned, he finds places like that

repugnant. Charlie notes that didn't stop him joining it. Cochran's outraged at Charlie's gall and demands to speak with his supervisor. Charlie says that would be the President, and he's about to shove Cochran out the back door. Bartlet says he *knew* Charlie knew Cochran.

Continuing in the day's tradition of pissing people off, the President meets with Senator Lobell (David Huddleston), who's in the Roosevelt Room with fourteen staffers. Apart from campaign finance, they agree that they agree on absolutely nothing.

> LOBELL: You know why?
> BARTLET: 'Cause I'm a lily-livered, bleeding heart, egghead communist.
> LOBELL: Yes, sir, and I'm a gun-toting, redneck son of a bitch.
> BARTLET: Yes, you are.
> LOBELL: So we agree on that.

Bartlet wants them to work together on soft money. Lobell says Bartlet doesn't have the votes in the House to do what he wants to do. Bartlet says he doesn't need 'em. In 1978, the FEC opened the loophole to soft money, and now they can close it again with four of the six votes. He has the two seats that just opened, plus Haskel, and Toby will take care of the fourth. Bartlet asks if he can count on Lobell's support to confirm his candidates. Lobell asks what he gets for this, and the President says he gets his thanks.

In his office, Toby meets Ross Kassenbach. Toby says the President thanks him for his work on the FEC and offers his congratulations. Kassenbach asks on what. Toby replies on being named the next ambassador to the Federated States of Micronesia.

C.J. is still feeling vulnerable. Josh tries to comfort her by explaining that Bartlet thinks of her like a daughter, but she's unmoved. C.J.'s going to retrieve the poll numbers and bring them into the Oval Office. The staff sits around waiting nervously. As they bite their lips and twiddle their thumbs, Josh can't give up his argument with Joey. He says making English the official language would safeguard against ethnic strife, wouldn't it? Joey blows a raspberry at him. Joey states that 72 percent of Hispanics strongly oppose any law on English. The Republicans will never put it on the table for fear of alienating such a large block of voters. She says, "It's ludicrous to think that laws need to be created to protect the language of Shakespeare." It is what he wanted to hear. Now everyone just sits back to await the polling results.

C.J. comes in with an envelope. She tells everyone, "I was wrong." Everyone prepares for the bad news when she says, "We went up nine points."

"Okay," says Bartlet, "what's next?"

WHAT KIND OF
DAY HAS IT BEEN

The President is holding a town hall meeting at the Newseum in Rosslyn, Virginia. It's just Bartlet, a stool, and a microphone. A moderator sits at a small desk to the side, pressing Bartlet about apathy among young voters. At the last election, only 32 percent of eighteen- to twenty-five-year-olds voted. Bartlet asserts that indifference toward politics has always been a problem, but in the end, decisions are made by those who show up. As the President winds up the meeting, Gina Toscano surveys the audience from a catwalk. Sam receives a call from a guy called Peter Jobson. Sam sees Toby across the atrium, sitting alone, very much wrapped in his own thoughts. Sam makes a gesture with his hand like a plane taking off. Toby calls over to Josh and motions the same. Josh passes the message on to Leo, though Leo's not even sure what the signal means anymore.

In the press area, Danny's tapping away at his laptop when someone hits him on the back of his head. C.J. is finally presenting Danny with a peace offering, a tip about the space shuttle *Columbia*. In front of the theater, Butterfield whispers to Gina that the President wants to watch a softball game after the meeting, so he's going straight to the car, no rope line. The President is announcing that his aide, Charlie Young, gave him a report from the Center for Policy Alternatives that says 61 percent of young people think politicians have failed their generation. Charlie's delighted that Bartlet used his material. He remembers something Josh told him on his first day in the White House.

> **CHARLIE:** (pause) You were right.
> **JOSH:** What do you mean?
> **CHARLIE:** It doesn't go away.

The town meeting comes to a close and the audience slowly disperses. There's a large crowd outside, gathered on either side of the exit route, chanting for the President. Floodlights illuminate the area. Always observant and on edge, Gina's looking all around. Something's caught her eye, but she's not sure what. Zoey falls in with her, chattering about her father's inability to stay away from rope lines. Gina's wracking her brain. She murmurs, "I saw something . . . " She realizes what she saw, whips around 180 degrees, and looks up . . .

The twelve hours before the town hall meeting had been intense. An F-117 *Nighthawk* didn't return from patrol of the no-fly zone over Iraq. The President has been in a pretty good mood until that point, joking as he rehearsed for the town meeting.

> STAFFER #4: Good morning, Mr. President.
>
> STAFFER #5: 'Morning, sir.
>
> BARTLET: Hey, Steve. Hey, Mikey. (to Charlie) Listen, have I gotten any of the names right so far?
>
> CHARLIE: No, sir, but you came damn close on a couple of 'em.

Bartlet corrals Sam to ask him why the space shuttle *Columbia* didn't land last night. Sam doesn't know, and Bartlet refers him to Toby, whose brother is a payload specialist on the flight. Sam asks Toby if he knows why the shuttle didn't land.

> SAM: You know that not only did I not know you had a brother on the space shuttle right now, I didn't know you had a brother.

Josh needs to see Vice President Hoynes, but the only time he has open is when he's jogging. Josh sighs. Not exactly the meeting he was hoping for.

Leo pulls Bartlet out of his speech rehearsal to go to the Situation Room. They've established the *Nighthawk* pilot is probably alive, but is grounded only about ten miles from the Fourth Corps of the Republican Guard. Fitzwallace has devised a rescue scenario using low-altitude helicopters. The President asks the pilot's name—Captain Scott Hotchkiss from Rhode Island. Bartlet knows there's a bounty on American planes or pilots. He says if Fitzwallace has to call this kid's parents, he's invading Baghdad.

Leo briefs C.J. on the F-117, but demands that she lie to the press

Blanche Sindelar (Property Master)
Even if the script doesn't specifically call for something, if they talk about it, we like to get some research so that everyone's walking around with their files or their stuff on the desk. The actors really appreciate it when we have real paperwork out there. The episode with Richard and his brother and the space flight, he wanted more information and more pictures to help him get in the mood of the character at that point.

about the risky rescue plan. C.J.'s immediately on guard lest they rehash what happened over India/Pakistan. It wasn't lying to the press that made C.J. uncomfortable, it was being lied to by her colleagues. Leo's putting her in the loop this time.

Sam tells Toby one of the payload bays on the shuttle wouldn't close. After researching, he knows Toby's brother is Dr. David Ziegler, who holds postgraduate degrees in physiology and biology. With this recitation of information, Sam knows more about Toby's brother than he does about Toby. Sam says the shuttle has a minor problem. Toby asks him to keep in touch with Peter Jobson at NASA and to let him know as soon as the shuttle lands.

Josh is jogging with Hoynes, with agents in front and back. Josh says that soft money is legalized bribery: over a hundred businesses gave more than $125,000 to both parties at the last election. Josh knows Hoynes has been meeting with opponents of finance reform. Josh stops and says Hoynes is backing the wrong horse. Bartlet's approval's at 51 percent. National TV exposure from

the town hall, that's another five points. If they bring the pilot back alive, it's in the high sixties. Josh says they're off to the races and Hoynes'll be wondering where everyone went.

JOSH: You've had some experience battling Jed Bartlet when he's right. And you've had some experience battling him when he's popular. Why in the world would you want to try it when he's both at the same time?

HOYNES: (pause) Josh, sometimes I wonder, if I'd listened to you two years ago, would I be President right now. (beat) You ever wonder that?

JOSH: No, sir, I know it for sure. (beat) I'm done. I appreciate the time, sir.

C.J. delivers her briefing on the *Nighthawk*. Inevitably there are questions about a rescue. Danny asks the pertinent question, speaking slowly as if to spell it out. "There've been no military moves?" C.J. says, "No."

The President's prepping again for the speech when he sees Zoey. He asks her to join them tonight at the news station. Zoey balks, saying he'll just talk about her. She changes the subject,

confessing that Charlie has something he wants Bartlet to look at. When the President confronts him later, Charlie denies that he has anything to show his boss. Sam says they should have a signal for good news of the pilot if it comes through when Bartlet's on TV. Ignoring his colleagues' rolling eyes, Sam demonstrates his liftoff gesture.

Leo congratulates Josh on catching up with Hoynes. He's hopped on board. But Leo says the President would jump out of his skin if he knew Josh had discussed a political upside of getting Hotchkiss back from Iraq. The pilot and the rescuers are in real danger. "As a guy who flew planes in a war, I was really offended too," Leo says. Josh apologizes and steps toward Leo as if they're going to hug, but Leo backs away. "*Man*, did you read that wrong."

Charlie pulls Zoey into Josh's office. He's upset at her for divulging to her father that Charlie had any agenda in the White House. Charlie says he doesn't have the same relationship with the President that Zoey and the staff do. Zoey calls Charlie a chicken. Charlie says no, these people are the smartest people in the world. With that, Josh sits down where his chair is, or would have been if there'd been a chair there. "Donna!"

Sam informs Toby there's a problem with the space shuttle door. Sam says if it were really that bad, they'd have called the President. Toby admits he reacted the way he did before because he forgot his brother was even in space.

The President demands Charlie tell him what Zoey was talking about. Charlie begins to say it's a report he's been looking at. Fitzwallace is there, so Bartlet tells Charlie to stick the report in his briefcase. Fitzwallace will wait with the President for news on the F-117. Fitzwallace comments on the presidential seal in his carpet. It's an eagle with arrows in one hand, an olive branch in the other. Usually, the eagle faces the olive branch, but when Congress declares war, the eagle faces the arrows. Fitzwallace wonders aloud if they just have another carpet lying around. The call comes and Fitzwallace picks up the phone. They have the pilot on the line. He's safe. Bartlet's thrilled and promises to look into Fitzwallace's carpet question.

C.J.'s having to deal with press queries. Carol tells her she did a good job. C.J. says she did, too. Saudi Arabia was spelled perfectly. But there's only one "l" in Tel Aviv.

As news of the rescued pilot drifts in, Danny's furious with C.J. She

John Spencer
You find out things after the fact. I didn't find out until the end of the first season that Leo was a fighter pilot in Vietnam. So that was kind of new news. I got a wife, then she left me. One's character's history accumulates in an hour drama. You don't necessarily go in with all the information like you would in a movie or a play.

looked directly at him and flatly said there was no military action. C.J. says if lying misdirected the Iraqis for even half a beat, then she can sleep fine. Danny's more upset because she called on him and made him the fool who clung to the wrong answer. He's not staying in the penalty box forever.

Before he heads for the meeting, the President finds Toby staring out of a window. Bartlet says he just talked to the shuttle mission commander, and they're trying to fire something called an RCS. If that doesn't work, the space program is full of brilliant scientists, so they have thirty-nine other things they can try. Bartlet tells Toby not to be a horse's ass; he should go to Edwards when the shuttle returns safely and talk to his brother. Toby thanks Bartlet for his concern, but recognizes that no problem in space is small.

But when Sam gets the call from Peter Jobson at the Newseum, he knows the shuttle is returning safely and Toby's brother is okay. Sam does the takeoff gesture and Toby breathes a sigh of relief. Bartlet gives his closing speech. He's been called a liberal, a populist, and a socialist tonight,

but in actuality he's an economics professor whose great-grandfather's great-grandfather was Dr. Josiah Bartlett, New Hampshire's delegate to the Second Continental Congress in the summer of 1776. Together those men wrote a document that stated, "We hold these truths to be self-evident, that all men are created equal." That was the first time anyone had thought to do that. "Decisions are made by those who show up," he says.

The mood is energetic and upbeat as the President and his staff exit the Newseum. Gina nervously scans the crowd, sensing that something is not right. In a small dark room overlooking the crowd, two handguns are being loaded. Bartlet is drawn toward the rope line, unable to ignore his supporters. Gina's looking, turning in small circles as she hunts through the crowd and the students on the horizon. Then she remembers. She sees a young man look up at a window. She looks up, too.

GINA: *Guuuuhhhn!!*

A window is open in the building across the street and GUNSHOTS begin hitting the sidewalk as three AGENTS dive for BARTLET and GINA grabs ZOEY to the ground. The STAFF instinc-

Melissa Fitzgerald (Carol)
Aaron Sorkin knows my husband, obviously he knows me too. When I read the script, I said to my husband, "This will be the best show ever on television." I ended up getting an audition and I went in and read for Staffer #2 for the pilot. A few weeks later I came to work and Aaron said, "We're going to make you C.J.'s assistant and this is going to be your desk." That was really exciting for me. It was actually a nice progression from Staffer #2 to Carol, being C.J.'s assistant. And I was so happy to be able to work with Allison. Allison is an immensely brilliant actor and she's a wonderful woman. I feel like coming to work, for me, working with her, is kind of like going to acting class, except I get paid for it.

tively look to see where the shots are coming from as the CROWD starts flying. Even the SCREAMING crowd doesn't drown out the rapid pops of GUNFIRE as we:

DISSOLVE TO

END TITLE CARD

We continue to HEAR the screaming of the crowd and the GUNFIRE along with agents shouting, "*Get down on the ground!*" We HEAR the sound of panic and finally the crackle of a radio: "*Oh, God, we've got people down.*" "*Who's been hit, who's been hit . . .*"

FADE TO BLACK

END OF SHOW

A TOUR OF
THE WEST WING

Lobby

The high-traffic, high-security area used by employees and guests of the West Wing is the Northwest Lobby. While several rooms of the main building of the White House are open to the public, the West Wing is closed to public tours. Private groups or guests are admitted to view the offices of the staff, although personal tours are only conducted after the President has left the Oval Office for the night, usually around ten o'clock.

The Roosevelt Room

As Leo's daughter Mallory pointed out to Sam, the conference room in the West Wing is named for the twenty-sixth President of the United States, Theodore Roosevelt, although it does stand in honor of all the Roosevelts. A bronze bust of Teddy Roosevelt sits on the mantel across from busts of the thirty-second President of the United States—and distant cousin—Franklin Delano Roosevelt and his wife, Eleanor. Also on the mantel sits Josiah Bartlet's Nobel Prize for Economics.

The Roosevelt Room has witnessed meetings ranging from general staff to union contract negotiations to gatherings with legislators and heads of state. It is also the formal meeting room for the President's cabinet. Traditionally, the President sits in the middle of the table, with the vice president seated on his right. Many of the staff can be found in the Roosevelt Room during informal late-night meetings, where take-out food is often brought in, which is known to attract Ainsley to any get-together.

Upper Press/Staff Bullpen

The combined bullpen of the staffs of the press secretary and the deputy chief of staff is considered off-limits to the press, but it is not unusual to see one or two members of the fourth estate milling about as they have grown close to the President's staff. Surrounding this area are the Offices of the Legislative Liaison, Political Liaison, and Inter-Governmental Affairs.

Throughout the West Wing, sets of four clocks hang on the walls representing the following time zones:

1. POTUS: Set to the time zone in which the President is currently.
2. D.C.: Set to the current time in Washington, D.C.
3. ZULU: Set to Greenwich Mean Time.
4. HOT SPOT: Set to the time zone of a military "hot spot" in the world, in this case it is Haiti.

Communications Bullpen

Formerly the offices of the White House counsel, this area was commandeered by the Communications Department upon their arrival. The first assistant or communications aide to report for work—often either Ginger or Bonnie—"opens" the communications bullpen every morning with a phone call to the switchboard, alerting them that someone is in the area to receive calls.

Press Briefing Room

The Press Briefing Room is the most public face of the White House. From this room, C.J. updates the media on the general events of the day, as well as breaking stories. The room is also the site of most presidential press conferences. Often filled with the corps and various members of the media, room capacity is only eighty-six people allowed by law. Larger press gatherings are often held in the East Room.

The room, built over the White House pool, was originally created to give the press greater access to the administration. Sam and Josh recently considered moving it across the street—into the OEOB—to free up additional space in the overcrowded West Wing. The plan quickly died when the press got wind of the idea.

The Mural Room

Named such for the artwork depicting Revolutionary War scenes covering the walls, the Mural Room is the formal reception area for guests of the White House. This room has hosted many

photo ops for the President and foreign dignitaries, such as Indonesian President Siguto. Most notably, this room served as the backdrop for the interview in which the President announced to the world that he has MS—a fact that he has been covering up for years.

According to the plaque on the wall, the fireplace in the Mural Room was a favorite of President Andrew Johnson's, who would sip whiskey from a charcoal keg while reading by its light. The flue has been welded shut since 1896. Unfortunately, Sam and Josh discovered this information too late and accidentally set fire to the room one night when the heat was out in the building.

Sam's Office

Less cluttered than his boss's office, Sam's space is an eclectic mix of formal law office and informal living space. His bookcase is filled with law books, as the former corporate lawyer often finds himself in the position of informal counsel for White House staffers. Both Josh and Toby have come to their friend in this capacity on various occasions. His desk accessories include the extensive assortment of medicines and candies of a self-proclaimed nut about dental hygiene.

Although Sam does have a computer in his office, he prefers to use a laptop, as he is often working on the run. Never is this mobile office more necessary than when he and Toby are working on the annual State of the Union—known to keep changing up to moments before it is addressed to the public.

C.J.'s Office

Though an integral part of the Communications Department, C.J.'s office is not located in the communications bullpen. This is likely due to the lack of available office space in the overcrowded West Wing. As press secretary, C.J. needs to keep tuned into world news, which accounts for the multiple televisions at her disposal. Sitting in a bowl on her desk are reminders of the lighter side of her job, in the form of decorated eggs from the annual Easter egg hunt and Easter egg roll.

C.J. also keeps a pet goldfish named Gail in her office that was a gift from reporter Danny Concannon. Josh had led Danny to believe that C.J. liked pet goldfish, when in reality her interest leaned more toward the cocktail crackers of the same name and design. C.J. decided to keep the gift anyway.

Toby's Office

Toby's usually cluttered office reflects the typically busy day of the White House communications director. An activist in his youth, his office reflects a proud history of civil disobedience—reminiscent of the days he spent protesting with his older sisters. An Amnesty International painting hangs on his wall; his bulletin board is littered with bumper stickers calling for peace and world harmony. For inspiration he has a photo of John F. Kennedy, his brother Edward, and Theodore Sorensen by his desk. Sorensen is considered arguably the most talented presidential speechwriter in history.

The couch in Toby's office has been known to double as a bed for busy staffers, such as Sam, who have not had the time, or desire, to go home. As a stress reliever and aid to his thought process, Toby has recently started bouncing a rubber ball against the wall of his office. If his neighbor, Sam, minds, he certainly hasn't said anything to this point. The pair shares a glass wall between offices. This helps when they need to get each other's attention during crunch times.

Donna's Office

Situated in the staff bullpen is the desk of Donna Moss, assistant to the deputy chief of staff. Her boss, Josh, can often be heard yelling out to her from his office that is conveniently located only a few steps away. She rarely answers when bellowed to in this manner. Donna has personalized her desk area with numerous mementos and photos of herself with Josh. This is just one example of their close working relationship.

Josh's Office

Josh considers his office a sanctuary and often tries to hide in there even though this is the first place people, like C.J., would go looking for him when he is in trouble. The room, however, is not truly a safe haven, because the ceiling did once nearly fall in on him during construction in an upstairs office.

Josh often conducts meetings in his office with most of his staff. Donna always has fruit and danish for the meetings, causing other staffers, such as Sam, to sometimes interrupt on a food run. Josh's office looks out toward the Northwest Executive Entrance to the West Wing and Donna can often be found waiting there, looking out to be ready for his return to the building.

Leo's Office

With the exception of the President's outer office, this is the only "room" in the White House with direct access to the commander in chief, which comes in handy during times of crisis, both national and personal. Leo's assistant, Margaret, makes sure the doorway between the two rooms is closed during private meetings. The room also serves as an informal meeting room for Leo's staff and guests. The senior staff can often be found adjourning to this office following meetings with the President.

Leo has decorated his office largely with a nautical design reflected through the model ships and paintings throughout the room. Model airplanes also accent his office as a reminder that Leo served in Vietnam with pride as a pilot.

President's Outer Office

Directly off the Mural Room is the President's outer office. This is the shared office space of the President's secretaries, including the late Mrs. Landingham, and his personal aide, Charlie. Mrs. Landingham filled the office with photos of the President and artwork sent to the White House by children. The centerpiece to the room, and often the largest conversation piece, is the U.S. flag made of children's handprints hung on the wall.

Across from Mrs. Landingham's desk sits the workspace of Charlie Young. Though much of the decor of the outer office was set before Charlie joined the staff, he has personalized his area with photos and artwork of jazz musicians. Charlie moves back and forth between the two desks on his side of the room.

The Oval Office

The centerpiece to the Oval Office is the famous "Kennedy desk," so nicknamed as JFK was the first to bring it into the room, as each President chooses his own decor. Many will recall the famous photo of President Kennedy sitting behind the desk while his son, John Jr., peeked out from the open kneehole. The desk, also known as the *Resolute* desk, was built from the wood of the *HMS Resolute* and given as a gift from England in appreciation for the U.S. finding and returning the missing ship years earlier.

The French doors, fitted with Restoration glass, open out onto the portico leading to the Rose Garden. When the right combination of doors is open in the West Wing, a wind tunnel is created that ends in the office, blowing open one of the glass doors. The President usually leaves for the residence every evening by way of the portico, as opposed to walking through the West Wing.

The Oval Office is, by far, one of the most famous rooms in the world. Yet, even with its public face, it has seen its share of private moments. One of the most formal rooms in the building, the President is often able to relax his title when the doors are closed and treat his staff as

the family they have become. However, even in the most relaxed setting, the room still stands as one that demands respect. Mrs. Landingham was always the first to police the language used in the room, making sure offensive words like "klutz" and "geek" were never spoken. Bartlet himself insists on the use of his title "Mr. President" while in the Oval Office, even by longtime friends. For in this room he is not just a man, he is the leader of the free world and is often called upon to make decisions that can be too much for a single man to bear. In the Oval Office, Jed Bartlet serves as the full embodiment of the President of the United States.

When some of the staff from the Clinton White House came to visit *The West Wing* set, they wanted their pictures taken at the *Resolute* desk, because they said it looked so real and they wouldn't be allowed to sit at the real desk.

SEASON TWO

" . . . in order to form a more perfect union . . ."

IN THE SHADOW OF TWO GUNMEN, PART I

It's a matter of minutes after the shooting. The President's limo speeds over the Arlington Memorial Bridge at eighty miles an hour. Inside, Butterfield tells Bartlet that Zoey's safe but he can't speak to her, she's vomiting in her car. The men are stunned and expressionless, breathing hard. The President asks if anyone died and the agent doesn't think so. Bartlet just noticed that Butterfield has a blood-soaked handkerchief wrapped around his hand. He tells the driver to get to a hospital but Butterfield says he has to secure Potus in the White House. Suddenly, Butterfield sees blood on the President's mouth. He reaches around the back of the President's coat to check him out. He looks at his hand and it's covered in blood. Butterfield shouts to the driver, "GW! *Blue! Blue! Blue!*"

Outside the Newseum, the chaos has subsided but only a little. Witnesses are giving statements and paramedics attend to the wounded. C.J. hit her head; she says someone pulled her down to the ground. Sam tells her Bartlet's on his way back to the White House. Gina talks to the ID agent. She says there were two shooters and they got them from the roof. But there was a signal from the ground. That means someone's still out there. She describes a white male, twenty to twenty-five, five foot ten with a baseball cap. The agent needs to know what kind of cap but for the life of her, Gina can't describe it. The agent barks orders: fix a perimeter, close the airports, get the harbor patrol and the Coast Guard.

Toby's looking for Josh. Charlie thinks he got in a car with Leo but Toby says he didn't. Finally Toby sees Josh sitting to the side, leaning against a low wall. Toby asks, "Did you hear me shouting for you?" Toby gets closer. When he's in front of Josh he sees why he hasn't answered. His chest is covered in blood.

In the George Washington University Hospital Emergency Room it's a fairly light night. The phone rings, the duty nurse picks it up but there's no one there. She sees it's not the ER phone but the second phone, a special red one with a single line. When she picks it up, Butterfield says, "We're coming in." The nurse is asking if it's a drill when motorcycles roar outside in a scream of sirens. It's not a drill. She hangs up the phone and shouts, "Blue, blue!" Staff and Secret Service agents flood the ER. Eagle's two minutes away.

Blissfully unaware, Hoynes is doing a photo op with the USC women's volleyball team when an eight-man Secret Service detail just about kidnaps him.

The President is wheeled into the ER. He's been shot in the abdomen. Entry and exit wounds are visible. Vitals are read off: BP 134 over 78, pulse 108, pulse ox 98. Bartlet has to talk to Leo before he's given any anesthesia. He runs down the drill: Get the cabinet and the Security Council together and suspend trading on the stock exchange. Bartlet knows the next hours are perilous.

Abbey Bartlet is told about the procedure and finds the anesthesiologist.

ABBEY: There are fourteen people in the world who know this, including the Vice President, the chief of staff, and the chairman of the Joint Chiefs. You're gonna be the fifteenth. Seven years ago my husband was diagnosed with a relapsing-remitting course of MS. (beat) When this is over, tell the press or don't tell the press. It's entirely up to you.

Leo sees Gina standing by herself in the ER. She's beating herself up because she can't tell the troopers and field agents what they're looking for. Leo tries to help, saying Gina did her job by getting Zoey in the car. Josh is brought in. He's in much worse shape than Bartlet. A bullet collapsed his lung. Josh is losing pressure and he might be delirious.

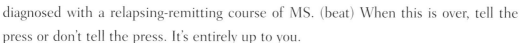

It's a flashback to three years before and Senator John Hoynes of Texas is conducting a big strategy meeting with about eighteen staffers, one of whom is Josh. Hoynes doesn't want to talk about Social Security thirteen weeks before the New Hampshire primary. Josh is a lone voice in the room who thinks he should. Hoynes pulls Josh aside. He says Josh has been pissed off at every meeting for a month. Josh says Hoynes is the prohibitive favorite

Stockard Channing
When Aaron first suggested to me that I'd be a doctor and about the MS, I said, "You're opening a can of worms." The first year, we sort of made it go away. Then this year, in the beginning, when he was shot, I bit the bullet. That's another side of Abigail's character. Though she despises politics, you wouldn't want to play cards with her. She went for high stakes when she tells the doctor, "You have a choice." It's a very tough-minded thing that I'm rather intrigued by.

for the nomination; he has $58 million in a war chest, but "I don't know what we're *for*." Hoynes says they'll run a good campaign and Josh is going to have a big role in the White House. Until then he should cheer up and get off his ass about Social Security.

Leo McGarry has come to see Josh, and from the way Josh calls him "Mr. Secretary," it's evident they're not pals. He wants Josh to come to Nashua to hear Jed Bartlet speak, but Josh, who works for Senator Hoynes, wonders why he should bother. " 'Cause that's what sons do for old friends of their fathers," says Leo.

JOSH: Leo, the Democrats aren't gonna nominate another liberal academic governor from New England. I mean we're dumb, but we're not that dumb.

LEO: (he smiles) Nah. I think we're exactly that dumb.

A few states away, Sam Seaborn is working on a deal to acquire oil tankers for a client. A dozen lawyers and executives sit around the table in a conference room at the law firm of Gage Whitney Pace. Sam's job is to limit the client's liability with a shield that masks the assets behind a wall of debt, and although it's not his dream job, he seems set. He's making partner in a month and getting married in September. Sam returns to his office to gather some paperwork and finds Josh standing forlornly in the hallway. The old buddies greet one another, and Josh gets right to the point. He wants Sam to quit the law firm to write speeches for Hoynes. Sam's not convinced: he doesn't think Hoynes is the real thing.

JOSH: If I see the real thing in Nashua, should I tell you about it?

SAM: You won't have to.

JOSH: Why?

SAM: You've got a pretty bad poker face.

*   *   *

A doctor tells Abbey that Bartlet's going to be fine, but a bullet lacerated Josh's pulmonary artery. Abbey tells the staff, who've gathered at the hospital, what's going on.

Leo is in the Situation Room. Fitzwallace isn't there—he was on his way to Manila but his plane has turned around. Hoynes comes in and some of the military have to be reminded to come to attention. Hoynes says he wants the shooters' accomplice in an hour or he's federalizing the National Guard. There's more. National Security Advisor Nancy McNally (Anna Deavere Smith) says satellite pictures show Republican Guard movement in Iraq. Leo's not worried; they do this every few months. But McNally says they're headed south and it's been only hours since Iraqi airspace was invaded rescuing the F-117 pilot. She recommends that Fitzwallace put the Thirty-second Tactical on ready alert and take them to Def Con 4. Leo says the President's under anesthesia and they have time. McNally says they don't.

> There's silence as everyone looks to HOYNES . . .
> HOYNES: (beat) Nancy, we're gonna follow Leo for the moment.

Leo wants to get a message to Iraq: "Don't mess with us tonight."

Josh's procedure is going to take twelve to fourteen hours, and the doctor suggests the staff leave. Donna's just arrived and she sensed something was badly wrong when she came in. Toby tells her Josh was hit. She can't believe it; the horror silently takes hold of her.

Everyone with any kind of credentials is jammed into the press briefing room. Danny asks C.J. if there has been any discussion of the Twenty-fifth Amendment. C.J. says, "No, the President's wounds are relatively superficial." She won't answer questions about the shooters or about a manhunt. Someone asks why the President was allowed to exit a building in the open air with no tent or canopy. She won't talk about that, either.

After the briefing, C.J. realizes she's lost her necklace in the chaos of the past few hours. She's trying to remember what happened last night. Danny says the President's been under anesthesia for an hour and there's been no use of the Twenty-fifth Amendment, so who's in charge? C.J. can't answer.

In Leo's office, McNally is arguing for Def Con 4. She says there was more than one shooter, plus a signaler on the ground. They have to assume they're under attack. Leo says counsel is advising that Hoynes might not be able to order the alert, because the President has to sign a letter handing over power to the vice president and he didn't.

> NANCY: Absent the Twenty-fifth, the Constitution doesn't give it to him unless the President's dead.
> TOBY: He's hemorrhaging, he's supposed to draft a memo?

Toby tells C.J. to hold off Danny, who's like a dog digging for a bone with his questions. She says she was asked about the canopy but she's not going to answer questions on protection procedure. Toby gives Ginger a big hug and asks if she's okay.

*   *   *

Flashback three years and Toby's in Hank's Tavern in Nashua at three o'clock in the afternoon. He's asked his fellow barfly to come hear his boss, Bartlet, campaign at the VFW tonight. She asks Toby if he's any good at his job. How many campaigns has he won? Toby adds them up. That would be none. She asks him why he's drinking and Toby says he's about to be fired.

A few stragglers file in as Bartlet is speaking at the VFW hall. The house is about three-quarters full and he isn't commanding its full attention. There's something about his manner that tells us he's not fully committed to the idea of doing any of this. Josh is there but even he hasn't taken his coat off. As Bartlet speaks, Cal, an aide, is trying to get Toby to tell him what he advised Bartlet to say if asked about the New England DFC. Toby says he told him to tell the truth. Bartlet is duly asked about the New England Dairy Farming Compact he voted against in Congress. The questioner says it hurt him. He's a Bartlet voter and he wants an explanation.

Bartlet says, "Yeah, I screwed you on that one." He says he hosed him and a lot of his constituents. But one in five children lives in poverty. Bartlet says there is an unwritten commandment: "We shall give our children better than we ourselves received."

> **BARTLET**: I voted against that bill 'cause I didn't want to make it harder for people to buy milk. (beat) I stopped some money from going into your pocket. If that angers you, if you resent me, I completely respect that. But if you expect anything different from the President of the United States, you should vote for someone else.

Bartlet gets polite applause at best. It wasn't his crowd and the last answer wasn't what they wanted to hear. Except for one guy: Josh is stunned. He looks over and sees Leo McGarry eyeing him, as if saying I told you so.

* * *

At 1:45 A.M., the President is out of his operation. He's already asking, "What's next?"

* * *

Bartlet is sitting with his aides after the speech at the VFW. He's cranky and disconnected. He can't relate to these guys. Once Bartlet's left the room, Cal says they have to talk about what happened tonight. Toby says he means Bartlet's last answer. But he's just guessing because he's pretty drunk. It looks like Toby is done. Cal tells him they can talk about it in his room. Leo says he has no time for such niceties. Then he fires everyone except Toby. All Leo says to Toby is, "Don't screw up."

When Leo tells Bartlet what he did, Bartlet says Leo kept the only one he didn't know. Leo says the others were worthless. He made the decision because Bartlet's a crappy politician. In his defense, Bartlet says New Hampshire sent him to Congress and made him governor. "Big deal," says Leo, Bartlet's family founded the state. Bartlet asks Leo why he's doing this. Leo's bigger in the party than he is. He asks, half-joking, if it's one of the twelve steps.

LEO: I'm tired of it. Year after year after year after year, having to choose between the lesser of who cares. Of trying to make myself get excited about the candidate who can speak in complete sentences. Of setting the bar so low I can't even look at it. They say a good man can't get elected President; I don't believe that, do you? I have skills and I'm gonna use 'em to get a man elected President. A *man*. A full-grown American man.

Leo says he's bringing in new people: Josh Lyman, Sam Seaborn, C. J. Cregg. He says that Josh is on a train deciding to join and he'll see Sam in New York. Leo's worked with him before. Toby's going to California to get C. J. Cregg. Leo says that Bartlet will admire these people. They'll inspire him and be loyal. Bartlet will lead them and they'll follow him wherever he goes.

* * *

Bartlet is looking at Josh being operated on. He says, "Look what happened."

IN THE SHADOW OF
TWO GUNMEN, PART II

A small television above the bar trumpets news of Josh Lyman's surgery, while the late-night clientele of the Dixie Pig Bar B-Q watches with mild interest. A young man scowls at the TV and grinds his cigarette into a plate, a swastika tattooed on his hand. He steps out the door, and dazzled by light and noise, is immediately surrounded by an army of law enforcement and military with enough firepower for a small war.

Still surrounded by a throng of reporters with notepads and flashbulbs, C.J. keeps the details to a minimum. She admits that a suspect is in custody, and reports that Josh will be in surgery another six to eight hours. Wearily watching the briefing from the vinyl chairs of the hospital, the staff huddles together and tries to sort out the tasks ahead. Sam has to return to the White House to talk to Nancy McNally about a letter the President was supposed to sign to release power to the vice president. Reporters are still inquiring why the President left the Newseum in open air rather than under the protection of a Secret Service canopy, and Toby volunteers to investigate. Sam eyes Toby knowingly, and says they were all in the meeting. . . .

*   *   *

Sam is back in a meeting in his law firm's conference room and the room is abuzz as lawyers are going over final details of the tanker deal. Sam sits silent until he can no longer bear it; he says when he was a congressional aide they used to say no idea was too stupid. In that spirit, he tells the client they shouldn't buy these obsolete, twenty-year-old ships with poor construction and even poorer steering and navigation devices. They should buy new ones that won't sink. The clients and lawyers stare at him with a mixture of surprise and disgust.

Meanwhile, Josh is at a pay phone in a downpour, trying desperately to remember the name of Sam's firm. Sam is telling his increasingly irritated clients they should spend the extra eleven million for a better ship. His passion is earnest: remember the *Exxon Valdez*, the *Amoco Cadiz?* His pleading trails off as he sees Josh at the conference room door, soaked through. Josh doesn't say a word. His unexpected arrival and bad poker face tell Sam all he needs to know. He's seen the real deal. Offering no explanation, Sam walks out of the conference room and away from his career in corporate law. Dumbfounded, his boss asks him where he's going and Sam replies, "New Hampshire."

*   *   *

The White House is a flurry of activity, and the chaos and questions seem never-ending. C.J. asks Sam if he saw who pulled her to the ground behind a police car as the bullets hailed down on them. Her necklace came off but her memory of the night is fuzzy. C.J.'s distraction is apparent, and Sam offers to do any morning shows for her. Danny still wants to know who was in charge the three and a half hours Bartlet was under anesthesia. C.J. can't offer an answer—she tells him they're working on it.

*   *   *

Three years before, C.J.'s jarred out of her sleep as her phone rings at 6:30 in the morning at her home in Los Angeles. She rushes to work, Triton Day PR in Beverly Hills, to find Roger Becker is one unhappy client. He complains his movie studio only got two minor Golden Globe nominations for its $20,000 a month. What's more, he fell from third to ninth on *Premiere* magazine's One Hundred Most Powerful People in Hollywood list. Yanked from her sleep, C.J. skips the niceties and moves straight to bluntness—Roger's movies were bad. Her boss, Isobel, intervenes, pulling C.J. into the hallway. Roger wants her fired and the firm needs his business. It takes a moment for C.J. to realize she's being canned. Swallowing the little pride she has left, C.J. asks for a taxi to be called; she couldn't get her contacts in that morning and broke her glasses as well, so she can't drive.

When she's dropped off at home, a box of her personal belongings in her hand, she notices a rental car in her driveway. She goes around the back of the house and calls out. Toby, relaxing in a lawn chair, responds, but C.J. can't make out who's lounging on her patio. She realizes it's Toby and starts to ask what he's doing there, but she's taken a corner too soon and falls into her pool. Toby's fairly unconcerned: he knows C.J. pretty well. C.J.'s wondering how her day could get any worse. She curtly tells Toby to avert his eyes because her clothes will be clingy.

Back on dry land, Toby tells C.J. the nice story he's concocted to reel her in. Jed Bartlet likes her work and wants her to join the campaign as his press secretary. C.J. is no fool—she knows Bartlet has never heard of her. Toby confesses he's there on Leo McGarry's instructions. He wants her.

C.J.: How much does it pay?

TOBY: What were you making before?

C.J.: Five hundred fifty thousand a year.

TOBY: This pays six hundred dollars a week.

C.J.: So this is less.

TOBY: Yeah.

RICHARD SCHIFF: It was my idea. Who did they write that for?

ALLISON JANNEY: They wrote that for Leo. For John Spencer.

RICHARD: I said, "You know it makes sense, given the way that we interact, that we have a history and that I went and got her." And they immediately agreed. John was great. "You know what, that makes sense."

ALLISON: Richard is so smart that way. He can think of things like that.

RICHARD: See, she's just being complimentary because I'm sitting here.

ALLISON: No I'm not! Shut up. That solidified our relationship more. There's a history before that moment that you saw poolside.

RICHARD: When someone doesn't have a strong reaction to someone falling in a pool, there must be a lot of history.

ALLISON: That's very true.

C.J. says she's worked statewide, never national. Toby says it's graduation day.

*   *   *

In the hospital, Butterfield's telling Bartlet what they know. Charlie is called into the room, and Bartlet tells him the guy they picked up is named Carl LeRoy; he and the shooters were members of West Virginia White Pride. Everyone gives Charlie a moment to absorb this. He asks if they tried to kill the President because of him and Zoey. Butterfield says the President wasn't the target and without another word, Charlie understands. He leaves the room and Zoey goes after him.

Leo is explaining to Margaret that before the President went under anesthesia, he should have signed a letter temporarily handing over power to the vice president. Margaret tells Leo she can sign the President's name. In fact, she has it down pretty good.

LEO: You can sign the President's name?

MARGARET: Yeah.

LEO: On a document removing him from power and handing it to someone else?

MARGARET: Yeah. (beat) Or do you think the White House counsel would say it was a bad idea?

LEO: I think the White House counsel would say it's a coup d'état.

Bartlet's new team—Toby, Josh, Sam, and C.J.—is watching campaign coverage on television at his storefront headquarters. Volunteers are working the phones, taking around coffee, being busy. On the TV, Bartlet is the top story with a surprisingly strong showing in a straw poll. The anchor says they're going to Bartlet, but he's not there. The failed TV interview is symbolic of the entire campaign: it's not a particularly smooth operation and Bartlet doesn't know who anyone is. His staff has a game plan. They want him to leave New Hampshire. He'll win his home state primary whatever he does and Hoynes can fight it out with Wiley for second. Toby says they should go to South Carolina and be the first ones in. If he beats Wiley, Wiley'll drop out and Bartlet will pick up his money at least. Then if they split the next four states, Hoynes has lost half the actual primaries going into Super Tuesday. Hoynes'll win the South, they'll win the North and Northwest.

TOBY: This race is gonna be decided a week later in Illinois.

C.J.: Illinois is gonna be High Noon.

LEO: Sam, if we win in Illinois, do we have a shot at California and New York?

SAM: If we win in Illinois, we're gonna run the table.

Bartlet deadpans, that the people are saved the bother of even voting. "What's next?"

JOSH: I feel bathed in the warm embrace of the candidate, Leo.

LEO: He's very easy to like once you get to know him.

JOSH: How many people get that far?

LEO: Not that many.

Josh finds a woman in his tiny office answering his phone. Donnatella Moss introduces herself as Josh's new assistant, though Josh is unaware he had an old assistant. Donna says she's a volunteer who drove in from Madison, Wisconsin. It turns out that she wasn't exactly assigned to Josh, she just showed up.

Donna says she's a college graduate with a degree in political science and government. Actually she's just a couple of credits short. At Wisconsin she majored in political science and government, but also in sociology and psychology. And biology for a while with a minor in French. And drama. She tells him the truth—she had to drop out. From the start, Josh is messing with Donna. He gets her to admit she left school to pay the bills until her boyfriend finished his residency. And he broke up with her? Josh asks. No, says Donna, she broke up with *him*.

Donna says she's serious about this job. Josh says there are no passengers. She wants to come to Charleston, she'll pay her own way. Donna's sure he'll find her valuable. The phone rings. Donna waits, then answers it. Josh dangles an ID tag in front of her.

*   *   *

Donna is watching Josh being operated on, her hand on the ID tag.

It's Tuesday morning. C.J. wants to see Sam. She tells him he was good on the morning shows, and admits she couldn't go on TV and talk about what happened, because she couldn't remember anything beyond being knocked down and the police car window exploding. She lost her necklace. But listening to Sam on TV, she says she knew.

> **C.J.:** I think you have my necklace.
>
> **SAM:** (pause) I didn't want you to feel beholden to me. I didn't want it to be like an episode of *I Dream of Jeannie* where now you have to save my life or the time/space continuum—
>
> **C.J.:** Sam—
>
> **SAM:** —or following me around with coconut oil and hot towels—
>
> **C.J.:** Sam. I don't—coconut oil?
>
> **SAM:** I'm just saying—
>
> **C.J.:** I don't feel beholden to you.
>
> **SAM:** (pause) Why not? I saved your life.

Toby is telling Ron Butterfield they both know that the Secret Service got a memo saying Bartlet didn't like being enclosed in a canopy or a tent. That's why he was out in the open at the Newseum. Toby wrote the memo and urged Bartlet to sign it. Toby says he doesn't want the Secret Service blamed. He wants to make the memo public. Butterfield says, "No, it wasn't anybody's fault. It was an act of madmen." They secured the President and Zoey in their cars and got the shooters in nine-point-two seconds. Butterfield says he'd never allow Toby not to let him protect the President.

Alternate scene:
Danny goes on to ask Leo what he's been bugging C.J. about. Who was in charge when the President was under anes-thesia? Leo says there was no constitutional crisis, but they did blow it on the letter. He didn't want the cabinet voting on the Twenty-fifth because it says the President is mentally incapacitated. And that's the only way the vice president could have gotten authority. Leo tells Danny it turns out the vice president isn't a power-hungry man. He says there were disagreements, but there was an unspoken assumption that he spoke for the President. "But if you're asking who was in charge, I was."

C.J. pauses during her briefing to make a point to the press about shooting victims. She says last night there were more victims than the President and Josh. There were thirty-six homicides, 480 sexual assaults, 3,411 robberies, 3,685 aggravated assaults, all with guns. Having a gun doesn't save you; the President was protected by the best-trained armed guards in history. Danny and Leo are watching. Danny says she's good and Leo agrees.

*　　*　　*

In a large suite at the Sheraton Centre Hotel in Chicago, Bartlet's team is watching the Illinois primary results. The room's stuffed with people, room service carts, and fax machines. Staff members are gathered around TVs in clumps. Josh is trying to call home, his dad had chemo that day. The exit polls are good but Bartlet is still shouting at people.

Josh tells Abbey her husband's a son of a bitch. She says he's not ready yet, he's terrified. Josh asks if he's gonna *be* ready? Right then, the primary is called for Bartlet. The room erupts in unfettered joy. Someone turns up a song on a tape deck and everyone starts singing and dancing to the music. Donna comes to find Josh. Josh tells her to get happy but Donna says no. She tells Josh his father died.

Josh sits alone at the airport, waiting for his flight home for his father's funeral. As he waits for his flight to be called, he notices a guy in a dark suit plant himself by a pillar. A few minutes later, another, wearing an earpiece. He hears his name and turns to see Bartlet. Josh tells him his father had a pulmonary embolism, which led to cardiac arrest. Quickly reentering political director mode, Josh tells the governor he should be back at the ballroom. Bartlet steps out of his candidate persona and into a more human one. He tells Josh his father was proud of him. *He's* a father, so he knows. Sighing, Bartlet admits he's been a jackass to Josh and all the campaign staff. But he knows what they've given up to work for him and how valuable they are. Bartlet offers to go with Josh, and Josh knows he would, but he insists that Bartlet get to California, and back on the campaign trail. When Josh has gone, Bartlet seems more reconnected, in touch with the reasons he wanted to be President in the first place. He turns to Leo and says confidently,. "I'm ready." The plan has played out; Bartlet is making his nomination acceptance speech before the massive convention crowd.

Aaron Sorkin

Martin and Brad just astonished me in that scene. It was beautiful.

*　　*　　*

Josh wakes up in the hospital after his operation, Bartlet and Leo huddled over his bed. Josh's expression is oddly undistressed, almost blank. The room is silent for a long time. Josh tries to say something, but it's barely audible. The President leans in to hear.

LEO: What'd he say?

BARTLET: (pause) He said, "What's next?"

THE MIDTERMS

C.J. is getting ready for a press briefing. Josh is on the speakerphone from his hospital bed. He must be recovering nicely because he's giving C.J. a hard time, trying to get her to lead with physicists announcing a model for the grand unified theory. C.J. keeps saying "psychics." Senior staff are coming at C.J. from all sides. Toby needs her to spin some inflation figures and Leo wants to focus on a housing regulation. Sam tells her Congressman Grant Samuels died. She leads with Samuels. Then C.J. starts to talk about psychics at Cal Tech and the Fermi Lab . . . Josh, watching on TV, bangs his head against his headboard.

It's August 14, twelve weeks before the midterms. At a meeting in the

Allison Janney
Starting it off, there were five scenes done together and I had to be the link all the way through. I just loved it. I couldn't get enough of it. It felt like I was on the stage. I just carried it all the way through. I just loved the opportunity to do that.

Roosevelt Room the staff is looking ahead to the elections. Toby says their approval rating is 81 percent. Sam thinks the numbers are soft, C.J. disagrees.

> TOBY: Still, eighty-one percent . . .
>
> SAM: You're moved by the show of support.
>
> TOBY: No, I'm thinking we got shot at and nineteen percent of the country still hates our guts.
>
> SAM: Well, you're a glass-is-half-empty kind of guy.
>
> TOBY: No, I'm a who-cares-how-full-the-glass-is-if-it's-filled-with-turpentine kind of guy.

Ed thinks they have a good shot at taking back the House. Larry says that they might possibly pick up two seats in the Senate. They look at specific seats. Florida nine? "No way," says C.J.

Toby wants to take advantage of their approval numbers and go after guns and hate groups. Leo tells C.J. if anyone asks about the linkage between approval numbers and the shooting, say the President is gratified by the support, but he wants to concentrate on the issues. Toby asks which issues and Bartlet says he'll let them know.

Later, C.J. tells Toby they're getting interview requests for pieces on how the staff is coping psychologically with the shooting. She doesn't want to do them. Bartlet tells Leo that Elliot Roush is running for the school board in Manchester. Years ago, Bartlet beat him in his first congressional campaign. Bartlet wants poll numbers on the school board contest.

Sam has a meeting with a well-dressed and clean-cut guy named Tom Jordan and his wife, Sarah. Sam studied law with Jordan at Duke. Sam is extremely matter-of-fact: They want Jordan to run for Grant Samuels's seat in Congress. Sam says Jordan's perfect: a graduate of Oberlin and Duke, he's a prosecutor with a great conviction record and the number one issue for the women voters is crime. He'll have the full weight of the DNC, the Congressional Campaign Committee, the minority leader, and the President. And he has five minutes to decide if he wants to run.

In the second act, Toby's excited. He tells Sam he knows how to go after hate groups without it appearing random and in violation of their civil liberties. The FBI can investigate *all* extremist organ-

izations under cover of investigating this one crime. He thinks he's found his vehicle, but Donna stops him in his tracks. Josh needs his recovery time, and rule number one is firm: no visitors.

Zoey's looking for her dad when she runs into Leo. She confides that Charlie's been down, he feels a lot of responsibility for the attack in Rosslyn. Yes, Leo says matter-of-factly, he's the reason the President was shot and Josh almost died. They both decide it would be better if they word that differently when consoling Charlie.

Bartlet is obsessed with Elliot Roush and the school board race in Manchester. The guy keeps popping up in Bartlet's life, and he makes the Spanish Inquisition look like Barbara Walters. He's currently polling 46 percent and Bartlet so desperately wants to pop his political balloon.

The wheels in Toby's head are turning. He wants hate groups to register their affiliation with the FBI. Sam points out that similar laws were passed in the South during the civil rights movement, much to the chagrin of the National Association for the Advancement of Coloured People (NAACP). They might have been unconstitutional but Toby thinks they might work now. C.J. pulls Sam aside to tell him there's a problem with Tom Jordan. It seems he has made a lot of preemptive challenges against black jurors during his law career. She tells him to look into it.

Dulé Hill

The scenes were hard for me to do because of Charlie's relationship with the President and even because of my relationship with Martin. It's hard even to come at Martin, for me to raise my voice to him, to be insubordinate to him, let alone the President.

Martin Sheen

Dulé is very special. People don't even know, he's one of the great tap dancers in the world. He's a class dancer. And now he's recognized as a talented young dramatic actor. To have watched him flower. He's become like a son in many ways. I just adore him. I adore the way the relationship has grown.

It's October 20, three weeks before the election. Bartlet's working in the Oval Office into the night, and he still has a few hours' worth of calls to make. A few of them are campaign calls which, he explains to Charlie, he technically cannot make from the Oval Office. His shoulders sagging with stress and exhaustion, Charlie asks the President why he doesn't just stay there and make the damn . . . the word "damn," the rudeness, and the insubordination came out before Charlie could censor himself. Bartlet pauses, recovers from his shock, and explains why he won't solicit contributions from the Oval Office, the power seat of the United States. Charlie quietly finishes up his duties and steps out.

Charlie's walking away from the Oval Office when he notices lights on in the Roosevelt Room. There's a little boy in there, his head barely visible above the table. Five-year-old Jeffrey Mackintosh has come with his dad, Andrew, who's installing software in the West Wing. Andrew explains that Jeffrey's mother works nights; Charlie's been in that boat before.

Leo has to break bad news to Sam about Tom Jordan. The papers are reporting that he was a member of an all-white fraternity. Sam's checked that out, they just happened not to have any black pledges. But you pair that with the preemptive challenges in *voir dire*, says Leo, and African American leaders have a problem. It's over; he is going to cancel the President's stop and shut down Jordan's money. Sam protests, explaining that he promised their full support. If they walk away now, then Jordan's a racist, and the White House said so. He's thirty-five and he's finished in politics and as a prosecutor. Sam walks out, slamming the door.

C.J. has been thinking about the aftermath stories everyone's wanting them to do. She goes to speak her mind to Toby. She acknowledges that there might be a psychological aftermath, and wonders if he should talk to someone. He's been ignoring his responsibilities so he can behave like the director of the FBI.

TOBY: Well, I'm waiting for the director of the FBI to behave that way.

C.J.: Toby—

TOBY: I'm waiting for the Justice Department, I'm waiting for Congress, I'm waiting for the White House to behave that way.

C.J.: You wanna lock up everybody with a white sheet?

TOBY: Yes I do. Yes I do. Who has a problem with that? Bring 'em to me right now. Yes I do.

The President tells C.J. he wants to talk about Elliot Roush on the record. C.J. chides him gently—he can't take sides in a school board election. Elliot Roush . . . Bartlet can barely bring himself to say the name. His loathing is palpable. Bartlet says he's known towering men, men of faith and peace, all kinds of people. Then there's Elliot Roush.

It's the day of the election. Tom and Sarah Jordan have come to see Sam. Sarah's incensed, more steamed than her husband. She knows they dumped Tom. Sam's not even going to try to deny it. "That's how we do it," says Sam.

Toby goes to see Bartlet in the Oval Office. Bartlet jokes with Toby about having his first-ever egg cream. Toby knows about egg creams, "we invented them in Brooklyn." Bartlet figures Toby wants to ask for a leave of absence. "No problem," Bartlet says, and Toby starts to leave. Bartlet says he can have fifteen minutes off. "It's time to get up off the mat, Toby." Toby says they could really go after the hate groups. But he's floundering.

TOBY: (pause) Why does it feel like this? (beat) I've seen shootings before.

BARTLET: This wasn't a shooting, Toby, it was a lynching. They tried to lynch Charlie right in front of our eyes, can you believe it?

An alternate scene. Tom comes back into Sam's office. Tom says he'll be fine. Sam wants to ask him something.

SAM: Do you really think black jurors are incapable of reaching a just decision based on evidence? (beat) Do you really think they're any less interested in walking down streets that are free of crime?

TOM: I'm a prosecutor, Sam. My job is to get a conviction.

SAM: Are black jurors less capable of reaching justice?

TOM: Yes.

SAM: (pause) Well, if nothing else good happens today, at least you got creamed.

Bartlet gets out some keyhole satellite pictures of the headquarters of the West Virginia White Pride. He says he could have had the attorney general take them out any time. But he hasn't because every day he's felt a little bit better. Toby isn't sure he'll come out the other side. Bartlet says he isn't, either, but he thinks they should go to work every day. Toby asks about Roush. Bartlet says he's going to win. Toby asks Bartlet how he beat him. Bartlet says he's been thinking about it for weeks but he can't remember.

There's a reception for radio talk show hosts. Pool photographers snap pictures as stewards pass around drinks and hors d'oeuvres. The President comes in and addresses them. He notices a woman sitting in a chair. Bartlet doesn't want to do what he wants to do. It's unprofessional. Unpresidential. The hell with it.

The President asks the woman if she's Dr. Jenna Jacobs. "Are you an M.D.?" She says she's a Ph.D. "In psychology?" asks Bartlet. "Or theology, social work?" No, English literature, she says. Bartlet wonders if her listeners assumed she had training in any of the disciplines he mentioned. He likes how she calls homosexuals an abomination on her show. Jacobs says she doesn't say it, "the Bible does, Leviticus 18:22." Bartlet commends Jacobs for knowing the chapter and verse. Okay then, he asks, how much he could get for selling his daughter into slavery as in Exodus 21:7? He asks if he should kill Leo for working on the Sabbath as in Exodus 35:2? How about touching the skin of a dead pig, Leviticus 11:7? Where does that leave the Redskins? Bartlet's on a roll.

BARTLET: Think about those questions, would you? One last thing: While you may be mistaking this for your monthly meeting of the ignorant tight-ass club, in this building, when the President stands, nobody sits.

As Dr. Jacobs gets to her feet, Bartlet tells Toby that's how he beat Elliot Roush.

Charlie's talking to Andrew Mackintosh again. Mackintosh knows Charlie's "the man who almost got the President killed." Charlie says his mother used to work nights, too. He says she was shot and killed. She wasn't supposed to be on that shift but she switched 'cause Charlie asked her to.

ANDREW: (pause) Hey, Charlie. You know what I think she'd say if she were here right now?

CHARLIE: What?

ANDREW: The same thing my father would say: "If they're shooting at you, you know you're doin' *something* right."

Zoey and Charlie are going out. Leo asks if he's taking extra protection . . . Secret Service protection. The staff goes to Josh's house to wait for the election results. They're sitting on the stoop having a beer. Josh is in the pajamas C.J. got for him, enjoying being outside. Sam has the results of the twelve races they keyed on. He says the incumbents lost them all. After four months and $400 million, Josh realizes the House stayed the same.

JOSH: I don't know, Toby. It's election night. What do you say about a government that goes out of its way to protect even citizens who try to destroy it.

TOBY: (pause) God bless America.

Martin Sheen
You can't play a President. The other players have to treat you like one. That's the only way that you have any credibility. So I'm very lucky that they treat me with a degree of respect. At least on camera.

DONNA MOSS
JANEL MOLONEY

It is just as well that someone with the intellectual self-confidence of Josh Lyman has Donna Moss to keep him grounded. Donna is clearly adept at bossing her boss, or at least in pointing out to him where the shallow water might be. Whether it be the disposition of the budget surplus or the economics of the Mexican bailout, Donna's relentless interrogations of Josh, often involving money and why she doesn't have enough of it, serve a more mundane practical purpose too. Donna often functions as the voice of the audience.

Aaron Sorkin

She's helpful in that regard, in that she is very bright, extremely capable, but has a lot of catching up to do in terms of here's the way the world works. And yes, she will ask, sort of "from the mouths of babes" questions in the show. I have to be careful there because I will sometimes rely on her too heavily for exposition. She'll sort of become Mademoiselle Exposition and you don't want to do that.

Janel Moloney reached into *The West Wing* and grabbed with both hands—she took what was initially a minor role and made something much more substantial.

Janel Moloney

I had already worked with Tommy and Aaron on *Sports Night*. I actually read for C.J.'s role first. And I read for Donna and I just loved the part right away; even though it was petite, it was fully formed. The character was there. All of the elements that are there now were there just like golden nuggets in the first show. Every week after that, I would have a little bit more, and I'd see a different side of my character, and then a little bit more. It just kept expanding. And then during Christmas they asked me to join the cast as a regular member.

Aaron Sorkin

Janel Moloney came to us via *Sports Night*. She did an episode of *Sports Night* in the first season and just parked it in the bleachers with one scene that really knocked me out. The role of Donna was a small, recurring, supporting role. That was its intention in the pilot. She was in every

episode the first year, then we made her a series regular. We simply put the proper title on her this year. She was a series regular in the first year, too.

Janel Moloney

I have a pretty dry sense of humor. My parents have very dry senses of humor and so does Aaron, so we all worked well together on that level. But I don't know. Ultimately Donna is pretty different than I am.

The dynamic between Donna and Josh was inspired by a woman Aaron Sorkin met researching the series. But however the parts are written, the actors still have to put flesh on the bones.

Aaron Sorkin

When I met him, George Stephanopoulos had an assistant, a beautiful, really brilliant woman named Heather Beckle. I remember talking to Heather, and simply in trying to say a nice thing to her, in trying to let her know that I was impressed with her, I said something brilliant, like "Wow, it must be incredible working for the President." And she said, "Oh, I don't work for the President. I work for George. George is my sunrise and sunset." And I thought, Now, imagine blowing off the President to say I work for him. I want to write that woman.

Janel Moloney

What I've always focused on from the first day is my relationship with Josh. That's all I really ever pay attention to. I think they're just absolutely mad for each other. I think it's probably something they both struggle with personally and they don't really know how to express it and they don't really

JANEL MOLONEY

On a personal note, it's been really fun to feel so appreciated as an actor. That's not something I've ever had before. It's really hard in Hollywood. You feel like you can work at a certain level but you never get the material and you never get the chance to work with the people. But everything came together here: an extraordinary cast, an extraordinary writer, directors and producers that are just absolutely top of the line. The classiest, most respectful people you could ever hope to work with. That is just an amazing change for me. I mean a really amazing change. And then you get noticed. People on the street come up to you and tell you how much they love the show. You get letters. You could do a movie that's pretty successful and nobody sees it, and you do two scenes on *The West Wing* and everybody sees it. That's a big difference between television and movies.

want to admit that they have the feelings that they have. So they just kind of are going and working and dealing with what they have to deal with and that's about as far as they've gotten.

I associate my time on this show distinctly with Brad. I really feel like that's my central relationship on the show. It's always a pleasure anytime I work with him. Any scene I do with Brad is particularly enjoyable.

Bradley Whitford

Donna and Josh are barely in check. It's very complicated. I think they're absolutely crazy about each other, but she's my assistant and it would be, of course, inappropriate. I think I know deep down that emotionally, as a human being, I can't function without her and I think professionally, as a human being, I can't function without her, either.

Bradley Whitford's gratitude on Josh's behalf is well founded. If for nothing other than the subtly indicated role Donna played in getting Josh help the Christmas after he was shot, she has been invaluable. And she gets it. She was instrumental in the happy conclusion of the Stackhouse filibuster. And as Toby said, if everyone reacted as Donna did to the news of the President's illness, the administration would be in much better shape.

IN THIS
WHITE HOUSE

Sam's going to be on the TV show *Capital Beat*. He's a regular but he's on with someone he doesn't know, Ainsley Hayes (Emily Procter). The host Mark Gottfried (Ted McGinley) says she's a young, blond, leggy Republican who's never done TV. When he sees Ainsley, Gottfried advises her not to overreach. He says Sam usually wipes the floor with whomever is in her seat. She shouldn't be scared. Sam says hello to Ainsley and the show gets going.

Gottfried asks Sam why the President's $1.5 billion education package is a better bill than the Republican one Bartlet vetoed last year. Sam gives an example. He says it provides enough money to buy textbooks for teachers in places like Kirkwood, Oregon. Ainsley argues that's not true, Sam's lying. She says the

Republican package had plenty of money, but gave it to communities to spend. Ainsley won't let Sam answer. She says Sam's right, textbooks are important. They'd help him realize Kirkwood is actually in California. The show goes to a break and Ainsley asks if she overreached. Sam knows he's been stuffed.

SAM: Please . . . oh please, let them not be watching.

JOSH pops his head into TOBY's office. It's Christmas morning—

JOSH: Toby. Come quick. Sam's gettin' his ass kicked by a girl.

TOBY gets up and follows JOSH—

TOBY: (calling) Ginger, get the popcorn.

C.J. is briefing on a summit of African nations and drug companies about Africa's twenty-six million AIDS victims. A questioner asks if the White House has declared war on the pharmaceutical companies. Toby may have taken that into his own hands. He says a drug that costs ten dollars and eighty cents in Norway where nobody needs it costs ninety dollars in Burundi where everybody needs it. Sam's been hearing it about *Capital Beat*. C.J. asks him if Geneva's in Switzerland or Oregon.

A new reporter introduces himself to C.J.: Bill Kelley, *Cleveland Courier*. He asks if she knows anything about Alamo Energy selling drilling equipment to Iraq. C.J. says she can't tell him anything. Kelley says if they were doing that, wouldn't they be violating sanctions? Grand jury investigations are secret, C.J. says. She can't tell him any more.

Bartlet asks Leo if he saw Sam get pureed by Ainsley Hayes on TV. He says they should hire her. Leo says good joke, she's a Republican, but Bartlet's serious. He's read three of her columns and he thinks she has a sense of civic duty.

Bartlet has a photo op with the African delegates. Someone asks President Nimbala (Zakes Mokae) what he wants to gain from the summit. "A miracle," he says. Bartlet again tells Leo to hire Ainsley Hayes.

Two friends of Ainsley's are watching a tape of her performance on *Capital Beat*. They're telling Ainsley she's going to be a star. An agent's going

Kim Webster (Ginger)
Richard [Schiff] has been a major, major influence on me. He has really shown me the way, he kind of has guided me. I think it was the second episode of the first season, I was sitting at a desk outside his office and he came up to me and said, "Oh, so are you my new secretary?" And I said, "Yeah." I was just an extra. I think he pushed that because he didn't really have an assistant on the show, but he said that he did. He's always been extremely generous as an actor: "Make sure Kim's in this shot."

It's mind-blowing. It's like the best graduate acting program that I could have ever gone to, just watching them work.

to call. Ainsley's trying to figure out her caller ID when the phone rings. Her friend thinks it's the agent but it's not. Ainsley knows this number already: 202–456–1414. It's the White House.

C.J.'s come to work late. She says she didn't sleep at all for worrying about something. She can't even muster the energy to have a dig at Sam's geography skills. Leo brings Sam and C.J. out to the corridor. He says he wanted to tell them something where there were people so they wouldn't scream. He's offering Ainsley Hayes a job.

C.J.: Are you kidding?

LEO: No.

C.J.: Are you kidding?

LEO: No.

C.J.: Are you kidding?

LEO: No.

C.J.: WHAT THE HELL MADE YOU THINK I WOULDN'T SCREAM WHERE THERE ARE PEOPLE??!!!

Josh gives Donna a primer. U.S. companies hold the patents on HIV medications. The drugs are so expensive, people in Africa buy them off the black market in violation of copyright treaties. Donna asks how much the drugs cost. "One hundred and fifty dollars a week," says Josh. A police officer in Kenya makes $43 a month.

Damson, a drug company representative, is telling President Nimbala it's not about profit, but Nimbala wants to know why one of his products is half the price in Norway it is in his country. Damson says prices are not the issue, and Toby interjects they should make it the issue. It's getting uncomfortable. Josh asks how much it would cost to provide free drugs to three countries. Damson says they don't know. They're getting nowhere.

In the third act, Ainsley comes to meet Leo. She's nervous as hell and puzzled, excited, and terrified all at the same time. Ainsley thinks she's been called in to be reprimanded for the job she did on Sam, but Leo surprises her by offering her a job. Ainsley misses the offer and Leo waits while Ainsley's brain catches up.

LEO: Here it comes.

AINSLEY: Did you say "offer me a job"?

LEO: Yes. Associate White House Counsel. You'd report to the deputy White House Counsel, who reports to the White House Counsel, who reports to me.

AINSLEY: (pause) I'm sorry, a job in *this* White House?

LEO: You want a glass of Scotch?

AINSLEY: Yes, please.

Ainsley tells Leo she's always been a Republican. He says he knows, he has her FBI file. Ainsley says she loathes almost everything they believe in, but she's wanted to work in the White

AARON SORKIN

These arguments aren't fun unless there's somebody on the other side who can argue something interesting right back. I wanted a bona fide Republican to come in there and give it that voice. There had been some discussion in the off season of bringing in another young, attractive female to complement the young, attractive females that we already have in the show. We wanted to attract more younger females. The easiest way to do that is tell stories about them.

There was a period of time where you couldn't flip through cable news without finding a young, blond Republican. It turns out most of them didn't know anything and got the reputation for not knowing anything and not really being much more than young, blond, and leggy. I thought it would be fun if we had a character who they assume was that and turned out to have more going on. So Ainsley was born. Emily's been wonderful. She's become a great friend and we're nuts about her.

EMILY PROCTER (AINSLEY HAYES)

It took me four auditions to get the part. The first time I read, I read with Aaron. I didn't realize Aaron was Aaron. Here is this great-looking guy and I thought this is some actor that they've hired to help me out. Afterwards I leaned in and was like, You're really good. Thank God I didn't know. My second interview I did know, so I was completely embarrassed that I had done it. I told them I was very nervous so when I left I cried. I thought, I'll never get that job. I broke rule number one. They'll never hire someone who admitted to being nervous. And that was, I think, my first realization of how great and how different they were.

House since she was two. Leo tells her Bartlet likes smart people who disagree with him and he's asking her to serve.

Josh tells Toby to ease up. He says that half of Congress was elected by drug companies so the patent treaties will be enforced. Toby says the pills cost four cents. The second one, says Josh; the first one costs $400 million. Josh asks about Nimbala. Toby says he was a great commander and he's a good President. He's holding his country together with both hands. "Then let's send him back with something," says Josh.

Ainsley has until the end of the day to think about the job. She's watching C.J. in the Press Room, and the new reporter who asked C.J. about Alamo is there. He thinks Ainsley is new, too. He tells her what he asked C.J. and says she's been weird about it. Ainsley is incredulous. "She told you there was a grand jury investigation?"

The drug summit has continued for four days. There are huge, fundamental differences. Damson says even if they gave away free drugs, it wouldn't make any difference. The drugs have to be taken at precise times. Josh asks what the problem is. Toby pipes in quietly: they don't have watches. And if the drugs are taken improperly, resistant strains of HIV could develop.

Ainsley sees C.J. in her office, cycling a stationary bike furiously in an effort to tire herself out. Ainsley introduces herself, and tells C.J. she's not taking the job. She confesses that she knows what C.J.'s been worrying about. She tells her attorneys and jurors can be prosecuted for confirming that a grand jury has been impaneled, but she's okay. Witnesses are free to say whatever they want.

Toby tells Nimbala he can put a deal together. They'll drop prices if he tries to stop black market drugs. Nimbala says 35.8 percent of his adult population is infected, why should he care about patent law? Josh says Congress could stop all aid if he doesn't. Toby says they might convince Congress to forgive their debt and get the Export-Import Bank to offer one billion for medication. Nimbala says, "It is a terrible thing to beg for your life."

Sam runs into Ainsley in a corridor. He tells her she forgot to mention that schools only got the money she talked about if they agreed not to distribute condoms. She says good, that's the last thing we need. Josh comes by and recognizes Ainsley. She tells them she's not taking the job. Ainsley says, "This White House feels government is better for children than parents and it loves the Bill of Rights, except the second one." Sam can't hold it in; he argues that Josh almost died.

He's so tired of the gun lobby talking about personal freedom. Ainsley says their administration just doesn't like the people who like guns and they should think about that the next time they make a redneck joke. The tension hangs but Sam and Josh know there was some truth to that.

There's a great bustle in the Oval Office. Doors are opening and staffers are coming in and out. The military is there; something's happened. The President tells Nimbala there was a coup in his country. Rebels have the capital, the radio station, the television station. Nimbala says he has to go home. Bartlet says he can't. He has to take asylum but Nimbala insists he has to go home. Bartlet is pleading: They'll shoot him the moment he steps off the plane. Bartlet tells him his brother and sons are dead, his wife is in Kenya. From just outside the Oval Office, Ainsley is watching.

Later, Ainsley's friends are gloating about her rejecting the job. One asks if she saw anyone who wasn't worthless. Ainsley says they're smug and superior, they like taxes, but don't call them worthless. She says they have commitment, they are righteous, and they are patriots. "And I'm their lawyer."

Saturday morning. The President's in Toby's office. Charlie comes in with a note. Bartlet and Toby both know what it's going to say. Toby asks if it happened and Bartlet says President Nimbala was executed in the airport parking lot.

AND IT'S SURELY
TO THEIR CREDIT

Josh is sitting at his desk, outraged. He's just received another letter from his insurance company, asking him for $40,000 to cover his hospital bills.

Donna is welcoming thirty guests to the White House to watch the President record his weekly radio address. She tells Sam the President once took eleven takes for a speech that's usually two or three minutes. Bartlet cracks up, comprehensively blowing the first take, and he's still going at take five.

C.J. tells Toby she's okay with Ainsley. When she first heard the news, she broke a door, but she's over it now. C.J. says it's sexist for people to stereotype Ainsley just because she's a good-looking Republican woman. Toby informs her

that Ed Barrie, a retiring three-star general, is doing all the Sunday morning shows. Worried that Barrie's going to beat up the President, C.J. tells Carol to get him to her office at once.

> **TOBY**: By the way, you are a beautiful woman and no one around here ever assumed you were either ambitious or stupid.
> **C.J.**: Toby?
> **TOBY**: Yeah.
> **C.J.**: Took two years.

Leo tells Ainsley Hayes that Lionel Tribbey (John Larroquette), the White House counsel, thinks hiring her was a great idea. Ainsley knows Leo hasn't told him. Tribbey comes in going full throttle, brandishing a cricket bat he says he'll kill people with. He's after two guys—Joyce and Brookline—who testified to Congress they couldn't produce the Rockland memo. Tribbey says he has the renegade memo in his hand. Leo introduces him to Ainsley. He asks if she's the girl who's been writing the columns. Leo says yes. "You're an idiot," says Tribbey, without missing a beat. Leo tells Tribbey Ainsley's working for him. Tribbey laughs a little and excuses himself.

The President is nailing the radio address when the door flies open and Tribbey bursts in, loudly complaining about the "blond and leggy fascist" they just hired. Bartlet tells Tribbey he might not have noticed the people in the room, all of whom have given the party significant amounts of money. They can talk about Ainsley later. The President tells his guests Lionel Tribbey is obviously a very brilliant lawyer they cannot live without. Otherwise, "there'd be very little reason not to put him in prison." And he starts the address over, take twelve.

Sam tells Toby about Josh's insurance woes. The hospital was "out of network," so only 20 percent of Josh's bills are covered. After he was shot, Josh neglected to have his life-saving operation approved. Sam asserts that he'll have to sue. Toby remarks that he likes a country where you can sue the insurance company but not the people who shot you. Something clicks in Sam's head.

SAM: Josh, this is our way in. A civil action. You could subpoena everything. Membership rolls, donor rolls, minutes of meetings, weapons inventories, computer downloads, and you depose every man and woman who's ever been to a meeting and every man and woman they name. (beat) Josh, the Southern Poverty Law Center wants you to sue the Knights of the Ku Klux Klan for a hundred million dollars.

Abbey Bartlet wants to see her husband. He's tied up so Charlie takes a message. Abbey says the President's blood pressure is 120 over 80; all his signs are good. "So we can have sex now." Not Abbey and Charlie, Abbey and the President. She tells Charlie to find him, and Abbey waits while Charlie gives him the message. Bartlet flies into the Oval Office and he wants to get down to it right there; it's been fourteen weeks, he says. They can't have sex in the Oval Office so they coordinate their schedules. They'll find an hour sometime before six.

General Barrie sends an aide to see C.J. The aide admits Barrie has some concerns about the readiness of the armed forces, and Barrie feels it's his patriotic obligation to voice them to the public before his retirement. C.J. says it's called ring and run. She wants Barrie.

C.J.: Go back to the Pentagon. Right now. Tell General Barrie C. J. Cregg says he's a coward.

Leo and Ainsley are trying to find her office in the bowels of the White House basement. Ainsley thanks Leo for being decent. He says the others will come around. He tells her she's in the administration foxhole now and her colleagues are under siege. Leo says when he announced his alcoholism he faced radio, TV, magazines, cameras in front of his house, editorials, op-eds. People said he's a dangerous drunk, he should resign. Ainsley says she wrote one of those op-eds. Leo says he knows. They find Ainsley's office. It's a little room with various widths of pipe running everywhere and a desk and chair just stuck in. Trying to sound upbeat and professional, Leo explains that it's the steam pipe trunk distribution venue. Welcome to the White House.

Tribbey lumbers into the depths of the White House basement and finds Ainsley's "office." He demands to know what she's doing here. She sweetly professes that she's serving her country, she feels a sense of duty. He asks if she stepped out of *The Pirates of Penzance*? "He *is* an Englishman. That's *HMS Pinafore*,"* she says knowingly, without a hint of annoyance. Tribbey brushes her off; if she wants to prove herself so badly, she can go to the Hill and talk to the associate majority counsel at governmental affairs. It's time to deal with Joyce and Brookline, the guys in the Communications Office that Tribbey had earlier threatened to kill. As Tribbey's about to leave, she declares that Bartlet's way too moderate for him. She's done her research: didn't he leave his practice with its seven-figure income out of duty, too?

*Ainsley is correct, as confirmed by Sam. The song is from *HMS Pinafore or The Lass that Loved a Sailor*, words by Sir William Schwenck Gilbert (1836–1911), music by Sir Arthur Seymour Sullivan (1842–1900), which was first performed in 1878.

Sam is delightedly showing Josh the evidence he's gathered to start deposing witnesses in his lawsuit: racist books and videotapes inciting violence. . . . Leo interrupts to update Sam on the situation with Joyce and Brookline. Sam is prepared to talk to governmental affairs, but Leo explains that Tribbey sent Ainsley Hayes already. Sam's clearly disgruntled that he's been trumped, and bitterly announces that they better hope she doesn't leak the story. Toby admits he's not wild about the developing lawsuit against the hate groups. They can file equally harmful depositions, asking Leo about drugs, Sam about prostitutes. But Leo assures Josh if he says the word, they'll all take a leave of absence and join his legal team.

The President is trying take twenty-one of the radio address in front of a new audience. He glances at his watch and sees it's 5:45 P.M. He races out of the Oval Office on reason of "a special meeting of the government," but Charlie stops him short. He tells the President his wife had to leave early for a trip to Pennsylvania, so there will be no residence rendezvous this evening.

General Barrie (Tom Bower) bursts into C.J.'s office shouting about his service record. When she called him a coward, she said the one thing guaranteed to get him down there. Barrie goes at C.J. hard and she gives it right back. She says jumping up and down on the commander in chief and leaving town is an act of cowardice. She has an answer for all his charges about readiness. Barrie says he's going to tell Tim Russert. She says he isn't. C.J. calmly tells Barrie she notices he wears a Distinguished Combat Service Medal he won when he served on the *USS Brooke*. But she found out the *Brooke* never saw action. He wears a medal he never won. The blood is gone from Barrie's face. "Debate is one thing," says C.J., "but I don't allow drive-bys."

Fresh back from the Hill, Ainsley goes to see Brookline and Joyce. They're immediately rude and hostile. Ainsley says Tribbey asked her to take care of the false testimony they gave about the Rockland memo. They could face a grand jury. And some of the Republican committee members take their attitude as a sign of disrespect. She says just apologize, it's easy. A short note, it's done. Joyce tells her they're busy.

That night, Bartlet races to the residence. He says Abbey has two minutes to get ready for him or he's going to get Mrs. Landingham drunk. As Abbey's changing, Bartlet asks her why she was in Pennsylvania. She says she was dedicating a statue to Nellie Bly. Bartlet says she didn't have to do that, she can pass that kind of thing along. Abbey stops undressing. He's blown it. Abbey tells her husband Nellie Bly pioneered investigative journalism. Then she tells him about other women overlooked for memorials: Elizabeth Blackwell, the first woman M.D., Amelia Bloomer . . .

Sam is reading off lists of precedential cases for Josh. He sees Ainsley and says he should have

been the one to confront Brookline and Joyce because they work for him. Ainsley asks if there's any chance Sam could be rude to her tomorrow. One more disappointment today from this place she used to worship and she's going to lose it. Sam watches her walk away and tries to resume his conversation with Josh, but thinks better of it and follows her down to her office. He finds her staring at a vase of dead flowers on her desk, complete with an envelope addressed with the word "BITCH."

Without pausing to think, Sam flies into the office Brookline and Joyce share with a bunch of staffers. He grabs a blotter, scattering stuff off Brookline's desk. In a heat of impassioned anger, he tells them when he writes something, he signs his name. Do they understand how big a harassment suit they exposed the White House to? Do they realize that whether or not they like it, she works here? He grabs a black magic marker and scrawls on the back of the big blotter.

SAM: Which is more than I can say for either one of you.

SAM shows them the blotter: "You're fired. S. Seaborn."

BROOKLINE: Sam, I don't know who you think you are around here, but you can't fire us.

LIONEL: (O.S.) Ohhhhhh . . . yes he can.

They turn to see LIONEL standing in the doorway.

LIONEL: (pause) Leave here and don't ever come back. It's time for you both to write your book now.

On Saturday morning, Bartlet is recording his radio address in front of Abbey, who's watching him very closely. Bartlet, clearly inspired, catalogs more women deserving of public monuments, only fifty of which have been built with public money. He does the address in one take. Before he can follow Abbey up to the residence, he tells C.J. to let Barrie out of the box. "The man's earned the right to say whatever he wants," he says.

Josh tells Sam the lawsuit would tie up the staff indefinitely, that he's using his position for a personal agenda. He thinks a lawsuit's too small, like he slipped in someone's driveway. He doesn't want to sue the West Virginia White Pride. But he'll sue the insurance company—no problem.

Ainsley's coming to her office but the lights are all out. She feels around for a light switch and the sound of a fanfare blares forth. The walls of her office are decorated with posters from *The Mikado*; *The Pirates of Penzance*; *HMS Pinafore*. Sam, Josh, Toby, C.J., Charlie, and Donna are all there. They welcome her with a toast, singing along: "For he himself has said it/And it's greatly to his credit/That he is an Englishman/That he is an Englishman."

THE LAME
DUCK CONGRESS

C.J. is running through business at a routine daily briefing. She wants to make it clear that the visiting Ukranian dignitary Vasily Konanov will meet with advisors; no cabinet-level officials and certainly not the President. A reporter asks C.J. to comment on Senator-elect Morgan Mitchel, who's announcing he's seeking a seat on the Foreign Relations Committee. From there he'll block the Comprehensive Test Ban Treaty getting to the floor. C.J. says the treaty will be ratified. Danny asks if the President has considered a lame duck session of the Senate to vote on it. C.J. says not that she knows, and Danny asks her to check.

Donna is lecturing Josh on statistics from the Occupational Health and Safety Administration. She says 600,000 Americans a year get carpal tunnel syndrome.

Josh doesn't care. Sam says they *should* consider a lame duck session. Musical chairs with the committee seats may fall Mitchel's way. If there's a vacancy at the Department of Foreign Affairs, Mitchel will get it 'cause no one else wants it. Toby says that without lobbyists, there's no money in it. Sam thinks they have no chance with the new Congress, but C.J. says bringing the old Congress back looks like politics. But, as Toby says, "It *is* politics."

In the Oval Office, Toby says the world is waiting for the U.S. to ratify the treaty first. But Sam says if they lose the vote, it'll hang around their necks. Josh chimes in. Congress'll be pissed off and could stall confirmations. C.J. doesn't think it's justified. They argue and everyone's talking at once. Leo wants to take the temperature, and Toby says C.J. should leak that Bartlet's considering it.

Leo informs Toby, Josh, C.J., and Sam a *Post* editorial is going to say the President's time isn't used well, schedules are abandoned, and the West Wing is like a high school yearbook office. And based on what he just saw in the Oval Office, the *Post* has a point. Leo institutes new rules: anyone who wants an answer on anything from the President must put a two-page summary on Leo's desk first.

C.J. tells Danny she can't believe his paper's doing another editorial. Then with Danny in her office, C.J. asks Carol to call the spokesperson for the senate majority leader's office. So they *are* considering a lame duck session, Danny says. C.J. says he can write it but he should attribute it

down the food chain. Danny leaves. Carol has the spokesperson on the line but C.J. confesses she didn't really need him.

All of a sudden, Vasily Konanov shows up. Charlie tells Josh he's sitting in a car in the driveway refusing to move unless he sees the President. And he's drunk. Leo instructs Charlie to put him in an office and explain why he can't see the President. He's a member of the Ukrainian parliament. Leo says he's crazy, but our kinda crazy.

Sam asks Ainsley to summarize a twenty-two-page position recommendation paper per Leo's new regulations. In return, she wants to go with him to the Test Ban Treaty meetings. "I want to learn from the master," she says. Sam says women think that kind of thing works, but it doesn't . . . but she can come. Ainsley wonders if Sam has any lunch she could eat, she's finished hers already.

Toby has a meeting with a couple of aides. They say their guy isn't going to vote for the treaty. One of them tells Toby to check his own backyard first. Toby doesn't have all the votes he thinks he has.

After failing with Josh, Donna tries to interest Leo in the OHSA guidelines. He says they can't afford it and tells Donna to type slower. Leo tells C.J. that Danny wants access for a three-part feature. C.J. says no, the *Post* has burned them four times in two weeks.

In the corridor, Toby tells Leo the bad news: they lost a vote. Toby's counting on Tony Marino to tell him who jumped the fence. Marino spent four years of his life on the treaty and he lost his seat to Mitchel in a bad race before the fight was really over. Toby thinks Marino will help; he can stick it to the voters and Mitchel at the same time. Toby walks into his office, and much to his deadpanned surprise, Konanov is sitting at his desk, and he is not happy. Josh comes to the rescue, taking Konanov to his office. Josh explains on the way that their administration deals with the Ukrainian president, not with Konanov, but Konanov is adamant that he's going to see Bartlet.

Still fighting for the Test Ban Treaty, Sam meets three Senate aides, reluctantly letting Ainsley sit in. Sam asks what it'll take to get their boss to loosen his grip. One aide points out that lots of people, six ex-secretaries of defense included, are against the treaty. Sam counters 82 percent of citizens are for it. Sam pleads, asking if there's room for movement, admits that they'd consider attaching reservations to push this through. The aides scoff; they've wasted a trip. Ainsley, unable to stay silent any longer, asserts that politics should stop at the water's edge, but all the aides are interested in is beating the White House.

> **AINSLEY**: You're a shmuck, Peter. Today, tomorrow, next year, next term, these guys'll have the treaty ratified, and they'll do it without the reservations he just offered to discuss with you. (beat) Can I take this muffin?

Margaret is typing hunt-and-peck. When Leo protests, Margaret says he told Donna to type slower. Leo tells her to look at his face. His thunderous visage is enough to get Margaret back to 120 words per minute.

Leo suggests to Josh that Konanov can meet President Bartlet accidentally. Konanov just wants to say he met the President. Josh should have a low-level meeting and keep the door open. Leo says he did it with the Dalai Lama once. Josh tells Donna she's wasting her time with the typing slowdown because Congress and the White House are exempt from any workplace-related laws they pass. But Josh has a job for her. He needs Vasily Konanov to meet with someone of absolutely no consequence, and she's his girl.

> **DONNA**: So I'm a beard.
>
> **JOSH**: Yes.

JOHN SPENCER
Margaret's my gal Friday. All of the good and the bad comes with that. I'm certainly comfortable enough, at times, not to treat her very well, and kind of abruptly. "Cut to the chase, Margaret, just do it." And I think that kind of thing comes only out of a comfort of a long-term relationship where you get to know and feel comfortable with someone. We have worked together a long time. She's very important. She's kind of the caretaker behind the man. Not necessarily on a romantic or intimate level, but certainly on a personal level.

NICOLE ROBINSON
I think that for every ounce of oddness or quirkiness that Margaret has, she makes up for in efficiency. I feel like she's probably the first one there and the last one to leave, and Leo would expect no less. There's not a lot of people who are that way. She's completely dedicated and devoted despite her weirdness.

DONNA: I'm being used.

JOSH: Yes.

DONNA: As a dupe.

JOSH: Yes.

DONNA: How am I supposed to feel about that?

JOSH: How do you usually feel about that?

Back at the White House, Sam tells Ainsley the muffin line was not the best closing. She gives Sam her two-page summary and waits for him to come back to her, which he does only after a moment's hesitation. He says she reversed his position.

Toby arranges to meet Tony Marino at a bar, and Marino jumps right to the point—he's heard they're thinking about calling a lame duck session. Toby wants to know if they lost someone. Marino says it's true. It's him. He can't vote for the treaty in good conscience. He was defeated in his district largely because he supported the treaty, and he's going to respect the people who voted against him. Toby looks at Marino. He knows he's not screwing around. They're sunk.

The air's equally heated in the White House. Ainsley has been arguing with Sam about the position paper for two-and-a-half hours. She argues that employee fraud constitutes the failure of a third of small businesses. Furthermore, she says her stance is not because the violators fit some kind of Republican lineup stereotype. Eighty percent are white and more likely to be better-educated, male, managerial types.

Timothy Busfield
If I ever come back and play Danny Concannon—it could be in year ten—I'm in love with C.J. That's the driving force behind any scene I have in the White House. The writer comes second.

C.J. is waiting outside the Oval Office to see Bartlet when Danny arrives. C.J. goes in first and before she can protest, Bartlet says he wants to let Danny do his feature. To deny him access would be petty and petulant, and their administration is above it. He ventures to ask if C.J.'s reluctance is personal. C.J. shoots back, "Absolutely not." Bartlet says he's heard things. He continues, he's a great reporter and she's a great press secretary and it wasn't going to work out when they had those jobs.

Bartlet tells Danny the *Post* has had its head up its ass, but the White House can't afford to alienate it. However, Bartlet declares, "I'm canceling our subscription." Excellent, says C.J., the White House buys 1,100 copies a day. That's a clear message. No, says Bartlet, not the whole White House, just his personal copy. Bartlet grants Danny the access he wants and leaves the office. C.J. and Danny look at each other for a long moment, and the air between them is slightly awkward. C.J. says she knows Danny's been offered an editor's job, but Danny replies he's a reporter. C.J. wonders if he took a job outside the Press Room. . . . Danny interjects that he doesn't have a problem with a reporter dating the press secretary, but C.J. just can't do it.

Donna is testing the limited patience of Konanov, detailing for him the finer points of keyboard layout and RSI. Bartlet walks by as if by accident. Konanov is immediately all over him, but Bartlet refuses to talk policy with him. He tells Konanov to go home and say he met the President.

Sam invites Ainsley to join his meeting with Leo. Sam reports that the Commerce Department wants them to help small businesses with fraud prevention and employee theft and he recommends the provision. Sam explains that 85 percent of workers will commit fraud in the right circumstances. Leo thought Sam was going the other way on this issue, but Sam admits he got turned around. Leo ends the meeting, and Ainsley asks Sam if that's it. Sam replies yes. He explains she convinced him, Sam convinced Leo, Leo'll convince the President. "We play with live ammo around here," Sam says.

Toby is relating to the President his displeasure about the earlier

meeting with Tony Marino. With a hint of resignation in his voice, Bartlet admits they have to respect the opponents of the treaty. In this particular case, he couldn't give a damn what the people think. He doesn't think 82 percent of people can be expected to reach an informed opinion. Toby knows they can't afford to call a session and lose. It's not going to happen.

BARTLET: You know what we forget sometimes. In all the talk about democracy. We forget it's not a democracy, it's a republic. The people don't make the decisions, they choose the people who make the decisions. Could they do a better job choosing? Yeah. But when you consider the alternatives . . .

Bartlet asks Toby to come up for a cigar. He tells him he'll beat his ass at chess.

THE PORTLAND TRIP

The President is flying overnight to Portland. His schedule is so full the assistant energy secretary is coming along just to get some time with the President on the way back. On the press bus C.J. admits she's been forced to go because she made fun of Notre Dame. The bus emits a collective moan: C.J.'s committed the one unpardonable sin in the Bartlet White House. Before the President boards, Leo tells him they stopped a tanker in the Gulf. They think it's carrying Iraqi oil so they'll board the ship. The President makes C.J. put on a Fighting Irish cap as they climb the steps to the plane. C.J. hopes no one can see her and Bartlet makes sure to stop for a photo op at the top of the plane steps.

From a phone at the White House, Josh asks Leo if the President looked tired.

Josh says Bartlet likes long plane flights. He gets to talk to people and think out loud. Donna scoots in his office and tells Josh it's time to go. She's in a knockout dress and she's getting the weekend under way, shutting off lights and clearing up papers. Josh says he has to meet Congressman Matt Skinner that night; did Donna have plans? Of course she did, look at her dress.

> **JOSH:** Did you steal that dress?
> **DONNA:** I bought this dress.
> **JOSH:** But you're returning it tomorrow.
> **DONNA:** Yes I am.
> **JOSH:** That's stealing.

Josh instructs Donna that she has an hour and five minutes for dinner. "And if you want to have sex, you better do it during dinner," he says. Donna protests, explaining that this is *the* guy. Josh shakes his head in disbelief—she has terrible taste in men.

On the plane, Sam confides to Toby he's not writing well. He wants this speech to make people feel passion, and he's not ready to hand it to the press pool yet. C.J. says it's too late, they already got it, but Sam insists she get it back.

The President stops C.J. He pretends to test her knowledge, but really he wants some good solid advice. They've flagged a ship they think is carrying petroleum in violation of UN sanctions. If the oil is black market, the company is fined. However, C.J. points out, the oil company still gets to sell the oil and the profit is much bigger than the fine. Bartlet knows that's true; he only wishes the sanctions would be the real disincentive. Charlie interrupts, handing C.J. lyrics for the Notre Dame fight song. Bartlet's pleased to inform C.J. that she'll be leading a rendition of it as the plane flies over South Bend.

Congressman Matt Skinner (Charley Lan) comes to see Josh for a late-night discussion about the Marriage Recognition Act over a few beers. Matt says the language of the bill doesn't prohibit same-sex marriage, but Josh argues it does. Matt replies that for federal programs, the government defines marriage as the union of a man and a woman, but laws don't prohibit it at state level. Josh points out ugly things were said in Congress by members of Skinner's party when this bill was debated. Josh can't wrap his brain around why Matt still supports the bill. "Congressman," Josh cries out, "you're gay."

In the Situation Room, Leo is told that the captain of the tanker refused to allow U.S. forces

to board his ship. As a precautionary measure, warning shots are going to be fired over the bow of the tanker. Leo sighs, "There's no way this ends good." He'll call the President.

Aboard Air Force One, Toby and Sam are grappling with the speech about education, but nothing is satisfying their high standards. Sam believes the oratory should blow the doors off, and he wants to write about a permanent revolution. Toby's not so sure they should be quoting Mao Tse-tung in a speech about education in a democratic nation. Toby would love to write about a radical new approach to education but realistically they don't have one. He suggests they walk up and down the plane to get their blood and ideas flowing.

Donna comes back from her speedy dinner, reporting to Leo that she chugged down two whiskey sours and a bowl of soup. She lingers for a moment and tells Leo that Margaret's worried he's going to drink because his divorce papers are coming through. Leo replies that Margaret worries that the sun won't rise.

Josh is in the mess with Matt, seeking out those beers they both desperately need. Matt says the bill passed the Senate with eighty-five votes, the House with 342, and 60 percent of people oppose legally sanctioned gay marriage. The President has to sign the bill; the minority can't impose its will or morals on the majority. Josh argues that the Marriage Recognition Act would

bring government into the bedroom. Josh has a little more time before he has to call the President with his recommendation, and their discussion is moving nowhere fast. They'll have another beer.

On the plane, a reporter asks C.J. why they took off so late at night, and C.J. believes it's because Bartlet had a budget meeting that might have run late. Hanging her head a little bit, she asks for the drafts of the education speech back. She explains that Sam and Toby are polishing it up but assures them there will be no policy shift. Charlie reminds C.J. the President likes the Notre Dame song at a brisk and steady tempo.

From the Situation Room, Leo learns that when American forces boarded the ship, the crew threw the log, registry, and manifest overboard. When Leo calls Bartlet for options on dealing with the tanker, Bartlet says, under his breath, "Ah, Leo, just take the damn boat."

To C.J.'s delight, the fight song will have to wait because Bartlet wants to analyze the opening on the Tokyo markets. When C.J. asks him why the plane took off so late, Bartlet drifts into a romantic version of the real story: late flights are good, because people cease to be earthbound and burdened with practicality. He says it's a time for burgeoning ideas, new thoughts, open attitudes. Sam takes his chance to mention the permanent revolution to him, and Bartlet says Mao took a lot of long plane flights too. He says, "Look out your window. Is there anything more romantic than this?" Quickly coming down from his dream, he admits they left late because the budget meeting might run over, but it would have been great if creative inspiration *were* the reason.

Back in the White House mess, Josh points something out to Matt, something he's well aware of. Josh slowly explains that gay partners will be permanently ineligible for survivor benefits and Medicare. "Well, the government can't afford them anyway," says Matt gruffly.

Danny refuses to hand his copy of the education speech back to C.J., although she guarantees there are no new policy initiatives. But Danny doesn't need a guarantee; he has the old copy right there.

The President is listening to his staff work on the speech. As they pass phrases and ideas back and forth, he asks, "What happened to that idea to make a hundred thousand new teachers?" Toby says they can't force people to choose teaching as their profession. Charlie's been doodling on a legal pad throughout the discussion. Sam looks over and asks what he means by "Send 'em to college." Charlie says people receive full scholarships for college if they commit to three years in the armed forces. He says why not do the same if they'll teach public school? Toby asks where's the money going to come from, but Bartlet likes what he hears and instructs them to kick the idea around.

Beer bottles are piling up on the table, and Matt is telling Josh that any veto to the Act will be overridden anyway. Josh argues the logistical issue: the Senate's not in session, so the President can stick the bill in his pocket and it's vetoed. However, he can't steer clear of the ideological, moral issue, and points out that the majority leader of Matt's party compared homosexuality to kleptomania and sex addiction. Matt simply says he told their leader he was wrong. Josh is about to burst;

finally he asks Matt what he's been waiting to ask throughout their whole conversation. *How* can Matt be a member of this party? Matt takes the question seriously, explaining that he believes in 95 percent of what the Republicans stand for. His whole life isn't about being gay.

Josh watches Matt leave. Matt tells a colleague Bartlet'll sign the bill. The congressman congratulates Matt, and puts his arm around him. Matt's response is brusque: "Get your hand off my shoulder, Congressman."

On Air Force One, Toby and Sam bat around Charlie's idea. Toby steadfastly declares that they're not floating a policy initiative. It's pie in the sky and patronizing to have Ivy Leaguers play teacher for three years. Sam thinks teachers can be role models. He disagrees with Toby, arguing that kids won't feel abandoned if teachers leave after three years: a fifth-grade kid doesn't care where his fourth-grade teacher went. Toby doesn't relent, asking where the money's coming from. The wind's gone out of Sam's sails. After a silence, Sam admits he was mortified that he froze on the speech. Toby knows they can pull it off together.

Over the phone, Josh tells Toby he's going to recommend the President to sign the bill. Toby tells Josh that the President is frustrated with everything: the education speech, the oil tanker, and the lack of romance on late-night flights.

> **JOSH**: You know, when he goes off on a thing, Toby, he expects you to bring him in. He wants you to do it so he doesn't have to do it himself.

Toby starts to mention Charlie's idea, but the plane's about to land, and he saves it for another night. As they close up shop in the White House, Donna tells Josh her night stank. She says the guy was full of himself without cause to be, and she wonders if she'll ever find the right guy.

> **JOSH**: (calling) You look really great in that dress, Donna. You should buy it for yourself.

Pacing the cabin of Air Force One, clearly Bartlet *is* frustrated. He tells Leo they should have sanctions that work, they should seize the ship and sell the oil. Leo knows you can't change the world in a single evening, and tells Bartlet not tonight.

In the press cabin, C.J. has to renege on her earlier statement, and explains that there *might*

Thomas Del Ruth

We have a mock-up from the film *Air Force One*. It sits on a stage about thirty miles out of town. We've chosen exclusively to shoot the mock-up at night. The reason is we simply can't afford to raise the aircraft off the ground to a level where we could put a day-blue backing or a projection screen with cloud formations going by outside the windows. Or any other things that would give a sense of flying.

I resort to a theatricalized version of what an airplane would look like at night. I use hot light coming down on a passenger in a seat when he turns on a light. At the same time I build in illumination in the cove ceilings, which gives a softer, warm glow. So there is a romanticized feeling of what flying would be at night. We don't have the opportunity to create passing sources of light. We can't create the effect of an aircraft banking. With daylight you can. Those are all really nice, interesting things to do, but we just haven't had a chance.

be a policy shift or initiative in the education speech. Toby steps in and puts the press at ease: no new policies tonight. Toby confides to Danny that Sam choked on the draft and he wants to burn it. "No problem," says Danny, and hands his copy over without a fuss. C.J. watches in disbelief, but she figures it out: Danny went to Notre Dame, too.

Over the phone, the President asks how he can sign a bill that is so blatantly gay-bashing. Josh says he shouldn't, and he suggests Bartlet put it away, use the pocket veto. Congress'll send it back when they're in session and he'll be making a symbolic gesture to the gay community. The President says it's just wrong, but he knows he's been beaten. He tells Leo to put it in a drawer and they hang up. As he's leaving for the night, Josh asks Leo about his divorce papers. Margaret told him, and he couldn't help but worry that he would turn to alcohol to blunt the pain. Leo assures him he's fine. He says good night to Margaret and tells her she's a good girl.

C.J. tells the President a reporter wants to know why he went to Notre Dame. She knows he was accepted at Harvard, Yale, and Williams. Bartlet explains he was thinking of becoming a priest, but then he met Abbey. After debating for hours, Toby tells Bartlet that Charlie's idea is a good one, and they should look into how to get money for a program with a hundred teachers. The President is pensive. The oil company's gonna make a profit and the Marriage Recognition Act is going to be a law. And he gets a hundred teachers, not a hundred thousand.

"Well, it's a start, I guess," he says.

SHIBBOLETH

A half-mile off the coast near San Diego, a container ship is being detained by the Coast Guard with at least a hundred Chinese nationals on board.

In the West Wing bullpen on a Sunday evening, Sam's got his feet up: it's time to relax for the holiday. He's reading a speech to Toby about Pilgrims seeking a place in the New World. C.J. comes to the office in a flurry, telling them she's in charge of the Thanksgiving festivities but she's not sure of the procedure. She was sick and missed last year. As Toby and Sam rattle on about Pilgrims, she accuses them of slacking off every holiday. Toby responds that no one's checked out. C.J. rolls her eyes and leaves, and Josh joins the guys. Donna interrupts, leading in a guy carrying a cage with two turkeys. Where should he put them? Toby, Josh, and Sam are

thinking the same thing. It's too good to be true. "C.J.'s office," they say in chorus. She's gone for the night so the turkeys can roam around free as they are meant to be. "Show her who's slackin' off," says Josh, the three men laughing hysterically like college boys.

On Monday morning Josh reports on the gravity of the Chinese refugee situation. Eighty-three were in the hold of the ship; thirteen died on the way. Josh asks Leo what he's doing for Thanksgiving. He says he'll be with the first family. Josh says he's going to watch football with Toby and Sam but don't tell the President, he'll insist they come over.

JOSH: I'm just saying we've been working hard and we'd prefer to watch football rather than listen to a history of the yam in Latin.

Josh tells C.J. that Toby wants to add a name to the list of recess appointments—Leo's sister Josephine McGarry. It's not a favor to Leo; Toby wants to stir up a fight on school prayer. C.J. wonders what's next in her "week of unendurable Thanksgiving nonsense." With a deep sigh, she walks into her office, throws her purse and briefcase on the couch, and starts to take off her coat. She stops when a flutter on her desk catches her eye. There amid the paper, cluttering her desk, stands a turkey. Another flaps languidly on the couch. Before C.J. can scream, Donna runs into the office, breathless and armed with explanations. She'd hoped to head off C.J. to warn her. The President pardons a turkey each Thanksgiving.* Two are delivered, and the press secretary decides which is the more photogenic. C.J. balks in silence as Donna continues warily, "This one's Eric, that one's Troy." C.J., who reminds Donna that she holds a masters in political science from Berkeley, asks to be left alone.

Charlie's a man on a mission, and he has bought a new carving knife for the President. It's not the first knife he's presented to his overly particular boss, but he's sure this is the one: the

*The practice of sparing a turkey at Thanksgiving by Presidential pardon was begun by Harry S Truman in 1947. The two turkeys who make the trip to Washington are given by the National Turkey Federation and traditionally come from the home state of its chairman. The turkeys, always the larger male birds, or toms, are about thirty weeks old and weigh fifty to sixty pounds. Toms pardoned in recent years have lived out their days at the Kidwell Farm at Frying Pan Park in Herndon, Virginia.

Chef's Choice. Bartlet likes what he sees: "It's an American knife. No German knives for us." He holds the knife, inspects it, pretends to carve a turkey and declares that, no, the balance isn't right. Bartlet asks, "You know what we need?" "A German knife?" Charlie suspects.

Toby tries to convince the President that Josephine McGarry is the ideal candidate for the cabinet appointment. Bartlet says an appointment made in recess assumes Congress won't have a problem with the nominee. Bartlet's known Josephine twenty-five years and he's not wild about the woman. Her confirmation could cause a controversy they're not prepared to fight.

When Leo hears about the plan he flat out believes it's a bad idea. He tells Toby they're not geared for a battle and there's no reward in pursuing it. Josh and Sam come to say the Chinese refugees claim they are Christian evangelicals fleeing persecution in their homeland, and they're seeking religious asylum in the United States. Bartlet knows what this will turn into. Josh encapsulates it: Christian activists will say they have to stay, China will say they have to come back, the INS will say the law's the law.

Josh and Sam arrange a meeting with Reverend Al Caldwell, Mary Marsh, and company. Marsh doesn't waste a moment: if the President doesn't urge the INS judge to grant asylum, he'll wish he had. Immediately, Josh's hackles rise. He tells Mary she's not going to get anywhere threatening the commander in chief. Sam tries to break the tension—do they know the refugees were actually persecuted in China? Caldwell paints a picture of the horror: Chinese Christians are put in labor camps, arrested for recognizing papal authority, tortured. Mary adds American Christians will not stand by when religious freedom is threatened. "Sure they will," says Sam, "just not this time." The Christian right protested the play, *Apostle*, in which Jesus is gay. Fine. But where were they when someone threatened to blow up the theater?

> **SAM:** So you're committed to religious freedom for all people unless you don't like what they have
> to say.
> **MARY:** That's not—
> **SAM:** Don't look now, but I think the playwright's headed to China.

Tempers are flaring, and Caldwell takes Josh outside for a word. Sam's right, he accedes, but this is too important to stand idly by. Caldwell's church will pay the bond for each refugee.

In the Mural Room, four Senate aides are attacking Toby about Josephine McGarry. Toby says she's qualified but an aide argues she's antireligion. Toby points out she's on the board of visitors of her church and teaches Sunday school. But when she was Superintendent of the Atlanta School District, she enforced the law against school prayer, and 70 percent of citizens believe that law is wrong. Toby almost chuckles at the naïveté of that argument. Laws don't work like that. Furthermore, the President gains in the polls every time he draws a line in the sand with the Christian right. The aides can argue all they want, but the Senate couldn't *not* confirm her if it was in session. Her qualifications make her a shoo-in. She's the perfect candidate.

TOBY: You'll have given us a second term and we won't even have to leave the building. Not because I'm right and you're wrong, though I am and you are, but just because I'm better at this than you.

Not this time. An aide slides a manila envelope out of his briefcase and reveals a picture of Josephine McGarry, "enforcing the law."

Toby knows he's been beaten; he brings the photograph to Leo. It shows police breaking up a prayer at a high school football game. Two students are on their knees praying, locked in handcuffs. Leo's sister stands next to a cop whose hand is on his nightstick. One of the students is in his band uniform; another is black. The depiction couldn't be much worse. Toby begs, he can save it, but Leo pleads for him to slow down, they could live without an assistant secretary of primary and secondary education.

INS agents report to Josh that illegal aliens often pay up to $40,000 to be smuggled into the United States and work the debt off as indentured servants. Sometimes they are coached so they appear genuinely persecuted. The reality of it is grim: they had to want the freedom of America pretty desperately to spend two months in a container with dead bodies.

Charlie hasn't given up hope. He's armed with the Messermeister Meridian 3000 for the President, but with a second glance, Bartlet announces he doesn't like the handle. He's got more important matters on his mind: the Chinese Embassy says the people were not persecuted, and they left China illegally, so they must be sent back. Bartlet is aware of the coaching problem that often takes place, and therefore he's having one of the refugees flown in to meet with him. If the man is truly, deeply religious and not merely feigning faith to enter the U.S., Bartlet says, then he will have an innate understanding of "shibboleth." The word was originally a password mentioned in the Bible, a way for the armies to distinguish true Israelites from imposters sent across the River Jordan.

Leo invites his sister to the White House, but the air of hospitality ends there. He wants her

to withdraw her name from the list of appointments. He was willing to support her but the picture means, game over. Leo remembered, a few years ago he met a photographer on a campaign trip who told him Leo's sister had given him a heads-up on a photo-worthy event. Leo couldn't help but notice his name on the picture credit. Laws have to be enforced, Leo admonishes, but they do not strut while they do it. Toby admits that Leo's instinct about Josephine was right, but there would have been a reward to this fight.

> TOBY: It's the fourth-grader who gets his ass kicked at recess 'cause he sat out the voluntary prayer in homeroom. It's another way of making kids different from other kids. And they're required by law to be there. That's why you want it front and center. The fourth-grader? That's the prize.

It is the moment of truth in the Oval Office as Bartlet sits face-to-face with the Chinese refugee. He asks Jhin Wei (Henry O) to describe his faith, and he dutifully recites the names of the apostles, but asserts that religion is not about memorization of facts. Jhin Wei quotes Paul as saying man is justified by faith alone. "Faith is the true . . . " he struggles for the word. " . . . shibboleth." Bartlet smiles. He's heard the magic word.

After Jhin Wei leaves, Leo and the President discuss the imminent problem. Leo acknowledges that a healthy relationship with China is advisable. The U.S. wants to sell more 747s to China, have them protect copyrights, and negotiate on Tibet. The President wonders if they have to actually grant asylum to assure the freedom of the refugees. They are being guarded by INS agents and the National Guard. Surely, these guards will have to step away to celebrate their own Thanksgiving holidays. Surely, they will have to turn their backs at some point. Bartlet looks at Leo and smiles. The President tells Mrs. Landingham to get the governor of California on the phone.

The staff is more than ready to proceed with the holiday weekend. Toby asks C.J. what she's doing for Thanksgiving. She retorts it's about time he asked, she's been turning down other invites for weeks. Toby assures her, he just wants her to cook *for them*.

BLANCHE SINDELAR
I did all this research on carving knives of the period. We had to have the boxes for all those knives. Some were made, some I found. The final one, we took a flute box and had it remade to hold the knife and fork box. And the medallion on the top was carved with Paul Revere's initials. That's something special we made.

The turkey farmer has come to reclaim the unpardoned turkey. C.J. doesn't want to admit it, but she's gotten attached to Eric and Troy, and wants them both to go to a petting zoo. In a last-ditch effort, she tries to buy the condemned bird, but the farmer says they cost $275 each and this one's been sold already. Unable to bear the thought of Troy being eaten, C.J. wants to try to save it.

Charlie proudly presents a 1985 Komin Yomada, made in Japan from the best materials, but Bartlet says no. Bartlet tells Charlie this is so important because the Bartlet family traditionally passes on these knives from father to son. Bartlet needs a new set because he's giving his away . . . to Charlie. Bartlet removes a very old wooden box from his desk and lovingly hands it over. In awe, Charlie asks why "PR" is stamped on the lid. Bartlet explains that the knife set was made for his family by a Boston silversmith named Paul Revere, and has been passed down by proud fathers since. "I'm proud of you, Charlie," he says.

C.J. pleads with the President to pardon the second turkey in the spirit of giving. Bartlet is reluctant; he knows it's beyond even his powers to pardon a turkey. Rolling his eyes and humoring his press secretary, he drafts the flapping bird into military service instead.

Always the well of useless knowledge, the President tells Josh the Latin word for yam is *dioscorea*. Josh lets that one slip right over his head, and asks if Bartlet's heard that the refugees escaped. The President answers a bit too quickly, "Yes, can you believe it?" Bartlet ignores the questioning glances and reads from the Thanksgiving Proclamation. "A small band of pilgrims, strengthened by faith and bound by a common desire for liberty, sought out a place in the New World." The words resonate loud and clear. When they're alone, Josh asks if the President requested for the governor to stand down the National Guard. Bartlet looks Josh in the eye. He wasn't going to send them back.

JOSH: So the guy passed the test, huh?

BARTLET: You think I would send him back if he failed catechism? Let me tell you something: we can be the world's policeman, we can be the world's bank, the world's factory, the world's farm . . . what does it mean if we're not also . . . (pause) They made it to the New World, Josh. (pause) And do you know what I get to do now? (beat) I get to proclaim a national day of Thanksgiving.

VOICE: (O.S.) over the singing

ANNOUNCER: Ladies and gentlemen, boys and girls, the President of the United States.

BARTLET: This is a great job.

Martin Sheen

I love the funny stuff. I loved the turkeys—that was C.J. Anything with C.J. is precious. I love to crack her up. I think if all of us had our druthers, she would be the most favorite of all. We cherish scenes with each other, but when we get a chance to play with C.J., there's something real special about working with that dame. Every one of us knows it.

TOBY ZIEGLER
RICHARD SCHIFF

Is White House Communications Director Toby Ziegler the conscience of the Bartlet administration? He often stands on the moral high ground. He's there on capital punishment and it informs his opinion of census sampling. Toby is moved to arrange the funeral of a homeless vet and to publicly criticize the Indonesian president on human rights.

Toby's speech on the basketball court in "The Crackpots and These Women" shows this side of Toby best. As the President refuses to take a breather at game point, Toby sees a metaphor before him. Bartlet could have been a leader of men, "but the voices of his better angels were shouted down by his obsessive need to win." Bartlet is too pragmatic; not idealistic enough.

Toby argues with the President about the watered-down gun control bill, among other things. The President would like to emphasize it will save lives; Toby wants him to say the bill is worthless. Although Bartlet tells Toby at the end of the episode how much he relies on him, Toby's principles have gotten in the President's teeth.

This is nothing compared with Bartlet's anger at Toby's reaction to being told about the President's MS. Toby seems unable to get past the fact that the President has done something wrong. He has deceived, he has defrauded; people are going to get subpoenaed, deposed, court-martialed. Initially, it looks like Toby's not going to be able to overcome his indignation.

But Toby gets over it. Toby couldn't force his morals on anyone else if he wanted to. But he is willing to go the extra yard to achieve something he believes in. When Bartlet's second State of the Union address has to be written, Toby shows his true colors. More than anything, perhaps, he resembles a New Deal Democrat. Government exists to effect change for the good. Toby's convictions are his politics; not the other way around.

The last person who wants to see Toby exemplify an administration conscience is Richard Schiff.

Richard Schiff

George Stephanopoulos was on the set. He was asking me a bunch of questions and something about Toby didn't seem to jive with his idea. He said, "But Toby's the conscience of the White

House." That's what people are saying. My response to that is that I don't like to label it because then you are beholden to the label. And then you start getting limited.

Toby wants to win as much as anybody. When it came to the Mendoza confirmation, Toby was a pit bull. Mendoza was Toby's personal crusade. Perhaps Toby sees how much the two men have in common. When Mendoza is sitting in his Connecticut jail cell ready to jeopardize his nomination to beat a bogus drunk driving charge, Toby won't let him risk throwing his opportunity away. While it might morally be the right thing for Mendoza, as a jurist, to use the system to exonerate himself, the pragmatic approach is justified by the result—the win.

Messrs. Ziegler and Schiff would agree this is the priority. As Richard Schiff says, it's not as though the Bartlet administration had such a great first year.

RICHARD SCHIFF

I heard about the pilot, and the agents and managers were saying this is the one this year. This is the really well-written one. I didn't want to do TV at all. The only reason I was even interested was because a movie fell through. I went in and I knew Tommy Schlamme—I worked with him a couple of times and I knew John Wells. I didn't know Aaron's stuff very well. They were all sitting there and I knew I had a take on this character. I just happened to grow a beard for the other part. I went, "Wouldn't it be interesting if this guy Toby had a beard?" Who knew that I'd have to keep it for seven years or whatever.

I kind of knew they were interested, but other things were happening and I didn't know if the dates were going to work. And then I didn't want to test. The year before, I turned down four series because they asked me to test and I wouldn't. Going to the network was a big deal. I didn't want to do it. I told them I might not show up. And if I did show up, then I might do really badly. I decided that this project was worth it. I did show up and I did really badly. But I think Tommy and Aaron prepared the network and said, "He's gonna do really badly." I think they just wanted me.

AARON SORKIN

Competition for all the roles on the show was intense. We were really lucky, we got to pick from a universe of the best actors in town. A lot of people wanted to do this show. We cast it earlier than the other pilots so that nobody was already committed to something. Even with that, I think that the competition for the role of Toby was most intense. Richard Schiff really beat out the best actors in town for the part, to become the best actor in town. Once Richard did the pilot—I didn't know Richard at all before the show—I felt the same way that everybody else did, which was "get the ball in this guy's hands as much as you possibly can."

Richard Schiff

One of the things I certainly want to do, and I hope that we do as a group, is mix it up a little bit so that we throw some curveballs. Toby can't be too good of a person. None of us really should be too good of a person, or too smart or too cocky. And we're not, because if you look at the whole first year, we had very few successes. We had one. It was Mendoza. It's funny that people call us the ideal White House and not the idealistic White House. We're pretty lame as a group in terms of what we accomplish. It's very accurate and very realistic because so much of government is compromise.

GALILEO

ASA is great at naming things, says President Bartlet. He's yakking at C.J. as they head to the Briefing Room. He tells her about *Galileo* 5, a Mars lander. Sixty thousand schoolchildren are going to see its first transmissions from the surface on closed-circuit TV, and Bartlet will moderate a panel of experts to answer their questions. He tells C.J. she's not saying *"Galileo"* right. C.J. knows Bartlet will try to show off and answer all the kids' questions himself. In rehearsal Bartlet sees a sample question: What's the temperature on Mars? He says it's from 15 to minus 140. C.J. says, "No, it's 60 to minus 225." The President smugly tells her he converted it to Celsius in his head. The introduction prepared by NASA is awful, so Sam rewrites it in his head and nails it the first time. Bartlet smiles and turns to C.J.: Sam said *"Galileo"* right.

In the first act, Toby and Josh are dealing with a couple of issues. Neither looks huge. The *Milwaukee Journal* is quoting an unnamed White House source as saying the President doesn't like green beans. Leo says the Citizens' Stamp Advisory Committee is recommending Marcus Aquino be put on a stamp.* He's the former resident commissioner of Puerto Rico and a Korean War hero who advocated statehood. Leo wants a recommendation from Toby by the end of the day. Josh mocks him for getting the stamp assignment, so not surprisingly, Toby unloads the task on Josh.

C.J. advises Toby green beans aren't a story. Toby tells her to come see him in three hours. The President wants a clear schedule after 6:30 P.M. to read a couple of books on Mars and another on Galileo, but Mrs. Landingham dutifully reminds him he won't be reading. Leo put him down for a concert at the Kennedy Center by the Reykjavik Symphony Orchestra. Leo committed Bartlet because he canceled the Icelandic ambassador the day before; Iceland is threatening to defy the whaling ban, and they can't afford to offend them.

Intelligence reports a fire at a Russian oil refinery. Except it's not a refinery, as the Russians claim, it's a missile silo and it's beginning to look suspicious. Bartlet tells Charlie about Galileo Galilei, who deduced a physical theory observing a lamp at a church service. He went against Aristotle, which was a big deal in the seventeenth century. Bartlet ponders out loud: he wants a broader theme for the Mars classroom.

C.J. shows up in Toby's office after two hours and twenty minutes. He was right. Green beans are news. Everyone picked up the story. In Oregon, a big bean-producing state, the story is huge and they won Oregon by less than 10,000 votes in the election. Leo says C.J. and Sam have to go to the Kennedy Center to discuss the broader theme. C.J. says she can't go. She hired a new deputy and most of the people she rejected will be there. And Sam can't go, either, because Mallory's going and he never called her after his photo with Laurie appeared in the newspaper.

*Among the twelve eligibility criteria outlined by the U.S. Postal Service and the Citizens' Stamp Advisory Committee governing individual stamp honorees is that they should be dead for ten years. The exception is for Presidents, who may have a memorial stamp on the first birth anniversary after their death.

SAM: Screw the moment, I can't go.

C.J.: Well, I'm afraid, as we used to say in my hometown, that's just hard cheese.

SAM: Yeah, that was a real Algonquin Round Table you grew up with, C.J.

C.J.: Hey, that is like the fourth time I've been called dumb today.

In the Situation Room, the President hears that the Russians are still saying the fire was in a refinery. The U.S. knows an SS-19 missile blew up but the warhead didn't detonate. Bartlet wants the Russian ambassador fetched at once. Someone hands Bartlet a note. Bartlet reads it and shakes his head in subtle disbelief and even almost laughs. He shows the note to Leo. Bartlet sighs, "We lost the signal from *Galileo*."

Toby tells Josh they lost the signal eleven minutes before *Galileo* was due to land. They run into C.J. dressed up for the concert. Toby inquires where she's going.

C.J.: I have to go to the Kennedy Center and be with people who don't like me.

TOBY: You can do that right here.

The Russian ambassador, Nadia Kozlowski (Charlotte Cornwell), tells Leo he's looking more handsome every year. Leo's not going there. He says the Russians have a fire in a missile silo and the U.S. has satellite pictures to prove it. She says she can't comment on national security. Leo implores her to ask them for help.

The President is in his tuxedo being driven to the Kennedy Center. His bad mood gets even worse when Charlie tells him the concert is modern music featuring anvils and castanets. Bartlet says anything written after 1860 sucks. The whole program—Samuel Barber, Stravinsky, Schönberg—sucks. And to top it off, Charlie tells Bartlet there's a premiere of a piece by an Icelandic composer who was still rewriting it at six o'clock.

BARTLET: If he wants more time, I'm happy to take a raincheck.
CHARLIE: I thought you liked classical music.
BARTLET: I do. But this is not classical music if the guy finished writing it this afternoon.

Before the concert, trays of champagne are being passed among people in formal evening dress. Sam is standing by a railing, trying to make himself inconspicuous. Mallory surprises him and he launches right into his defense. Why did he need to call her and explain himself? Mallory

says he could have called. She has a new boyfriend, Richard Andrewchuk. The hockey player? Mallory's got the upper hand and throws in that they're having lots of sex. Sam says they'd have to. What would they talk about? She says he's terribly bright. "Well, good," says Sam, " 'cause he's a *really* bad hockey player." An aide hands Sam a note.

Sam has to tell the President about the Russian rocket, which exploded when liquid hydrogen was being drained. Bartlet knows what that means and he just can't believe it. There's no news about *Galileo*.

C.J. has discovered the source of the quote about the President's eating habits: Charlie. There were some food writers visiting the White House and Charlie said the President likes steak, lobster, spaghetti, ice cream. And he doesn't like green beans. Charlie tells C.J. she's crazy to think this is serious.

CHARLIE: Education's a serious thing. Crime. Jobs. National security. In eighteen months
    I've been to Oregon four times and not a single person I've met there has been stupid.
C.J.: Everybody's stupid in an election year, Charlie.

CHARLIE: No, everybody gets treated stupid in an election year.

Okay, but from now on, C.J. says, the President likes everything.

C.J. walks onto the terrace to take a call from Toby. She tells him one of the people she turned down for the deputy position just saw her and he booed. Toby's telling her about *Galileo* 5, when another one of the rejects, Tad Whitney, starts walking toward her. C.J. begs Toby not to hang up, but he does, and C.J. talks into the dead phone for a second.

Tad approaches C.J. and he wants some answers. People at State thought he was a lock, was it because he stopped seeing her? No, they dated for six weeks five years ago. He thought she might want an explanation. It wasn't because she was bad in bed. "I'm *great* in bed," C.J. shouts. A group of people a few yards away turns and looks. Tad says he thinks it's personal and C.J.'s got a problem. She says he's not close to being a problem. When Tad asks what he can do to improve his chances next time, C.J. says he should vote for somebody else at the next election.

Sam is sitting in one of the motorcade's sedans getting an update from Josh. Mallory sneaks up on him again. Now she wants to complain to him about the cost of *Galileo*. It cost $165 million to lose, how much to make sure they won't find it again? Mallory says the money would be better spent on food, housing, education. She asks if they really need to go to Mars. Yes, says Sam.

SAM: 'Cause we came out of a cave, and we looked over the hill, and we saw fire, and we crossed the ocean, and we pioneered the West, and we took to the sky. The history of Man is hung on a timeline of exploration. And this is what's next.

Mallory actually agrees. We're supposed to be explorers, she says. She likes hearing him talk about it. She's still pissed, she assures him, but he shouldn't worry about it tonight.

The President gets back to the White House, and Leo and the ambassador are still mid-debate. She wants to set limits for an inspection team. The President asks where she gets the nerve. He says their missile regiment is a mess and he knows deserters were draining the hydrogen so they could steal the warhead. "When were they going to mention that? How could they not

ask for help?" Bartlet insists the inspectors will go in, no limits. The ambassador tells Bartlet where Russians get their nerve: "From a long, hard winter."

The staff regroups in the Oval Office. The probe is not responding. C.J. says they're left with the stamp, green beans, and the chance that one of the people who heard her say she's good in bed will make a story of it. After people suggest remedies, C.J. says the President just doesn't like green beans, don't they think the people of Oregon will understand that? Furthermore, can't they honor a man without necessarily subscribing to his politics? The government should trust its citizens to understand and respect personal differences. It's an unusual diatribe from C.J. and the room is slightly awkward for a second. Josh says he was going to recommend putting Aquino on the stamp anyway.

C.J. is left alone with the President and they walk out onto the portico. The President tells C.J. the new piece of Icelandic music was magnificent, genius. He's going to wait up and see if they hear anything from *Galileo*. C.J. says he should do the televised classroom either way. He has a captive audience of schoolchildren and some of them don't go to the blackboard or raise their hands because they're afraid to be wrong. C.J. tells Bartlet he should say, "You think you get it wrong sometimes?" He should say he hasn't given up hope, but in the meantime he's telling NASA to build *Galileo* 6. "It's about going to the blackboard and raising your hand," C.J. says. That's the broader theme. The President tells C.J. she said it right that time.

C.J. leaves and Bartlet takes a puff of his cigar, puts a hand in his pocket, and looks way up into the sky. "Talk to us," he says.

NOËL

On Christmas Eve at 9:05 A.M., Josh visits Dr. Stanley Keyworth (Adam Arkin) and Kaytha Trask (Purva Bedi) in a little-used room somewhere in the White House. Keyworth introduces himself and says Trask is training as a traumatologist. Josh has a bandage on his hand and Keyworth asks what happened. Josh says he cut his hand putting down a glass. Keyworth explains that they're from the American Trauma Victims Association. They're called in by the government for the victims of bombs and plane wrecks. Josh is belligerent. He knows who they are.

JOSH: Dr. Keyworth, I'm the deputy White House chief of staff, I oversee eleven hundred White House employees, I answer directly to Leo McGarry and the President of the United States, did you think you were talking to the paper boy?

Josh asks Keyworth why he lied to him right off the bat. Josh points to Kaytha and says she's not training. Keyworth says she is. But that's not why there's two of them, says Josh. One of them watches him everywhere he goes: to his office, even the bathroom. Stanley admits that Josh is right, and he asks if Josh is going to lie to him. He persists, asking again how Josh cut his hand. He says Josh isn't "talking to the paper boy, either."

A few minutes in, Josh is not cooperating. He's pacing the room, barking at the doctor. Stanley is trying to get Josh to tell him what happened three weeks before, when some of his colleagues were becoming concerned with his behavior. Josh realizes they're asking him about the pilot. Josh says there was a lot going on. . . .

* * *

A flashback to three weeks earlier: a brass quintet is playing loudly in the West Wing lobby. Toby asks Josh if he likes it. No, he answers, this isn't the Paramus Mall. Toby is always being accused of not being in the spirit so he's arranged for live music in the White House for the next three weeks. Josh covers his ears and tells Toby that Ben Zaharian said that tapping into the Strategic Petroleum Reserve had a lot of merit. Toby passes it on to C.J.

C.J. is conducting a standard briefing, and she's asked an unusual question about a woman going crazy during a White House tour, after she saw a painting. Sam passes Carol a note to give to C.J. just as she's asked a question about Zaharian, the energy secretary, and C.J. finesses an answer. "Good save," Josh tells her.

In the Situation Room, the President is hearing about an F-16 Falcon that left its group during a training flight. An officer says the pilot isn't responding to radio calls. They don't know whether the pilot is defecting, or if his intent is something more malicious. The air force will intercept the plane, see if the pilot's conscious, and order him to land. If he is alive, and he doesn't respond, they may have to shoot him down.

* * *

Keyworth's asking Josh about the pilot. Josh doesn't want to go deeper into this conversation and asks how long they're going to be. Stanley says he'll be as long as he wants, Leo McGarry asked him there. Josh finally relents and says he was asked to look at the pilot's personal records. There's a knock at the door. Josh flashes back. He's in white tie, there's blood on his hand. . . .

Leo tells Josh the pilot broke off ninety minutes before. He wants Josh to figure out how the pilot passed psychological screening and was given an $18 million war plane. Donna asks Josh if she can go to the Congressional Christmas party because Yo-Yo Ma's playing. Josh just says yes. There's no joking around. Josh says pensively that the pilot has the same birthday as him.

Bernard Thatch (Paxton Whitehead) of the White House Visitors' Office reports to C.J. that a woman screamed when she saw a Gustave Caillebotte painting outside the Blue Room. Thatch says the painting was on loan from the Musée d'Orsay to the National Gallery and was given to the President when he took a liking to it.

The President says he doesn't like the autopen so he's going to sign all his Christmas cards this year. How many can there be? Charlie tells him he's sending 1,110,000. There's a thousand names on the first family's list, 100,000 campaign workers and contributors, and a card for every person who wrote a letter to the White House. That's minus the death threats.

*　　*　　*

Josh tells Keyworth when the air force found him, the pilot was dead. His name was Robert Cano. Keyworth asks Josh what he'd found out. Josh said nothing, he had only twenty minutes. "How'd he die?" asks Keyworth. He crashed into a mountain, didn't he read about it?

*　　*　　*

Leo is relaying the information on the plane crash to Josh. They know the pilot was conscious before the crash because he made a radio communication: "It wasn't the plane." Josh tells Leo what he found out—that Cano was from Tallahassee, trained at Laughlin. Not much.

*　　*　　*

Keyworth's asking Josh, "What else?" They had the same birthday, but what else?

*　　*　　*

Josh tells Leo that Cano received a Purple Heart when he was shot down over Bosnia. The plane caught fire, and he ejected with some injuries.

Toby's next musical presentation is a raucous bagpipe band, and Josh seems agitated.

JOSH: I can hear the damn sirens all over the building. (beat) The bagpipes.

He and Toby are not talking, but there seems to be a conversation going on in Josh's head. Finally, he grumbles aloud that the bagpipes can't play in the lobby. He goes into his office but he can't concentrate on anything. He comes out and demands some peace and quiet in the bullpen. C.J. asks Toby, "What's been the matter with Josh? You know what I'm talking about, right?"

*   *   *

Keyworth asks Josh if he knew people were worried about him. Josh says he should ask them. He already did, Keyworth answers. He asks Josh what happened on the nineteenth. Donna wouldn't shut up about Yo-Yo Ma, for one thing.

Keyworth brings up a meeting in the Oval Office, why didn't Josh mention that? Josh says he doesn't know what Keyworth heard about that. Josh was there to provide political perspective, to say that tapping into the reserve would be a bad idea. Keyworth asks Josh if he raised his voice to the President. No way. Josh knows there's a line that can't be crossed, ever.

*   *   *

Bartlet wants to set up the meeting to talk about the Strategic Petroleum Reserve. Josh says it's a bad idea; the Reserve and the IMF debt are related through someone called Didion, and the politics of it are bad. Leo tries to stop Josh before he goes too far. The President says they aren't related. "Of course they are," says Josh. He's talking loudly. He's right on the edge.

JOSH: You need to listen to me, you have to listen to me. I can't help you unless you listen to me. You can't send Christmas cards to everyone, you can't do it. Forget the SPR, let's get the IMF loans like we *said* we were going to, listen to what I have to say about Didion *and please **listen** to me!*

This is a horrible moment. Josh has lost control but he can't back down for fear it might be worse. He tries to make a comeback and says they should move on, but Leo doesn't give him a chance—he orders Josh to go to his office. When Leo comes in, Josh is as white as a sheet. He still wants to go back to the Oval Office. Leo asks Josh if he's heard of ATVA, because he wants him to sit with a guy.

> JOSH: If this is because of what I just said in there, I wasn't at my best when I was saying it—
>
> LEO: I'm not sure you were fully conscious while you were saying it.

*   *   *

"Thank God for Leo," says Keyworth, "Leo's an alcoholic, he knows what he's talking about." Again he asks Josh how he cut his hand. Josh is still saying he put a glass down too hard on a table, causing it to shatter. He's back at that night in his white tie, sitting in his apartment, a glass in his hand. He puts the glass down and it smashes in his fingers.

> KEYWORTH: You missed the coaster with quite a bit of force.
>
> JOSH: I work out when I can.
>
> KEYWORTH: I swear, I'm completely unimpressed by clever answers.
>
> JOSH: And I was so hoping we'd have a second date.
>
> KEYWORTH: You're in nine kinds of pain, you don't know *what's* going on inside of you, and you are so locked into damage control you can't—
>
> JOSH: You diagnosed me in eight hours?
>
> KEYWORTH: I diagnosed you in five minutes. Talk about the party.

*   *   *

Josh is at the Congressional Christmas party. And then, someone's knocking repeatedly on his apartment door, asking if anybody's there.

Bartlet is in classic white tie, which he reintroduced for the Christmas party. C.J. steps out of the party to meet Rebecca Housman, the woman who got upset on the White House tour. C.J. has learned that her father was Augie Housman, a French Jew who died in Auschwitz. The Nazis stole his art, and this painting ended up in the White House, where she recognized it. Rebecca's son says his grandfather paid about $300 for it. Bernard says it's worth $400,000 now and the longer it's in the White House, the higher it will appreciate. They'd be honored to continue hanging it. But her father's painting is worth more than money to Rebecca. She looks at her son and nods a small "no" in response to Bernard's offer. The Housmans leave with their painting.

Kenneth Hardy (Production Designer)

For Josh's apartment our location scout in D.C. went around to a number of people's apartments who had similar socioeconomic traits as Josh—working in that type of government position. Then we spent a lot of time talking to Brad Whitford about how he felt about his character and some habits and things we could put in. We got personal photos of his that we framed and put in the set. Aaron has established a lot about that character, obviously. We try to work those into the set, as well.

"So what's the diagnosis?" asks Josh. Keyworth says he has posttraumatic stress disorder. "Probably not something you can have when you work for the President," says Josh. "Can't it be something else?" Keyworth says they need to get Josh to remember the shooting in Rosslyn without reliving it. That's what happened at the Christmas party. Keyworth presses Josh. Josh says he was fine but he's remembering. Yo-Yo Ma, the Bach Suite in G Major. Keyworth asks how it started, and Kaytha says, "You tasted something bitter in your mouth."

KAYTHA: The bitter taste was the adrenaline.
The music continues . . .
KEYWORTH: What happened then?
The music continues . . .
JOSH: (pause) I couldn't make it stop.

Josh is trying to listen to the music but instead he hears gunshots. Then the screaming and the sirens. There's an explosion in his head and he's hit.

But still Josh can't tell Keyworth what happened when he went home. He says he made a drink and sat down on the couch. Keyworth asks if when the pilot killed himself, did Josh wonder if he were suicidal, too? Josh says he didn't. Stanley thinks he's lying, with all they had in common. It's more than just the birthday. The pilot was shot down, his plane caught fire, he ejected. . . . Josh says he made a drink, he pushed a magazine aside. No, says Keyworth, Josh pushed a curtain aside.

KEYWORTH (V.O.): How'd you cut your hand?

JOSH's fist goes through the window.

JOSH: Yeah.

KEYWORTH: And you broke a window?

JOSH: Yeah.

JOSH is looking at his hand.

JOSH: (quietly) Oh boy. Oh God.

Keyworth says, "Okay then." Josh asks if he's cured. No, no, definitely not, Keyworth will recommend a therapist. Now Josh wants to keep talking but Keyworth says they're done. But what if there's another pilot? Keyworth tells Josh it wasn't the pilot, he had been cooking already. Usually with a gun victim it's a car backfiring or something. With Josh, it was the music, the brass quintet. Music is the same thing as sirens. Josh continues talking but Stanley and Kaytha are putting on their coats and leaving. Josh wishes them a merry Christmas.

Leo's waiting for Josh in the lobby. It's almost deserted on Christmas Eve. Josh admits he didn't cut his hand on a glass, he broke a window. Leo's sympathetic. He's been there. He says he knows the way out.

LEO: Long as I got a job, you got a job, you understand?

Josh nods his head. Leo says Donna's going to take him to the emergency room to have his hand looked at. Josh says, "Donna knows?" She was the one who guessed. Donna fetches Josh and they leave the White House. He's trying to tell her he doesn't need a doctor but she's having nothing of it. They stop by some carolers. Josh listens for a second and then they walk off together.

THE LEADERSHIP
BREAKFAST

I t's late on a freezing cold night in the White House. Josh and Sam are starting a fire in the Mural Room. C.J. and a bunch of staffers have been making a seating chart for a breakfast in the Roosevelt Room. C.J. finishes. "See," she says, "that only took seven-and-a-half hours." Toby comes in. He says they missed one. It takes some time but C.J. realizes she forgot to seat the President.

Josh and Sam's fire fills the hall with smoke. Too late, Sam reads an information card off to the side of the fireplace that says the flue's been welded shut since 1896. Charlie comes in and says if the alarms go off, he has to wake the President. In a matter of minutes, Charlie is hurrying to the residence where he rouses

Bartlet to his bedroom door. "Mr. President," Charlie says, "you know how you told me not to wake you up unless the building was on fire . . . ?"

Leo and Toby discuss the guidelines for the Congressional/White House breakfast. It's supposed to herald a new era of bipartisanship so the idea is they can only discuss things they agree on. Nothing about the minimum wage or tax cuts. Toby proceeds to talk about issues, but Bartlet is fixated on the fact that Vermont maple syrup is on the menu. He lays down the law. In his White House, they only serve New Hampshire syrup.

Leo asks Josh if he's okay. He's going to ask him once a day. Next, he hits Josh up for a favor. Can Josh go to a dinner party and apologize to Karen Cahill, a columnist for *The New York Times*, for a joke Leo made about her shoes? He says if someone else does it, Leo appears thoughtful; if he does it himself, he'll seem effeminate. Josh farms it out to Sam.

C.J. and her staff are discussing the breakfast with Ann Stark (Felicity Huffman) and her staff. The conversation centers on the language for the remarks afterward. Carol lays out the game plan. Congressional leaders will talk to the press at the northwest entrance to the White House; C.J.'ll take questions in the Briefing Room twenty minutes later. "No," says Ann, "The majority leader will brief in front of the U.S. Senate, they need to be on equal footing." Toby comes in and leads Ann outside. The rules are crap, he says, they'll talk about them over breakfast.

Toby informs Leo he's meeting with Ann Stark. Toby believes when they have everyone in the room for ninety minutes, it's cowardly not to talk about real issues.

TOBY: This is what my ex-wife and I did for years. We had these rules. We could talk about anything but why we couldn't live with each other. I could have been two years younger right now.

Leo says he doesn't like people trying to impress him, and Ann Stark's only been the Senate majority leader's chief of staff for two weeks. He couldn't talk about real issues with his ex-wife, Jenny, either. They loved each other and they knew it was never going to change.

Sam's been kicking around a new idea. The White House is jammed and they could free up space by moving the press corps to the OEOB. It's a bad idea and C.J. fights back. They can't exile the press like that. It's as if they're trying to hide things from them. However, Sam and Josh persist by adding a question to a poll: If the White House moved the Press Room, would people object?

Donna asks Sam how it went with Karen Cahill. He'd worried about it beforehand but he believes he made some good points about nuclear weapons in Kyrgyzstan. There's a pause, and Josh says, you mean Kazakhstan. One is four times the size of Texas and has silos, the other is on the side of a hill and has nomads and sheep. Sam thinks he got it right. . . .

When they meet, Ann brings Toby a can of New Hampshire maple syrup as a present and peace offering. Wouldn't it be a lot more productive to talk about the minimum wage, Toby asks. If they do, Ann says, twenty senators will call and complain they moved without them. But Toby thinks their plan is not to move at all. His side has the votes and if there's no straight vote, they'll offer the wage hike as an amendment on everything. So Toby wants to talk about issues. Ann offers him a trade: fifteen minutes on dropping the litigation shield in the Patients' Bill of Rights in exchange for holding the press conference on the Hill. Toby takes it. What about C.J., Ann says, she'll object. Yes, but Toby points out C.J. works for him.

Now Sam is sure he mistakenly rambled on about Kyrgyzstan to Karen Cahill. He thinks she must have special powers to make people behave at their worst. Sam begs Donna to talk to her and to apologize for his silly error.

Toby breaks the news to C.J. about his deal with Ann Stark. She's furious. "It makes *us* look small and it makes Congress appear to be the seat of power." C.J thinks Toby took her legs out from under her with Ann Stark. Is Toby ordering her to move the press conference? Toby doesn't want to order her but C.J. says he's going to have to. "Do it," Toby says, and walks out of C.J.'s office.

C.J.hands over the reins of the press conference to a staffer. While she's waiting for it to start, a reporter asks her if they're thinking of moving the Press Room. Another reporter was asked by a pollster about it. At the press conference, the majority whip is talking to the assembled press. The breakfast is finished and the whip's reeling off the language C.J. and Ann discussed. He's saying the majority leader has a sore throat and went back to his office. C.J., watching on TV, knows something is up. She says Ann "took the majority leader off the board." They're about to get hit.

Ann Stark is watching, too, waiting for it. "Call on Simon," she says.

The whip duly calls on Simon, a reporter. He's nicely set up. He quotes "a senior White House aide" as saying that unless they get a straight up-and-down vote on the minimum wage, they'll attach it as an amendment to everything that moves. It's what Toby said to Ann. Toby's watching on TV as Congressman Shallick steps to the podium.

Kevin Falls (Co-Executive Producer)
We had been trying to find a place for Felicity [Huffman] all year, and Ann Stark, the chief of staff for the Republican majority leader, we felt would be perfect for her.

> SHALLICK: (on TV) This is disgraceful, and I think the record should show that a spitball contest was begun *behind* our backs, *through* the press, and before the one hundred seventh Congress was even gaveled into session. You want some quotes, open your notepads.

It's a train wreck. C.J.'s saying this wasn't part of the deal. Toby calls C.J. and tells her he's the senior aide they're quoting. Shallick's saying they've been ambushed so the minimum wage will be kept in committee and there'll be no up-and-down vote in the foreseeable future. It's a partisan disaster. C.J. has her deputy, Henry, on another phone. He's due to follow with their press conference. Toby says, "Don't let Henry take the podium." C.J. will take questions in the Briefing Room in twenty minutes. C.J. tells Henry to get home. Toby slams his phone down.

Leo storms up to Toby and asks what the hell happened. Toby reveals he gave the quote to Ann Stark and she fed it to a reporter. When he spoke to her it wasn't a quote, he was letting her know they had the votes. Leo says Toby misunderstood his relationship with Ann Stark, and now it looks like their administration went straight to the press.

> LEO: It was a breakfast. It was a damn photo opportunity. The year is one week old. The legislative session hasn't begun, and we can't put a forkful *of waffles in our mouth without coughing up the ball*. (pause—to TOBY) You got beat.

As for C.J.'s press briefing, Toby says they can't be passive and the high road doesn't go where they need. He tells C.J. to be cool and funny, then smack 'em down hard. "The majority leader's tragically out of touch," says Sam. "Why wasn't *he* at the podium," asks Josh. He has a sore throat. Josh answers, "We know how tough that can be, thank goodness he has health insurance." C.J. says that's the sound bite and the new story.

Sam asks Donna about her evening with the *Times* columnist. Karen confided to Donna that she wasn't really listening to what Sam was saying. Donna says she, on the other hand, "had a most stimulating conversation." She was pithy and erudite, no need for next day follow-up. Josh opens a recently delivered package and in it is Donna's underwear. Josh knows it's Donna's, her name is sewn in the back; they'll be discussing that later. Sam figures Donna wore the same pants twice that week; her underwear was stuck in the leg and they fell out on the floor in front of Karen Cahill, who kindly sent them back with a note.

C.J. asks Sam and Josh if a question was added to the monthly DNC tracking poll. Sam replies, "The poll's private, the only way the press would know would be if a reporter were called by a pollster." Well, C.J. says dryly, one was. Sam wonders what the chances of that are. He's thinking about the size of the odds. C.J. just wants him to fix it. Before this crucial press briefing, Josh has something he wants to say to C.J.

> JOSH: You had a lot of opportunities to say I told you so and score some points with Leo. You're a class act.
>
> C.J.: Why were you holding women's underwear before?
>
> JOSH: I've never really needed a reason. (beat) Eat 'em up.

Later on TV, a newscaster reports C.J. saying there was no intent to ambush Republicans with something that's been on the table for a year. Ann Stark is watching in her office when Toby comes in. She tells him he'd better get used to the idea that his party isn't in the majority. And the Constitution doesn't endow the White House with sovereign power. Ann's positively frosty, and she tells Toby never to walk into her office without an appointment again.

TOBY: (beat) You think this could wait until an election year.

ANN: When is it not an election year?

TOBY: Ten years ago? We used to be able to sit down. We'd order a couple of bourbons and talk about health care and the minimum wage. (pause) He didn't have a sore throat.

ANN: No.

TOBY: You kept him off the board so he'd come back on and fix it.

ANN: Yeah.

TOBY: When are you gonna announce?

ANN: Announce what?

TOBY: That he's running for President.

ANN: I'm pretty sure we just did.

Charlie asks the President, Donna's wondering if he could tell Karen Cahill she wasn't making a sexual advance when she left her underwear at her feet. No, he couldn't. Charlie says Toby's outside but the President doesn't want to see him. He packs up and heads out to the residence.

Toby walks into the Oval Office. He knows Bartlet avoided him. Toby admits he made a blunder he could have avoided if he'd listened to C.J. or Leo. Toby says their opponents are coming for them. Leo knows. If Toby only knew what it was like to get Bartlet to run the first time. "It was like pushing molasses up a sandy hill." If Leo has to tell him it's time to run again, Bartlet's gonna get crazy.

TOBY: So we gotta do it *for* him. (beat) We'll keep it away from this office, but we gotta get real now. (beat) Leo, Ann Stark's a wartime consigliere. That's why she was bumped up.

LEO: I'm a wartime consigliere, too, Toby.

TOBY: Yeah.

LEO: I was just hoping it'd be peacetime a little longer.

TOBY: Yeah.

LEO: Son of a bitch.

TOBY: Yeah.

LEO: Shake my hand.

TOBY does . . .

LEO: We just formed it.

TOBY: Formed what?

LEO: The Committee to Reelect the President.

THE DROP-IN

The nuclear missile defense system is being tested. In the Situation Room several officers and civilians are looking at a big screen that is displaying a detailed radar projection. As the target is launched from an atoll in the South Pacific, Leo announces that he's going to get the President. President Bartlet is accepting the credentials of a new ambassador of Thailand in the Oval Office. There's a bit of banter, the official presentation, and some photographs. When Leo comes by, Mrs. Landingham knows they're testing what she calls "the preposterous contraption." The President rolls his eyes and tells Leo it's not going to work. Leo's the "Charlie Brown of missile defense," he says.

When the President reaches the Situation Room, he's told an interceptor has been fired at the simulated nuclear warhead and they should collide seventeen miles up. There's a countdown to impact followed by a long silence. An announcement is made: "Negative intercept." There are gestures of frustration. Leo asks how much they missed by. "By one three seven," says a colonel. "That's 137 feet?" asks Leo. "No," the colonel says, "they missed by one hundred thirty-seven miles." That's not bad when you consider the size of outer space, quips Bartlet.

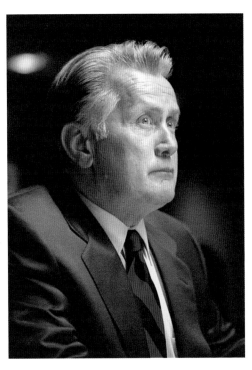

C.J. is telling the press the President will be meeting four new ambassadors this week, including an as-yet-unnamed British one. No one cares. Sam has something for C.J.'s afternoon briefing. He tells C.J. she should mention they've accepted an invitation to address the Global Defense Council. The President was going to be in South America but his trip fell through. Now he can use the event to announce the Clean Air Rehabilitation Effort (CARE).

Sam goes to work in the Roosevelt Room, priming the staff for the CARE initiative. He says their position is going to be that global warming is a clear and present danger to the health and well-being of the planet. Sam makes sure everyone knows the benefits are $22 trillion versus half a trillion in compliance costs.

Toby checks in; he's been on a trip. He wants to know when this decision was made. Sam thought they had a consensus; they'd been looking for a chance to announce it. But, Toby argues, it's not as easy as that. The AFL-CIO's not going to be happy. Bartlet blew them off to go to South America, instead of which he's speaking to labor's good friend, the environmental lobby. The

President is nobody's understudy. But Sam told the President there was an opportunity, and Bartlet said yes.

Later Toby tells Leo they should screw the environmental lobby a little to show that the President isn't beholden to them. Toby wants them to be admonished for failing to condemn acts of ecoterrorism like the burning of a twelve million acre Colorado ski resort that threatened the habitat of a breed of lynx species. Toby says he doesn't want the criticism in the advance text; it should be a drop-in. "I don't want Sam and his fourteen objections," Toby says.

Josh tells C.J. he hears that Cornelius Sykes is going to be asked to host the Will Rogers dinner. C.J. knows it's a problem: at the last benefit, his jokes bordered on off-color. Because C.J. knows Corey Sykes, Josh recruits her to see him in New York.

The President is regaling the Swedish ambassador with his knowledge of all things Swedish, holding his country responsible for the fall of the Roman Empire. Leo tries to persuade the skeptical President that the missile test wasn't as bad as it looked.

LEO: Nine out of the ten criteria that the DOD lays down for success in these tests were met.
BARTLET: The tenth being?
LEO: We missed the target.

Leo tells the President about Toby's drop-in. "Can't they take it for granted that people oppose arson?" says Bartlet. Leo reminds the President that a year and a half ago he took Al Caldwell's head off because the Christian League hadn't admonished extremists. Leo says they have to hold their friends to the same standard. Meanwhile Bartlet is enjoying Leo's discomfort at the fact that the new British ambassador is Leo's old adversary, Lord John Marbury.

Sam and Toby are going over the CARE speech. Sam is determined to nail it. He's on the twelfth draft. Sam knows the difference between a good speech and a great speech is the audience's reaction, and he wants this one to make them jump out of their socks.

Josh tries to break it gently to Leo: he's not going to turn the President around on the missile shield. Leo knows he won't today or tomorrow, but as long as there's money to keep trying, he's fine. Lord Marbury arrives on his usual high horse, addressing Leo as "Gerald." Marbury's an expert on NMD and Leo wants his support on it, but Marbury says it's a wasteful military boondoggle that'll never work and violates the ABM Treaty.*

C.J. meets with Corey Sykes (Rocky Carroll) in New York to convince him to decline the dinner gig. She's concerned the press will just revisit what happened two years ago, no disrespect intended. Corey's insulted, insisting he's raised money, registered voters, and loyally voted for Bartlet. He tells C.J. it takes a special kind of arrogance to pretend her request isn't disrespectful.

It turns out that Sykes made a joke when he hosted the last dinner about New York City cops shooting black people. Corey puts his own spin on what happened. He's a black man talking to a roomful of rich Democrats, he's going to talk about airline food? C.J. says there was huge pressure on Bartlet, who was running for President at the time, to disavow the remarks for their racist undertones, and he didn't. Corey's supposed to be grateful he wasn't disavowed when the Bartlet administration wouldn't even defend him when he was called a Hollywood sleaze? Corey's most angry at what they did say: that the candidate didn't laugh at the joke. Corey tells C.J. he won't cause the President any trouble, but he did laugh at the joke.

The President's CARE speech is winding down to a close. Sam calls Toby to tell him that Bartlet went off the speech and slapped the environmentalists down, something about ecoterrorism and a ski resort. Toby tells Sam to say to the environmental lobby that friends are honest with each other, and the President has always spoken out on moderate groups not taking responsibility for extremism. Bartlet finishes and there's polite applause from the audience. Toby asks Sam what's happening in the room and Sam says they're not standing; no one's coming out of their socks.

In the West Wing lobby, Sam runs into C.J., who's just back from her meeting in New York. C.J. also feeds Sam the line about friends being honest with each other. Sam asks if she's spoken to Toby tonight, but C.J. responds that she hasn't. Sam confronts Toby about the uncanny similarities in his and C.J.'s responses. It's as if people knew what was going to happen. Sam's caught on that the line was dropped in without his knowledge and he's beyond furious. He tells Toby to get away from him. Sam tries to get in to see the President in the Oval Office but from the doorway, Toby signals to Charlie, who in turn tells Sam he can't get him in. Sam storms away.

At a reception in the Mural Room, Lord Marbury is telling Donna about eligible members of the British royal family. Leo interrupts to talk to Marbury about the missile shield. Marbury

*The Anti-Ballistic Missile Treaty between the U.S. and the USSR was signed in Moscow in May 1972, and ratified by the U.S. Senate in August. Each superpower was limited to two ABM deployment areas (after 1976, one) and was barred from developing a national version that could stop the other's missiles. The U.S. originally had an ABM system around a complex of silos in North Dakota, and the Soviet Union, one around Moscow.

admonishes Leo that he's forgotten it violates the '72 ABM Treaty, the Allies don't like it, the Chinese will increase their nuclear forces, not to mention the basic fact that it doesn't work.

LEO: You know what I haven't forgotten?

MARBURY: What?

LEO: That we opened a big can a whup-ass on you at Yorktown.

Toby's found Sam and tries to calm him down, reminding him that no one should ever go to the Oval Office mad. Sam thinks the drop-in's the story now rather than CARE, but Toby counters, insisting that it doesn't need to be a story, it'll be a law. In his view, the environmentalists should grow up—they got the package and the President. Toby didn't tell Sam because he didn't want to discuss it with him endlessly.

TOBY: I didn't want the discussion.

SAM: Then what are you doing here talking to me?! (beat) *Now* you want the discussion. (beat) You and the President may think they deserved it, but the cynicism of attacking your friends for political protection offends them. And it offends me. And it offends you. And there's really nothing I can do to make you feel better about that.

TOBY: We can't govern if we can't win.

Sam's not completely convinced and his ego is wounded. Toby doesn't want to leave it like this with Sam. He'll sit with him awhile to go over the numbers again.

In the Oval Office, Bartlet tells Leo and Josh a whole gaggle of people have been telling him he's been manipulative. One told him if he keeps this up, they'll encourage Seth Gillette in a third-party bid. Leo persists to the President that the missile shield will work. There's a time when every great invention in history didn't work. The President consults Lord Marbury on the effectiveness of the shield.

MARBURY: I think it's dangerous, illegal, fiscally irresponsible, technologically unsound, and a threat to people everywhere.

BARTLET: Leo?

LEO: I think the world invented a nuclear weapon, I think the world owes it to itself to see if it can't invent something to make it irrelevant.

MARBURY: It's the right sentiment. Certainly a credible one from a man who's fought in a war. You think you can make it stop. You can't. If we build a shield, somebody'll build a better missile.

And with that, the President accepts Lord Marbury's ambassadorial credentials and Leo offers him congratulations. "God bless America," says Marbury, to which Leo replies, "God save the queen."

Allison Janney

This group of actors is like my sports team. You have to have somebody to throw the ball to who's going to throw it back to you. This group of actors is just as concerned with making sure you have your moment as well as their own, which is just lovely and unselfish. You have to be unselfish in an ensemble like this and really just work for the end product.

It's not just about your performance. It's about making sure you're telling a story. I think we're all good storytellers and we've all been around the block. We've all come from the theater and we all have a common language, and we're all sort of around the same age. We've been at it a long time and we're not taking this for granted. It's really kind of a special thing to come to after all our years struggling.

JOSIAH BARTLET
MARTIN SHEEN

In the course of talking to Millicent Griffith, the surgeon general, about his daughter Ellie, President Bartlet makes a comment about *King Lear*. He says it's a good play, a deliberate understatement by many degrees of magnitude. [Griffith is meeting with the President, expecting to be fired over controversial remarks about marijuana.] Griffith is Ellie's godmother and she is able to enlighten Bartlet. Ellie spoke out courageously. She spoke truth to power and Bartlet had not seen it for what it was. An act of love. He is able to go back to Ellie and articulate his love for her, perhaps for the first time.

Shakespeare set his dramas among kings but they resonate for everyone. The classically educated Bartlet wields more power than any monarch. He knows his Shakespeare and he knows where it applies to him.

The foundation of the play is Lear's decision to divide his kingdom among his three daughters—Goneril, Regan, and Cordelia—in anticipation of his own death. He bases the division on how much his daughters say they love him. Goneril and Regan outdo each other in the florid telling of it, while Cordelia will not join in the charade. What will she say? Nothing. She knows the others are scheming. She knows that in the end, the heart will triumph over the games and she holds her insight in silence.

Lear's sufferings are immense. His daughters Goneril and Regan plot against him and reduce him to a shell. Every material possession and human relationship is lost. As he rails against the gods during a tremendous storm, Lear understands enough to realize he is losing his mind.

> *Blow, winds, and crack your cheeks! rage! blow!*
> *You cataracts and hurricanoes, spout*
> *Till you have drench'd our steeples, drown'd the cocks!*

In other words, bring it on! You can do no more to me! But, Lear says, "I am a man more sinn'd against than sinning."

Bartlet's extraordinary peroration in "Two Cathedrals" brings nothing other than Lear to mind. After all, Bartlet makes reference to it. The President even has his own vicious storm

brewing outside his warm White House. But Aaron Sorkin is more forgiving than Shakespeare, at least in the short term. Sick, debilitated, and assailed he might be, Bartlet is still standing at the end, all eyes on him, every ear cocked.

As the protagonists recall, the focus of *The West Wing* was originally going to be on everyone other than the President.

Aaron Sorkin

At the beginning the President wasn't supposed to be in the show at all. I wanted to get away from *The American President*. I didn't want to do that again. If the President is a character, he's going to take up all the oxygen in the room. But then I thought that was going to seem silly. We'll have always just missed him as he rounds the corner. We'll see the back of his head. I thought, this is going to be like the next-door neighbor on *Home Improvement* if we do that. So we'll use him once in a while.

Martin Sheen

My son Ramon and I were over in Charleston doing a film and Aaron calls about this show. He said, "Look, we can do the pilot now. I don't know where we're gonna go with this character. We just need you for half the season." I'd appear once a month and that's what I signed on to do.

Bradley Whitford

And then we realized after the pilot, or Aaron realized, that the reality of it is that these people are in constant contact with the President.

Llewellyn Wells (Producer)

Martin had such a great time doing it and loved the writing so much and loved the work experience so much that he said, "Where do I sign?" And then Aaron adjusted his whole thinking about the show based on the fact that this guy had come in and done such an incredible job on the project.

Both Martin Sheen and Jed Bartlet have become integral to the show.

Aaron Sorkin

I get asked, "Do you write for these specific actors?" The answer is, for the most part I do, now that we know each other very well. We've now done forty-four episodes of the show. With all of them, I'm really the first person to play the part. I'm saying it in my head, I'm walking around doing it, no one more so than Bartlet. This guy really lives inside me somewhere and I sort of do it and hand it over to Martin. A lot of the inspiration for Bartlet comes from my father, who is very much of another world. He's seventy-six now. He's a lawyer, a terribly wise and gentle man with a kind of "Aw, Dad" sense of humor. He's devoted to his family and filled with emotion about great men and women and events gone by. At times I'm writing my father, at times I'm simply writing a character I think my father would like. Oftentimes I'm giving Bartlet my kind of wise-ass sense of humor and oftentimes I'm giving him Martin's.

Bradley Whitford

The way our characters are supposed to feel about Bartlet is pretty much exactly the way we feel about Martin. Although Martin's politics are far to the left of Bartlet's, Martin is a guy who puts his money where his mouth is. He stands up for what he believes in and I think we all admire that. There's something we all love about him. He's a very humble guy. When Martin came on the show, then we got a father figure.

Martin Sheen

One of these comes along in a lifetime, let's face it. I'm sixty years old. I don't know how many years they do in these things, but we can get eight years out of it with Bartlet's presidency. Seven/eight years. I would retire at age sixty-five, sixty-six. Why would I want to look back? I mean, what am I going to do? What am I going to follow this with? I may as well go and do Shakespeare in Minneapolis or something.

BARTLET'S THIRD
STATE OF THE UNION

The President is only six minutes away from giving his third State of the Union speech, and Toby and Sam are still tweaking the text. Bartlet comments that the press is calling this the speech of his political life. There's a deal going down at the very last minute; Sam confirms it by phone and snares the news: they got the support for the Blue Ribbon Commission.

Meanwhile, Josh is supervising a roomful of pollsters, who are going to gauge public reaction to the speech. They're Joey Lucas's people but Joey's stuck on a delayed flight. Josh is very anxious and wants to get going.

The press briefing room is more packed than usual. There are several TV monitors on and the reporters are perusing copies of the speech. C.J. tells them

the President is going to announce a bipartisan Blue Ribbon Commission to study the long-term future of entitlement programs. They're reporting it late because the President wanted to make sure he had the support of the Democratic leadership. C.J. reminds everyone that *Capital Beat* is broadcasting a postgame show live from the White House for two to three hours after the speech.

At nine o'clock, Sam and Toby have finished making their revisions to the final draft of the State of the Union. In the Capitol Building corridor, right before he goes in, Bartlet prays and crosses himself. The doors are opened and the President is introduced to Congress to the traditional, thunderous applause. Bartlet approaches the podium with purpose and authority.

After Bartlet has finished, Josh and Donna, watching from the polling headquarters, congratulated each other on Bartlet's success. Josh is pumped. "That is his place of *business*." Suddenly . . .

JOEY (O.S.): Joshua Lyman, you have the cutest little butt in professional politics.

JOSH turns around to see KENNY interpreting for JOEY.

JOSH: (pause) Kenny, really, that better have been her talking.

Josh tells Joey the people need instructions. Joey calls out, "Is anyone chewing gum?" The pollsters shout no! She tells them they can get to work.

Live on *Capital Beat* with Mark Gottfried, C.J. gives Bartlet fourteen out of ten for his performance. He was interrupted with applause seventy-three times, Mark says. Deputy House Majority Whip Henry Shallick (Corbin Bernsen) points out that twenty-three of those were for co-opted Republican ideas. On air, C.J.'s her usual professional self. But, during a commercial,

Mark announces that C.J.'s not wearing any pants. In typical C.J. fashion, she sat on a bench in the sculpture garden that had just been painted and then showed up to go on air. Carol helps C.J. out by bringing a bathrobe from the women's locker room at the gym. Sam pipes in that the men don't get bathrobes, which is outrageous considering a thousand men and only fifty women work in the White House. "Yeah, and it's the bathrobes that are outrageous," says C.J. Sam has come to tell her that Jack Sloan, a Detroit policeman Bartlet just touted as a hero in his address, got an official reprimand for excessive force seventeen years ago after a criminal charge was dismissed. "Nobody has the story yet," but, as Sam says, they will.

Mrs. Landingham tells Charlie the President can't account for a five-hundred dollar check written by his wife that's never been cashed. The President balances his checkbook for relaxation, and he wants Charlie to ask the first lady about it because she would yell at Bartlet if he did.

In the residence, Abbey's watching the Blue Ribbon section of the speech over and over. When Charlie mentions the check she retorts, "Oh, how long has *that* been up his ass?" Abbey sent the money to a woman she read about in a newspaper, whose husband threw her out, set fire to the bed, and ruined the children's Christmas presents. Charlie tells her it was never cashed, but he'll look into it.

There's a reception after Bartlet's speech, and the atmosphere is excited and charged like the aftermath of opening night of a smash hit. Sam makes his entrance and is greeted like a hero. The crowd ripples with anticipation as they wait for the first poll numbers to roll in. As Leo's talking with Sam, Margaret urgently informs Leo he's needed in the Situation Room.

The mood in the Situation Room is grim. Five DEA agents have been abducted in Colombia. Leo wants to meet with the State Department, Justice, and the Pentagon, but the White House is crawling with journalists and there's a live TV show going out.

Joey patrols the phone banks as the pollsters ask questions and type responses into their computers. Josh receives new information about Jack Sloan. He tells Joey that Sloan was added at the last minute as one of the people recognized by Bartlet during the speech because of a heroic act at an elementary school. But he wasn't properly vetted, and now it is surfacing that he was officially reprimanded after he broke a suspect's leg making an arrest when he was with the Detroit PD. Josh thinks they're plagued. The numbers will be great but they will be dragged down by the negative spin on the cop story. Donna's mind is elsewhere. She says Josh should ask Joey out and "tonight's the night."

Margaret pulls Deputy Secretary Troop (Tony Plana) out of the reception. She tells him Leo wants him to "say hello to an old friend," the code for a serious problem. In the Situation Room, it's established that the agents were helping local police gather evidence at a cocaine lab when they were taken hostage. An officer reports they have nineteen guys in the area, while Troop knows they're in a Frente stronghold, and the agents will be guarded by a force of five to six hundred. Leo

says Fort Bragg Special Ops Command is going to submit three plans for a rescue.

Back on the live TV coverage things aren't running so smoothly either. Bartlet introduced an idea about compulsory school uniforms in the speech. Representing the White House on *Capital Beat,* Ainsley Hayes is saying that she's not 100 percent sure the position is constitutional. Mark asks her what the President thinks and Ainsley replies she's never met him. Off the air, Sam tells Ainsley he'd rather she hadn't said the constitutional thing. Sam didn't realize Ainsley has never met the President so he'll set it up. Ainsley admits she's scared and Sam, fountain of wisdom that he is, tells her not to drink anything.

SAM: And please don't forget you're a blond Republican girl and nobody likes you.

Abbey is giving a toast at the reception and getting big laughs. Then she quizzes Leo about the change in the Blue Ribbon language. She's clearly pissed about it and she knows who must have been responsible. Toby is introduced to the loudest cheers of the night. He's the MVP and everyone knows it. He makes his way over and embraces Abbey, but she doesn't respond with mutual warmth. She quietly tells him she wants to see him in his office in half an hour.

Donna is again encouraging Josh to ask Joey out. Josh brushes her off; he's just desperate for numbers. Suddenly, with a *thump,* all the power goes out and the emergency lights come on. In one swift moment, all the computers go down.

It's Toby's turn to face the camera on *Capital Beat.* Shallick is going on about gun control and the Second Amendment until Toby says he doesn't think the Framers of the Constitution were "thinking of three guys in a Dodge Durango. The combined populations of Britain, France, Germany, Japan, Switzerland, Sweden, Denmark, and Australia roughly equal that of the United States," Toby continues. The year before, there were thirty-two thousand gun deaths in the U.S. and one hundred and twelve in the others. Is it because Americans are more homicidal, or that the others have tighter gun controls? Toby excuses himself to pay a visit to Abbey Bartlet.

Abbey tells Toby the draft of the speech she read promised that ensuring Social Security and Medicare was the first fiscal priority of the administration, but now they're "setting aside partisan blinders, and not ruling anything out?" Toby counters that they gave the Republicans plenty to be annoyed about—the surplus, missile defense, capital gains. Yet, Abbey persists that she was thrown off by the last-minute changes.

Trying to keep a lid on the story, C.J. quizzes Jack Sloan in her office. He tells her he didn't break anyone's leg. Sloan says the guy was young, fit, and big while he himself is unathletic. He couldn't have beaten the guy up if he'd wanted to. Why didn't Sloan tell them, C.J. asks. Sloan assumed it was okay because of his recent heroic acts at the elementary school. C.J. tells him she'll have to alert the press so it doesn't look like they're hiding anything.

The power is still out but Joey says they're five minutes away from an East Coast sample. The President's back, and he's pleased he got a good reaction to some stuff he fought Sam on. Sam asks a favor in return. Could the President please introduce himself to Ainsley if he sees her? Sam advises him to say something along the lines of, "people assumed she was hired because she's a blond Republican sex kitten, they're obviously wrong, and keep up the good work."

Leo informs the President it's not the cop that's going to drag them down, they have an impending crisis in Colombia. The Situation Room's packed with people, and Bartlet is brought up to speed. The DEA agents will be killed unless a major drug lord, Juan Aguilar, is released from prison. Troop says Colombia won't agree to that. An officer outlines the military option, called Cassiopeia, but Troop wants to negotiate because a military intervention could escalate into a war. Leo says we're already *in* a war on drugs. The President tells his people to keep talking, but in three hours, special forces should be ready to kick in the door. Meanwhile, Bartlet says he'll be wandering the halls.

Sam goes to Ainsley's office and finds "Blame It on the Bossa Nova" playing full blast. Ainsley's having a great time. She's in a bathrobe drinking a pink squirrel, singing and dancing to the music. She says she sat on the same bench as C.J., and is thus relying on a bathrobe for coverage. Then she sees someone at the door and she shrieks, her arms flying up in the air, her drink sloshing everywhere. It's the President. "I never even knew we *had* a nightclub down here," he says.

BARTLET: Ainsley, I wanted to say hello and to mention, you know, a lot of people assumed we hired you because you were a blond Republican sex kitten and, well, they're obviously wrong, and keep up the good work.

Mark Gottfried tells C.J. off the camera that he's known about Sloan all night but he didn't want to ambush her. Toby interrupts, using the "old friend" line on C.J. Before she goes, she pleads for twenty minutes from Gottfried before he breaks the story.

The President wanders his way into the White House kitchen, where he finds Abbey sitting at a table eating a sandwich. Bartlet asks the staff to step out for a second. Bartlet knows she's mad at him. She erupts: When did he decide not to mention the Violence Against Women Act? Things had to be cut, he responds.

ABBEY: You made a promise, we had a deal.

BARTLET: (beat) Abbey—

ABBEY: When did you decide you were gonna run for a second term?

BARTLET: That's not what tonight's speech—

ABBEY: That's *all* that tonight's speech was about. (beat) You kicked off your reelection campaign. And I'm sitting here, eating a sandwich . . . 'cause we had a deal.

BARTLET: That was three years ago.

ABBEY: Yeah.

Stockard Channing
One of my favorite scenes is the one with Martin in the kitchen when she says they had a deal. People didn't really know what I was talking about, but they know that something's wrong with her because she wouldn't normally get this angry.

Bartlet's apologetic but knows he now has to switch gears. He tells Abbey about the Colombian emergency. Charlie summons him to join the senior staff. Abbey relents and tells her husband he has to focus. She'll stay up with him. Abbey heads back to the reception and greets well-wishers. Meanwhile, on TV, Mark Gottfried fades into the background, touting that the State of the Union appears to be a blockbuster.

EMILY PROCTER
Of course, there's comedy in life. My grandmother passed away not too long ago. I went to her house. Everyone starts calling on you, so you clean a little bit. I have long hair and the only thing I could find to pull it back was these reindeer antlers. It was a headband my grandmother used to wear at Christmas. I forgot I had it on. Everyone kept showing up and their first comment was, "It looks just like Christmas." And I said, "Oh, I know. Everyone's together and this is how Grandma would have liked it." I realized at the end of the day, when I went to the rest room, that I had on the reindeer antlers the whole time. And I thought, you know, that's life. And that's Ainsley.

THE WAR AT HOME

Three hours after the State of the Union address, Leo finds the President sitting outside on the White House portico smoking a cigarette. Leo chides him about his habit but Bartlet protests he only smokes two cigarettes a day. The President is mulling over what to do about the DEA agents in Colombia. In the Situation Room, the rescue plan is carefully outlined. They'll spring the hostages as they're being moved to the Frente command center. Troop suggests they keep negotiating but Bartlet says he has reason to believe the agents will be tortured. He gives the go-ahead for the rescue.

On *Capital Beat,* Mark Gottfried wraps up the live broadcast from the White House. He reminds C.J. she'd said she'd be gone twenty minutes and she was away for forty. C.J. tells Gottfried she found out that Sloan is innocent; he was cited for excessive force to calm the black community. To soothe Gottfried's temper, C.J. offers him an exclusive interview with Sloan for his show tomorrow.

Sam tells Toby that Seth Gillette wants a meeting with him. Toby replies with an emphatic no; he had his input. Besides, he's not the President, he's the junior senator from North Dakota. Too late. Gillette's important to the left wing and environmentalists, so Sam has set up the meeting already. C.J. joins them and says the *Post* is giving the speech good reviews. "Sleek, challenging, and oftentimes witty. Not unlike myself," she says. Toby thinks putting Sloan on TV is a bad idea. But C.J. believes he's not a brutal cop and has a right to clear his name.

Meanwhile at the polling banks, the power is still out. Donna is telling Josh he's missing all the romantic signals from Joey. Much to Josh's chagrin, Joey says they should pack in the polling till tomorrow.

The President's outside on the portico, playing chess with himself, waiting. He can't shake the image in his mind of dead soldiers being brought back from Vietnam. He knows the operation in Colombia is going down in the morning.

The next morning, Josh is telling Sam he thinks it's strange that Donna was pushing him to ask Joey out. Does he get jealous when Donna goes out with guys? Sam asks. Of course not. He just doesn't like it and usually does everything he can to sabotage it.

JOSH: —which is why it's curious that Donna would do nothing to discourage, in fact do everything to *encourage*, a date with Joey Lucas, who, quite frankly, is a very attractive woman.

SAM: Josh?

JOSH: Yeah?

SAM: You know your voice got just really high at the end of that?

JOSH: Yeah, sorry.

The President asks Sam and Josh to meet him for breakfast. Bartlet is extremely anxious about the hostages and the building crisis in Colombia. He says Nelson Guerra, the Frente head,

Emily Procter

Ainsley and Sam's relationship has evolved. It's a really thorough friendship between a man and a woman. I think Sam and Ainsley trust each other. They like each other. They have a similar sense of humor and a similar sense of being put in the embarrassing situations. They have a lot in common and they've become friends because of it. If it will move forward from there, who knows?

wants him to tell President Santos to release Juan Aguilar but he's not going to do that. They're not winning the war on drugs. He says last year it cost sixteen billion dollars and 60 percent of federal prisoners are incarcerated on drug charges. They have one-point-eight million people behind bars, a higher percentage than Soviet Russia or apartheid South Africa, and Just Say No isn't working. The President presses Sam and Josh for any thoughts they might have on the subject.

Ainsley wants another chance to meet the President. Sam says she had her chance last night; he's not the one who had her jumping around like Joey Heatherton.* Ainsley pushes and convinces Sam into arranging another introduction.

Toby reluctantly takes his meeting with Seth Gillette (Ed Begley Jr.) in a hotel restaurant. Gillette thinks he should have been given a heads-up on the announcement of the Blue Ribbon. Toby asks, "Where's the danger in studying options?" Gillette proposes the White House support his bill, which would divert general revenue into the trust funds instead, a proposal that has already garnered eighteen votes in Congress. Gillette makes a threat: if the commission recommends raising the retirement age one day or cutting benefits one dollar, he'll publicly condemn it. Gillette points out that the Bartlet administration lost friends admonishing environmentalists, and this morning they defended a cop who beat a black kid. He warns them that they're alienating seniors, environmentalists, and African Americans.

> SETH: Tell me which you think has a greater chance of happening: my reform bill getting passed . . . or the President getting reelected without the three groups I just mentioned.
>
> TOBY: You've named three groups that will never desert the President.
>
> SETH: Not unless I run as a third-party candidate, no. (beat) Those eighteen votes are lookin' a little bigger now, aren't they, you patronizing son of a bitch.

Toby tries to make light with a joke: "With friends like these, who needs anemones." Then he tells Gillette if he comes at them from the left, Toby's gonna own his ass.

Mrs. Bartlet is packing for a trip but she sends her staff out when the President arrives. She isn't in the mood to talk about what they discussed in the White House kitchen. Abbey tells her husband he's a jackass but he should deal with his crisis. Then they'll talk.

---

*Bartlet would recall Joey Heatherton's heyday in the sixties better than Sam. She was a sexy and dynamic dancer and singer who appeared in numerous movies and TV shows from *The Virginian* and *I Spy* to *The Mike Douglas Show* and *The Jackie Gleason Show.*

The electricity's back on, and Josh is waiting for poll numbers to return from five congressional districts. He tells Donna the President announced a five-day waiting period for a background check for gun buyers and those five congressmen are on the fence. If the idea polled well, he says, the bill will probably pass. If not, there'll be no bill, or they'll lose the seats. Josh changes the subject to what's really on his mind. Why is Donna trying to hook him up with Joey?

In Leo's office, an extremely professional-looking Ainsley is preparing herself to meet the President again. Ainsley asks if she can use the bathroom, and when Leo says yes, Ainsley walks straight into a closet. Before Leo can rescue her, Bartlet arrives. Sam relishes telling the President that Ainsley's in Leo's closet, she thought it was a bathroom. The President calls on Ainsley to come out.

BARTLET: How you doin', we met last night. You were singing and dancing in a bathrobe.

AINSLEY: Yes sir.

BARTLET: Why were you in the closet?

AINSLEY: I had to pee.

BARTLET: (to SAM) They won't let me smoke inside but you can pee in Leo's closet?

The President moves into the Oval Office. He's told the hostages weren't where they were supposed to be, that the radio communications they'd intercepted were wrong. It was an ambush. A shoulder-mounted SAM shot down a *Blackhawk* with nine people on board and now they've got nine more guys on the ground they have to get back. Bartlet wants a second *Blackhawk* to go in to get the bodies of the rescuers. But Leo breaks the bad news. The men are dead. Bartlet screams, get the president of Colombia on the phone at once. He storms out the portico door and rails outside in the rain. Leo comes out and the President is raging; no one thought they might try that? "IS THAT HOW I JUST LOST NINE GUYS, TO A DAMN STREET GANG WITH A HAM RADIO??!!!"

Back in the Oval Office, Bartlet tells his Colombian counterpart what happened. President Santos confirms the hostages are alive and says he respects and appreciates Bartlet for not asking him to release Aguilar, although he will if Bartlet requests.

Later, Toby argues that if they give in to the Frente's demands, that's the ball game. Sam agrees, but lives are at stake. Bartlet is firm in his belief—he'd rather sit in jail with Aguilar than let him out. He wants military options. Troop tells the President that to wipe out the Frente, they need a ten-to-one ratio like they had in the Gulf War. The Frente has twenty thousand soldiers, so they'd need two hundred to three hundred thousand men and they'd lose half. Bartlet wonders out loud, "What's the point of being a superpower anymore?"

Bartlet decides to make peace on the home front, and goes to see Abbey in their bedroom. Aides are helping her with suitcases again. Once they're alone, Bartlet shares the tragic news about Colombia. Then he says he hasn't decided to run again, he wouldn't make that decision without her. She says he already did. Abbey points out, "The whole place is in reelection mode."

BARTLET: That's what we do, Abbey, we run for things. From the day a congressman is sworn in, he's got to raise ten thousand dollars a week so he can get reelected. A President gets to govern for eighteen months. We try and get people to vote for us and in the process we hope the people force us to do good things.

ABBEY: We had a deal.

BARTLET: Yes, we had a deal.

ABBEY: Yes, Jed, look at me. Do you get it that you have MS?

Abbey reminds her husband that relapsing/remitting MS can turn into secondary progressive MS ten years after diagnosis, which is where they'll be in two years' time. She says he'll be fatigued, he'll lose the ability to think clearly, to reason. She says their deal is how Bartlet justified keeping

the MS a secret from the public. How he justified it to God and to her. Now, Abbey has to leave. They both say "I love you" before she walks away.

The polling numbers on gun control are in and they're bad. Josh asks, "A person can't wait five days to buy a gun?" Joey adds the waiting period tested well nationally. Josh thinks they'll have to dial it down but Joey suggests doing the reverse. Numbers lie all the time.

JOEY: If you polled one hundred Donnas and asked them if they think we should go out, you'd get a high positive response. But the poll wouldn't tell you it's because she likes you and she knows it's beginning to show and she needs to cover herself with misdirection.

JOSH: Believe me when I tell you that's not true.

Joey says the numbers just show Josh he hasn't persuaded people yet. He should lead, not follow.

Leo is in the Oval Office advising the President not to go to war in Colombia. Leo's fought a jungle war and he's not doing it again. If he could be anywhere in time, it would be the Cabinet Room, August 1964, when U.S. ships were attacked in the Tonkin Gulf. He'd speak up and say don't commit the troops. As far as Leo is concerned, the war's at home, the casualties are in American prisons and hospitals. The government is spending the same in Colombia fighting drugs as American consumers are spending buying them. They're funding both sides in the war and they can never win it that way.

Bartlet doesn't think he can call President Santos and ask for the release of Aguilar, but Leo says someone else can take care of the logistics. The people who heard Santos make the offer will keep the secret. Bartlet fantasizes about a Black Ops mission to kill Aguilar but he knows he can't do it. "We lost this one," Leo says. Bartlet instructs Leo to get the DEA agents out. The President is going to Dover to meet the bodies of the nine rescuers who died trying to free the hostages.

C.J. briefs the press on the Colombian crisis. She's spinning the story about how Aguilar was released from prison on a direct order from President Santos.

The President is standing on the runway at Dover Air Force Base at four in the morning. A transport plane stands on the tarmac with its cargo door open. Two lines of Coast Guard sailors in dress uniform make a path leading from the ramp. The two lines snap to attention. The President meets the honor guard accompanying the flag-draped coffins as they are brought from the plane and returned to American soil.

Martin Sheen
To have watched the flowering and recognition of talent. Richard Schiff, for example, he's been at this for, how many years? *Boom!* He's suddenly recognized as an actor. And people begin to discover him from all these other things he's done over the years. John Spencer, my God, he's been a known player in New York, and for *L.A. Law*, and any number of things. I've seen him for years. *Boom!* There he is. Brad Whitford, I mean, you look at him and you start laughing. He's got my number and all of us. He looks at you and you're finished. Then you get the first lady. You know, I'm a fan. I almost asked for her autograph. We've become really very close. These people have just been remarkable. It truly is an ensemble. I love the way Aaron spreads it around. Because any one episode to another, it can be about you one week and about any one of us the following week. Everybody gets in and supports it.

ELLIE

Dr. Millicent Griffith (Mary Kay Place), the surgeon general, is doing an online chat about the safety and legality of marijuana. She says there's no evidence it hurts reproductive systems permanently. From her office, Donna is following on her computer. Josh notices Donna's still working and tells her his memo on efficiency and professionalism is in effect—it's nine o'clock and time to pack up. Josh touts his message: Stay on the reservation, do the job. Donna draws Josh's attention to her computer screen: Griffith is asked if she supports decriminalization. Griffith says it's not for her to say. But marijuana poses no greater health risk than nicotine or alcohol and is not as addictive as heroin or LSD. The surgeon general thinks it's bizarre that marijuana is a schedule one narcotic while the government puts its seal on packs of cigarettes. Donna tells Josh, "Somebody didn't get your memo."

This is going to be big news. Once Josh has told her what happened, C.J. plays out the media response. Los Angeles and San Francisco will have it in the morning, and the *Today* show will lead with it. Toby comes out of a Blue Ribbon meeting in which Labor is yelling at him, and is accosted with the news about Griffith. Trying to fashion a defense strategy, the staff gets caught up in figuring out exactly when the President will return from his trip to Tokyo.

The problems don't end there. Sam says the Family Values Leadership Council has taken a full-page ad in twenty-two papers. He says it thanks a list of people for denouncing the movie *Prince of New York*. The problem is the President is one of them, and he's never even heard of the movie.

The next morning, Toby is throwing a Spalding ball against the wall in his office, trying to work through something. Sam is roused from his work and goes next door to see what's going on. Toby says the AARP and AFL-CIO want to put Gillette on the Blue Ribbon commission. That would neutralize Gillette, because he can't attack the commission if he's on it. It's a tricky situation though, because they can't afford to ask him and have him turn them down.

Josh asks C.J. if she can publicly support the surgeon general without endorsing her remarks. Josh will deal with Griffith himself. C.J. holds up her end of the deal at the briefing while Josh meets with Griffith. She's friendly and concerned about how Josh is recuperating after being shot in Rosslyn. But Josh is here on business: What was she thinking? Griffith indignantly replies that her answers were correct and it's her obligation as a doctor to tell the truth. She was only commenting on medical matters, not presenting an official White House stance. Josh regrets to tell her he's had three conversations with Leo and she has to resign. She flatly refused. Josh reminds Griffith that she serves at the pleasure of the President, and she says she'll continue to do so, right up until the moment he fires her.

At a briefing, C.J.'s asked about *Prince of New York* and she replies that Bartlet never denounced it to her. It turns out Charlie was offered a chance to screen the movie in the White House theater, but he passed. Morgan Ross, the producer, then went on television and declared Bartlet's a coward who's siding with puritanical censors. The Family Values Council took out the ad after that. C.J.'s incensed that Morgan Ross is getting free media by screwing them.

C.J.: I'm the enforcer, Sam. I'm gonna crush him, I'm gonna make him cry, and then I'm gonna tell his momma about it.

**Kenneth Hardy
(Production Designer)**
We got in the real surgeon general's office and took a bunch of pictures. Within twenty-four hours of knowing we needed a surgeon general's office, we had good photos of the real office. Often the real government offices are quite boring and not very attractive or interesting to shoot in. The surgeon general's office is a good example. It was in a new high-rise out in Rockville, Maryland. It had none of the trappings we liked. You need to help tell a story visually.

Martin Sheen

Oh, I love Kathryn Joosten. We all adore her. She's irascible, great fun. She's equally irascible to me off set. Wasn't she giving me the damn business the other day when I said hello to Jesse Jackson? "You won't be talking to Jesse Jackson." She and I are the oldest ones. I shouldn't have mentioned that. It's her own fault.

It happens that Morgan is due at the White House tomorrow for a meeting on voluntary ratings. Meanwhile, Danny is on the phone asking C.J. about the President's reaction to a comment in defense of the surgeon general. C.J. asks Carol, "Who made the comment?" "It was Eleanor," Carol tells her. C.J., thrown off for a moment; asks, "Eleanor who?" Eleanor Bartlet, replies Carol.

Josh tells C.J. to tone down her support for the surgeon general. But there's a wrinkle. Danny is quoting Eleanor Bartlet saying, "My father won't fire the surgeon general. He would never do that." It seems the middle Bartlet daughter is moving into the public eye.

Leo greets Bartlet at Andrews Air Force Base. He's getting off the plane and he wants to talk to the waiting press about the dangers of protectionism. Leo intercepts him with the startling news that Eleanor made a comment on the record. Bartlet says he must mean Zoey. By the time he's

back at the White House, Bartlet's steaming mad. "What the hell is Danny Concannon doing calling my *kids*?" He tells C.J. to suspend his credentials for six months, but C.J. reveals that Ellie called Danny, which Bartlet can't believe.

The President wants to dig deeper into the issues he's missed while in Tokyo. The Judiciary Committee, Government Reform and Oversight, Appropriations, have all come out against Griffith, and the Cannabis Society and others have jumped to her defense. Bartlet also understands he's denounced a movie he's never heard of.

> **BARTLET**: Well, I've got to hand it to you guys, you've pulled off a political first. You've managed to win me the support of the Christian right and the Cheech and Chong Fan Club in the same day.

He knows one thing for certain: he wants his middle daughter's ass down there right now.

Charlie is telling Mrs. Landingham why he chose *Dial M for Murder* over *Prince of New York*. The movie he turned down is about a Christ-like epileptic young man who embodies goodness but encounters sex, crime, and family dysfunction. Charlie mentions an erotic fantasy scene in a church in Long Island, and Mrs. Landingham gasps, "Please don't say the word 'erotic' in the Oval Office."

The surgeon general is called in to see Leo. He congratulates her, the interview was worth twenty to thirty million to right-wing causes. She argues that they're spending eight billion a year locking up forty thousand people, but Leo doesn't think that's within her jurisdiction. Leo knows she didn't say anything wrong but he can't have the government bogged down with this issue for two months. He wants Griffith to resign by eight o'clock or the President will fire her.

While Ellie (Nina Siemaszko) waits outside the Oval Office, she has a stilted conversation with Charlie about her medical school. Her dad casually reminds her she's at Johns Hopkins, which is forty-five minutes away, yet they never see her. She admits she called Danny and he explodes. "I've gotten reporters transferred to *Yemen* for approaching Zoey and Elizabeth. It is the *law*," says Bartlet. Bartlet won't let up; he asks if she cleared it with C.J. and party leadership and everyone else to make sure her comments fit into the press cycle. Ellie quietly says Griffith was only answering the question.

> **BARTLET:** *There's politics involved in this, Ellie, and you know it would make me unhappy and that's why you did it and that's cheap!*
>
> **ELLIE:** I didn't do it to make you unhappy, Dad.
>
> **BARTLET:** Well, you sure didn't do it to make me happy.
>
> **ELLIE:** I don't know how to make you happy, Dad. For that you gotta talk to Zoey or Liz.

Toby is consulting Congresswoman Andy Wyatt, his ex-wife, about the Blue Commission conundrum. Andy points out they didn't consult a lot of liberal Democrats before they made their Blue Ribbon U-turn. Toby explains that's the only way it's going to happen, they can't solve Social Security and run for office at the same time. He thinks if they put seven Democrats and seven Republicans and the President in a room with the door closed and have them make a recommendation, they can get results. But it will only work, Toby says, if people are confident in their representation, which is why the committee needs Gillette. Andy slyly changes subjects and tells Toby that she volunteered him for a benefit committee for the Child Leukemia Foundation. Andy didn't

ask him but she says if you skip over the first step and move right to the second, it's harder for people to say no. Toby ponders this and then tells C.J. to announce that Seth Gillette will be joining the Blue Ribbon Commission. She should say he is putting the party above his personal differences, and when asked to serve, he answered the call.

As the entertainment industry and politicians battle over the new ratings system, Sam pulls Morgan Ross out of the meeting for a face-to-face talk. Sam says the President never saw his movie but Ross knew he'd get more business from the ad than he lost, so he went on television to bash Bartlet. Sam makes his point clear: If Ross calls the President a coward for his PR purposes again, he'll be dealing with Sam, not C.J. Ross gets the message.

In the White House screening room, Josh and Donna are watching *Dial M for Murder* with a rather somber crowd. Josh says it's a bad sign when the President's not talking during the movie. Bartlet steps out to see Millicent Griffith, who's come to resign. He asks if she put Ellie, her god-daughter, up to calling Danny, but she insists she didn't. Does Griffith know why he's never been able to get Ellie to like him? Bartlet thinks she's mad at him, but Griffith tells Bartlet it's the other way around, he's mad at *her*. He's been the king of whatever room he's in his whole life. She says Ellie knows she's not his favorite, but Bartlet swears that's not true. He doesn't want to believe he's isolated himself from his middle daughter. If that's the case, Bartlet realizes that stepping forward to the press was an act of great courage. *"King Lear* is a good play," he says.

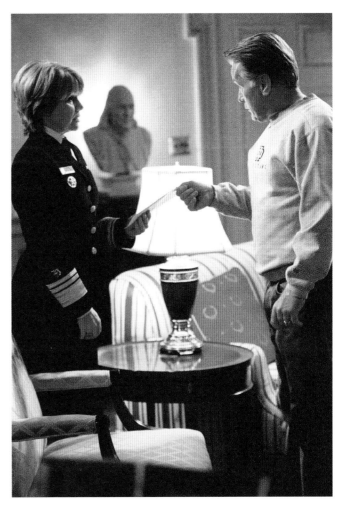

> **BARTLET:** "My father won't fire the surgeon general. He would never do that." I wanted to be so mad at her. (beat) But the truth is . . . (beat) . . . it's the nicest thing she's ever said about me.

The President does an about-face and refuses to accept Griffith's resignation. She says Leo's right, they should concentrate on the bigger things. Bartlet counters, "These *are* the bigger things." Griffith tells Bartlet he is an excellent role model to which he replies, "Yes, I know."

In the movie theater, Bartlet fills Josh in on what happened. He smiles. Josh says, people will think he just did it because his daughter asked him to. Bartlet replies if Josh ever has a daughter, he'll find there are worse reasons to do something. "Watch the movie," he says, "they're coming to the good part."

Bartlet moves down to the front of the theater and sits next to Ellie. Bartlet starts talking to his daughter. He knows no one will tell him to be quiet. He asks Ellie what she's going to study. He runs through as many medical disciplines as he can. "Pediatrics? Obstetrics?" Bartlet leans in. "The only thing you ever had to do to make me happy was come home at the end of the day," he says. Ellie's trying not to cry. She doesn't know how to react. Bartlet will let up. He's made up with Ellie. "Stop it, I'm trying to watch the movie." Now she's trying not to laugh.

"Okay," he says, "here comes the good part."

SOMEBODY'S GOING TO EMERGENCY, SOMEBODY'S GOING TO JAIL

Don Henley's "In a New York Minute" is playing on a radio in Toby's office. It's first thing in the morning and the bullpen is empty and sparsely lit. Leo comes to work and walks past Toby's office. He reappears, looks in the window, and walks in. Sam's asleep on Toby's couch. Leo wakes Sam and asks if he slept there. It takes Sam a moment to get acclimated. Yes, he says, he doesn't have a couch in his office. Leo offers his own explanation for his pre-dawn arrival—he came in early to avoid the World Trade Organization protesters clogging the city. He asks about the pardon recommendations but Sam's too wired to think clearly. Leo advises him to go home. Leo heard what happened with Sam's parents. Leo says *his* father had affairs.

SAM: My father didn't pick up a cocktail waitress, Leo, he's had a woman in an apartment in Santa Monica for twenty-eight years.

Sam confides to Leo he found out about it three days ago and it's been haunting him ever since. Ginger opens the Communications Office. It's 6:35 A.M. Sam thinks he's got a fresh shirt in his office but he doesn't. He heads home to change.

Leo's on his way to give his Andrew Jackson speech to a roomful of staffers but Josh moans at its uselessness; everyone knows about "Big Block of Cheese Day." In the Roosevelt Room, Leo starts in about Jackson and his cheese, but he's interrupted by people complaining about their assignments. Toby arrives late, cursing the demonstrators, who are protesting against the WTO and the World Bank. To Toby, they're amateurs, nothing like the glorified rallies of his day. Then Toby's told that his assignment is to meet the demonstrators. If it's any consolation though, C.J. adds she got the students to agree not to have cameras. Toby shakes his head—he can't believe they fell for that.

In the corridor, Donna greets an old friend, Stephanie Gault (Jolie Jenkins). She asks if Donna had a chance to mention her to Sam, but Donna hasn't; it's been a bad week for Sam. Donna realizes there's a larger issue behind Stephanie's urgency, and asks if Stephanie's dad is dying. He is. Donna reassures her friend that she'll get a moment with Sam, and suggests that she say she's heard Sam is the man with the ear of the President.

Charlie lets the President know his brother called to say they lost the site they'd chosen for Bartlet's Presidential library. He says it violates the Historic Barn and Bridges Preservation Act, a bill that Bartlet regrets ever signing. Charlie asks if they should green-light the second site but Bartlet tells him to wait.

ROB LOWE
Coming from movies, people were asking me, "How can you play the same character, day in and day out, week in and week out. Potentially year in, year out?" What I've discovered is the surprises that you get. Lo and behold, your father has been living a double life for twenty-eight years. That changes the way you look at your character and keeps the character fresh. These are the things that enable you to creatively engage, after playing this guy for forty episodes.

Aaron and I had been talking for a long time about finding a story for Sam. Sam's had so many great stories, but they've always been in service of someone else's. It was worth the wait because I think that it's some of the best writing that Aaron's ever done. It was personal, revealing, heroic, devastating, and yet about a grand national theme. Aaron and I and Tommy, and Jessica Yu the director, wanted it to be a very modulated, calibrated, interior piece. It was unlike other *West Wing* episodes. There are big gaps where no one's talking. Languid tracking shots where no one's speaking. So this was a very special *West Wing*.

Donna finds a moment to introduce Stephanie to Sam, and explains that Stephanie's grandfather was Daniel Gault. Sam recognizes the name: he was special economic assistant to FDR and special liaison to State for Eastern European affairs. Donna adds he was jailed for espionage and died in prison six months later, but Sam corrects her. Gault was jailed for perjury by HUAC. Donna says Stephanie wants her grandfather considered for a posthumous pardon, and Stephanie quietly mentions Sam having the ear of the President.

Sam knows Stephanie was fed the line but he lets it go. Sam says it's extremely difficult to demonstrate innocence but Stephanie interjects Sam already has. He's also addressed the need for a pardon in his thesis at Princeton, Stephanie states with confidence, a copy of which he sent to her father years before.

Sam explains that recommendations come from the Office of the Pardon Attorney. The President reviews the information and passes them to the counsel's office for further analysis. Sam promises to speak to someone at the FBI to give them a heads-up. Stephanie is grateful; she just wants some good news to give her father.

Toby is downtown preparing to meet the protesters and he is ready to enjoy himself. Rhonda

Sachs (Roma Maffia) is the police officer assigned to look after his well-being at the hands of the protestors. In the rowdy hall, a moderator struggles to keep control, but he is drowned out by chanting and yelling. Toby informs him it was stupid to give away the cameras. With them, Toby would have to try to control the crowd. Now he can just read the sports section and say he talked to them. With that, Toby tries to introduce himself from the podium but he's shouted down: "Global justice now!" He shrugs and ambles away, smiling.

Sam puts his own troubles aside, and arranges a visit to Special Agent Casper at the FBI. Casper tells Sam that even requesting the Gault file is wildly outside his authority. Sam believes he's just giving them a heads-up as a courtesy—he doesn't need permission to present the Gault case to the OPA or the press. Casper says Gault was named by Joe McCarthy as part of a huge conspiracy. Right, says Sam, along with General George Marshall, Owen Lattimore, I. F. Stone, Ring Lardner. Casper gives Sam the inside perspective: the FBI's failures are public, but its successes, like arresting a member of the West Virginia White Pride, are private. Casper tells Sam they even know it wasn't the Secret Service who ordered the canopy down at Rosslyn when the President was shot, but it wasn't publicized. Sam hopes that Casper isn't threatening Toby Ziegler, whom Sam knows made the canopy order. He indignantly insists he's putting Daniel Gault on the list.

Downtown, Toby is sitting, reading the paper with his feet up as the moderator tries vainly to get the vociferous crowd to listen to their guest. Toby's like a substitute teacher who doesn't care what his class is doing. Rhonda can see he's having a good time.

> TOBY: Well, it's not like being at a Yankee game, but . . . actually, yeah, it *is* like being at a Yankee game.

Rhonda asks what the protests are about. Toby observes that these people may claim to speak for the underprivileged but there are no black faces, no Asians, no Hispanics in the crowd. Rhonda fingers her handcuffs, and looks straight at Toby: "Lot in the Cabinet Room today?" she asks.

Sam tells Ginger to hold his calls; he's going to Toby's office to lie down and recollect his thoughts, but he's told the national security advisor's on the line. Nancy McNally asks Sam to come see her in the Situation Room, where she insists he drop the Gault case. Why? " 'Cause I just told you to." Sam protests about the lack of evidence in his conviction but Nancy affirms that Gault was a Soviet spy. It was proved by cables that were intercepted in the forties and only decrypted in the seventies. It's never been made public.

Nancy explains Gault was an agent called "Black Water." After Yalta he was given the Order of Lenin in Rostov. Sam denies this possibility but Nancy reaches down and drops a thick file in front of him. Sam's never seen one of these before: it's Gault's NSA file. Nancy could go to jail for showing it to him. She's assures him she's blacked out the code word sections Sam doesn't have clearance for, but nothing else. Sam stares at the file. He knows what he's going to find. He starts reading.

With the protesters chanting in the background, Toby tells Officer Sachs the students are merely playing at activism.

> **TOBY**: Food is cheaper, clothes are cheaper, steel is cheaper, cars are cheaper, phone service is cheaper, you feel me building a rhythm here? It's because I'm a speechwriter and I know how to make a point!
>
> **RHONDA**: Toby—
>
> **TOBY**: It lowers prices, it raises income, you see what I did with "lowers" and "raises" there?
>
> **RHONDA**: Yes.
>
> **TOBY**: It's called the Science of Listener Attention. We did repetition, we did floating opposites, we now end with the one that's not like the others. *Free trade stops wars.* (pause) And that's it. Free trade stops wars. And we figure out a way to fix the rest. One World, One Peace. I'm sure I've seen that on a sign somewhere.

Josh arrives on the scene to see what's up. Toby tells him the WTO *is* undemocratic and accountable to no one, and he's going to go back in to tell these people so.

Back in the White House, Bartlet is depressed by the thought of choosing a site for his memorial library. He tells Leo it is too soon to be thinking about the end. He has two more years and he feels he was just getting good at his job. Leo reminds him it's two years with an option for two more.

> **LEO**: (beat) Mr. President, is there anything we need to talk about?
>
> **BARTLET**: (pause) Not yet, okay?

Donna finds Sam in the empty White House mess throwing sugar packets into a spaghetti pot. Sam chastises Donna for telling Stephanie he was the one with the ear of the President. Then he says, "He was a spy," and lays out some of Gault's crimes: handing over Roosevelt's plan to enter the war, recruitment targets, lists of Communist sympathizers. Donna implores him not to tell Stephanie, but Sam insists he will, and he charges up the stairs to do it. Donna's right behind him. She begs Sam, "He's in a bad place, this was fifty years ago, what does it matter?" Sam whirls around to face her.

Martin Sheen
Rob, whom I've known since he was a boy, has never been better. I mean, never. My son Charlie and my wife and I were watching and after the scene where he's talking to the girl, Charlie said, "Just tell him for me, he's never been better in his life, and congratulations."

SAM: It was high treason and it mattered a great deal. This country is an *idea,* and one that's lit the world for two centuries. And treason against this idea is not just a crime against the living. This ground holds the graves of people who died for it . . .

Sam continues the tale: a woman was murdered in West Berlin in 1952 because she threatened to reveal Black Water's identity, and he can't keep the truth from Stephanie. "This girl's gonna find out who her father was." Donna interrupts, "You meant grandfather." Sam shakes his head; his thoughts are swimming. He finds Stephanie in his office, and looks at her for the longest time. He

can see Donna standing outside looking in at him. He can't do it; he can't disappoint her with the truth. Sam changes course and says he couldn't get access, and they'll try again in three months. Sam's measured response turns out to be the right one after all. Stephanie says that hope was all her father needed. She thanks Sam and leaves. Donna puts her arms around Sam. He says, "It's just there are certain things you're sure of."

Josh appears in the doorway, ranting that he nearly got killed at the protests. He was hit by a piece of banana. Josh reminds Toby that this is the second time this year he's almost been killed and both times he was with Toby—Toby needs a new wing man. Josh tells Donna they're taking Sam out and getting him drunk, and Donna invites herself along. Sam says he'll meet them there in a bit. He closes his door and sits at his desk. He picks up the phone and dials: "Dad, it's me . . ."

THE STACKHOUSE

FILIBUSTER

On a Friday evening the venerable Senator Stackhouse (George Coe) is reciting a recipe for deep-fried fantail shrimp from the Senate floor. The only other people there are the recording secretary and the chair of the session. Stackhouse is delivering a filibuster and his voice is raspy, both from a head cold and from speaking for a long time.

The staff's desperately trying to get out of town for the weekend. Sam has a house rented in Sag Harbor, Toby needs to be in Telluride first thing in the morning, and Josh is going to the New York Mets' spring training. He's determined that Mike Piazza will see him and call him, "*Dude*." All the reporters in the Press Room, who are itching to leave, are asking how long Stackhouse is going to be. C.J. doesn't think he'll be that much longer. Once he's done she tells the press there'll be a vote and the White House staff can give them comments.

C.J. is anxious to leave herself. She's trying to get to Napa for her dad's seventieth birthday. While she waits, she starts typing an e-mail to him. She writes that Minnesota Senator Howard Stackhouse has taken the Senate vote into his own hands. He can keep the floor as long as he desires, as long as he doesn't stop talking and he's not allowed to drink, lean on anything, sit down, or use the bathroom. He's protesting the immediate passage of the Family Wellness Act, which Josh had negotiated for weeks.

*　　*　　*

Flashback to the previous Monday, when Josh comes into a meeting of senior staff and announces they got the act. He's pumped. Leo congratulates him and asks how it feels to spend six billion on health care. Toby breaks the mood and reports that Philip Sluman, the chairman of the Petroleum Producers of America, says the administration's stricter emissions standards are to blame for the rise of gas prices. Toby says the energy secretary has to respond, and he'll approach the vice president about it.

Charlie seeks out C.J. to inform her that Hassan Ali is coming in at the end of the week. He gave the President a small ceramic statue of a cat on a trip to Cairo and it should be on prominent display for the visit. The thing is, the gift officer says C.J. has it.

Toby goes to see the Vice President, and not surprisingly, Hoynes thinks that Sluman has a good point. Toby tells Hoynes that tomorrow night Energy Secretary Bill Trotter is giving a speech, and they're going to write in a rebuttal of Sluman's statement. Hoynes points out no one listens to Trotter's rants but volunteers to issue his own refutation during his upcoming press conference on antitrust policy. The vice president is sure he'll be asked about gas, and if Toby thinks he's too soft in his response, Toby can still use Trotter.

*　　*　　*

C.J.'s fingers type furiously as she tells her dad via e-mail that Stackhouse is seventy-eight, he wasn't supposed to last fifteen minutes, and he just went into hour eight, droning on abut the circumstances of David Copperfield's birth.*

To pass the long hours, Sam is playing a game on his laptop. C.J. drops by his office and apologizes because she never had a chance to say she's sorry about his father's affairs. She lets that sink in and then mentions that she heard Sam got spanked by a fourteen-year-old intern from the General Accounting Office. She's nineteen, says Sam. Sam starts e-mailing his dad, too. He types, "Dear Jackass," but starts over. He has his own story to tell.

*   *   *

Earlier in the week, Josh was in his office handing out assignments. Sam wandered in looking for a piece of fruit, but ended up volunteering to compile a list of four hundred government reports to eliminate from the three thousand they receive.

Sam gets into his task with gusto, cutting redundant reports on Route 66 traffic and water pests. At each excision, Winifred Hooper (Cara Delizia) snorts. She's a nineteen-year-old intern who seems to be born mad at somebody. Sam feels her derision and asks her what's up. She says Sam's blowing through the files like they don't mean anything. One report is about career opportunities for garbage men. She knows about waste, she read the report. In fact, she's read *all* the reports, and there are real issues with waste management hiring. Sam's impressed. He steps out of his ego and tells her to look him up for a job when she's out of college. "No," she says, "you come see *me*."

C.J. searches for a co-conspirator, and tells Donna she was given the statue of a cat goddess called Bast in Cairo. Legend has it anyone who killed a royal temple cat was put to death. C.J. confesses that she broke the statue. The only words Donna can find is that C.J. is "monumentally screwed."

Donna has a message for Josh from Stackhouse. He wants an amendment to the Family Wellness Act to allocate money for autism care and research. Josh takes the message lightly—the bill's closed and Stackhouse doesn't really have a lot of muscle in Congress. Donna reads the message aloud, "You're gonna meet with me or there's not gonna be a vote while I'm alive. Stackhouse."

*   *   *

*The longest uninterrupted individual filibuster in Senate history was performed in 1957 by Strom Thurmond of South Carolina, who spoke for twenty-four hours and eighteen minutes against the Civil Rights Bill.

Eyeing the television in her office, C.J. watches in disbelief as Stackhouse reads on from *David Copperfield*. C.J. writes her dad that the senator's trying to make sure she misses the 11:00 P.M. print deadline, but there's no way he goes another two hours. . . .

Josh, equally plagued with downtime, composes a message to his mother. He writes that Leo ordered him to see Stackhouse but not to give anything away. He tells his mother he wore the new shoes she bought him, and he wiped out on the marble floor. He laughs as he types, but recollects his thoughts to tell her that the filibuster has been a part of parliamentary strategy for 150 years. . . .

* * *

Stackhouse is firm in demanding forty-seven million to fight autism. Josh protests that they can't do it. Of course they can, Stackhouse says. It was a two billion dollar bill that's now at six. Forty-seven million dollars won't make any difference. And it's a bill for children that also allocates money for Alzheimer's, glaucoma, and erectile dysfunction. Josh protests if they open up the bill, they'd have to postpone the vote. He admits they want to have the story before people leave for recess.

* * *

As the hours drag on, the news programs are picking up stories on Stackhouse. Donna watches one with particular interest, and asks for a dub of B-roll showing Stackhouse and his grandchildren. Josh writes to his mother that Stackhouse didn't really bother him. He was more interested in what Hoynes, who made his money in oil and champions the industry, was up to.

* * *

At his press conference, Hoynes is uncharacteristically tough on the oil companies. The government has ensured cleaner air while the oil companies are passing on the additive costs at outrageous markups. He hammers away. It's an impressive performance but the staff is haunted by one thing: Why did Hoynes volunteer to do it?

* * *

The President has a better idea to pass time; he asks Leo to have dinner with him. A famous chef is in town, and Bartlet tempts Leo with the menu: reinterpretations of classic Provençal cuisine, cassoulet, duck with green olives, Saffron chicken, tomate de Saltambique. Bartlet's not worried about the filibuster—he believes Stackhouse is a curmudgeon, a grouchy old crank.

BARTLET: He was all over me the first year. He called me "Bartlet the Inert."
LEO: It was pretty funny.
BARTLET: I'm a reformer. I'm the most liberal President he's ever served under. His hero, Hubert Humphrey, once, you know—
LEO: Shook your hand.

They walk to the private dining room. They see that the table has been set for a romantic dinner *à deux* with dim lighting and candles. Bartlet shrugs and says they thought he was dining with Abbey.

BARTLET: We'll just, you know, pretend there's no candlelight.

LEO: Or that we're not paranoid homophobes in any way.

Josh phones Leo to tell him there's no end in sight. Stackhouse is now reading from a rule book on casino gambling. Donna approaches C.J. and tells her she saw something on the TV footage that caught her attention. At two events, Stackhouse appears with his grandchildren, and while she knows he has seven of them, there's only ever six in the photos. Donna doesn't think he's being ornery, she thinks Stackhouse has an autistic grandson.

Over dinner, Bartlet decides to tell Leo the second secret he's ever kept from him. He says he made a deal with Abbey 'cause of "his thing." The two men look at each other for a long time. Bartlet's ashamed there was another secret. Leo guesses he promised to serve just one term. Bartlet nods his head very slightly. Bartlet whispers that's why Hoynes stepped up on oil.

LEO: 'Cause he thinks, maybe—

BARTLET: Yeah.

LEO: (pause—whispering) It was three years ago, she can't expect—

Leo's interrupted again by his cell phone. C.J. tells Leo the newest development—Stackhouse has an autistic grandson. Leo and Bartlet give up their dinner and head back to the Oval Office. While C.J. waits outside, she's wondering how to break the news about the shattered cat statue. She's certain she has the curse of Bast on her.

Pacing in his office, Bartlet is incredulous. He swears they'd have reassessed the components of the bill if Stackhouse had just said something. Leo thinks he didn't want to make capital out of his grandson. Bartlet declares, "The man's not stopping; never underestimate the grandfather." Bartlet asks C.J. what she'd do if he told her to ignore the press deadline. C.J. answers she'd try to help Stackhouse out. Donna raises her hand awkwardly. She knows that under Senate procedure, which Josh likes to explain to her, Stackhouse can yield for a question without yielding the floor. Leo says only senators can ask questions, and most have already fled the Hill. But Bartlet instructs Charlie to start calling around. They will find a way to make Senator Stackhouse's valiant and selfless act worthwhile.

Toby visits the vice president. He tells Hoynes he appreciates what he did, but he's curious why he'd volunteer for it. Toby says he got ahold of some private polling Hoynes had done and noticed that voters are concerned about his close ties to big oil. Not anymore, says Hoynes smugly.

TOBY: Mr. Vice President, what do you know that I don't?

HOYNES: (pause) Toby, the total tonnage of what I know that you don't could stun a team of oxen in its tracks. (pause) G'night.

After twenty minutes, C.J. finds a willing senator who barges onto the senate floor and raises a point of order: A silence fills both the chamber and the White House. Will Senator Stackhouse yield for a question? Stackhouse is confused and terrified of losing the ground he's worked so hard to get. Eventually, he yields. With a sigh of relief, the senator announces the question is in twenty-two parts, so perhaps Mr. Stackhouse would like to sit and have some water.

Because Stackhouse had blown the print deadline, there's no reason not to reopen the bill. Exhausted but exhilarated, the staff return to their e-mails. C.J. says there are so many days they just don't think anything good's going to happen. She writes her father:

C.J.: But I've seen a guy with no legs stay standing tonight, Dad, and a guy with no voice keep shouting, and if politics brings out the worst in people, then maybe people bring out the best. 'Cause I'm looking at the TV right now and damn if twenty-eight U.S. senators haven't just walked out onto the floor to help. I'll catch the first plane out in the morning and if you wouldn't mind not turning seventy until tomorrow, that'd be great. In the meantime, I love you so much. Your daughter, Claudia.

17 PEOPLE

Toby is incessantly bouncing his Spalding ball against a bookcase door in his office. He's just confronted Hoynes, demanding to know what's up his sleeve. Toby can't wrap his brain around Hoynes's strange behavior toward the oil industry. Two nights later, Toby is crumpling pieces of paper and throwing them into his trash can. Two nights after that, he's sullenly working at his computer when something strikes him. He looks out his window across the darkened bullpen and sees a light on in Leo's office. He heads over. Toby tells Leo he's been thinking about why Hoynes volunteered to slap down big oil. Has there been any discussion of Hoynes being dropped from the ticket in 2002? Leo says no. The next night, Toby's back to bouncing his ball.

The following morning, Leo finds Toby waiting for him in his office. Toby wonders aloud, if Hoynes is considering running for President in 2006, why is he conducting private polling now? That night, Toby persists, inundating Leo with more questions. He says a vice president would never challenge a sitting President for a nomination, right? So why is Hoynes giving a speech this weekend on Clean Air Industry at a semiconductor plant in Nashua, New Hampshire, President Bartlet's home state? Leo says if Hoynes were truly up to something, he'd mask his trip with a benign excuse. Toby informs Leo that Hoynes is speaking during a three-day camping trip to Killington.

TOBY: (pause) Why does Hoynes think the President isn't gonna run again?
TOBY has him in check . . .
TOBY: (pause) What's going on, Leo?
The two of them keep staring at each other . . . and staring . . .

It's toward midnight, and a terrorist threat is escalating on the Canadian border. In the Oval Office, the President tells Leo he closed the embassies in Tanzania and Brussels, and he's got an hour to decide what to do domestically. Leo can't shake his conversation with Toby; he advises Bartlet to let Toby in the know. Leo fills in Bartlet about Hoynes's suspicious speech in Nashua. Bartlet must have known this moment would come. Bartlet summons Toby. When he's alone, the President sighs and mutters, "Now it starts."

At the same time, Sam and Josh are taking a hack at a speech for the White House Correspondents Dinner, which seems to have evaded any semblance of humor. Josh, avoiding the task at hand, asks Donna if she received the flowers. Donna explains to the group that she started working for Josh in February, but he insists that he'll celebrate their anniversary in April, because that's when she started working for him without leaving to go back to her boyfriend. Donna gets in another dig by asking if Josh ever gets tired of the sound of his own voice. He says he doesn't.

Sam goes in search of some humor, and finds Ainsley in her office. She's researching for a brave visit to Smith College, her alma mater, for a panel dis-

Bradley Whitford

One of Aaron's most phenomenal qualities as a writer is his ability to pick up on an actor and what they might be able to do and then exploit the living hell out of it. Richard Schiff is a dear old friend of mine. His brother was my roommate in college, so I've known Richard forever. And Aaron didn't know Richard very well when he was cast. Man, did he pick up on some fundamental Richard-osities. We see it in Toby every week. The joy is that then it gets fleshed out and made more complex.

cussion on the Equal Rights Amendment.* Sam tells Ainsley he has never met one of the 40 percent of American women opposed to the ERA. Ainsley extends her hand and introduces herself.
Sam can't believe she's going to argue against the ERA at Smith, the cradle of feminism. She maintains she's a straight Republican from North Carolina—they hated her the first time around. All
differences aside, the lure of Chinese food persuades Ainsley to come help with the jokes for the
speech.

In a last-ditch effort to preserve some peace, Leo implores Toby to take it easy with the
President. Before he can respond, Charlie ushers Toby into the Oval Office, where Bartlet fixes
him a drink. The President banters for a moment about the Algerian terrorist who was arrested at
the Canadian border with explosives. He's closed the embassies and is talking to the FAA about
airport security. Then, without missing a beat, Bartlet dives in. He tells Toby during an eye exam
about ten years ago a doctor found unusual pupil responses and ordered an MRI. The radiologist
found plaques on his brain and spine. Toby's speechless at this information, but Bartlet is unnerv-
ingly forward: "I have multiple sclerosis, Toby."

*The first text of the Equal Rights Amendment was written in 1921 by Alice Paul. It had two parts: 1. "Men and
women shall have equal rights throughout the United States and every place subject to its jurisdiction." And 2: "Congress
shall have power to enforce this article by appropriate legislation." It has been introduced to every Congress session since
1923. It passed in a different form in 1972. It had to be ratified by thirty-eight states by July 1982 to come into effect but
fell three states short.

Silence invades the Oval Office as Toby tries to digest what he's heard. Within moments, he rapid-fires questions. "What does relapsing/remitting mean? Is it fatal? Does relapsing/remitting ever turn into secondary progressive?" Toby asks if he can stand up, and quickly hurries out onto the portico. Business proceeds with no mind to the drama unfolding, and Bartlet takes a call from the FAA in Leo's office.

The table in the Roosevelt Room is strewn with Chinese food cartons and copies of the Correspondents dinner speech. The staff is hard-pressed for jokes. Ainsley asks Donna about her flowers. Sam, always the spokesman, explains that Donna came back to work for Josh after she and her boyfriend broke up the second time. Josh encourages them to get back to the job at hand: making fun of Republicans. Sam says in a half hour he wants to make Toby laugh.

Leo joins Toby on the portico and gives him another drink. He tells Toby he found out about the MS a year ago when Bartlet passed out before the State of the Union. "That was an attack?" says Toby; he believed at the time that it was the flu. Toby asks who else knows. Leo tells him he's the sixteenth person and he can't tell Toby who all the others are, it's not entirely his business. He mentions the first lady, the doctor, the radiologist, the specialist, the kids. That's it for now. Putting the pieces together in his head, Toby asks about the President's physicals. Leo explains it doesn't show up in physicals. Nobody lied.

> **TOBY**: Nobody lied? Is that what you've been saying to yourself over and over again for a year?
>
> **LEO**: Look—
>
> **TOBY**: Leo, a deception of *massive* propor—I can't even—he gets a physical twice a year at Bethesda, his doctors are *naval* officers, are you telling me *officers* are involved with—
>
> **LEO**: Toby—
>
> **TOBY**: *These guys are gonna be court-martialed!*

Bartlet reenters his office, catching the end of Toby's impassioned remarks. "Nobody was asked to lie," Bartlet says. He fills them in on the terrorist threat but Toby isn't listening. Bartlet pauses, "What are *you* guys talking about?"

Josh, wandering the halls of the West Wing in search of inspiration, finds Charlie and asks how much longer Toby's going to be. What's going on? Charlie gives him a look that says you know better than to ask that. Josh leaves Charlie alone and meanders back to the Roosevelt Room where the jokes are still falling flat. Sam says they're fine, because Toby's going to come in and nail it, it's his thing.

Toby's alone with the President. "Didn't the President have an attack a couple of nights before the State of the Union?" he asks. Wasn't that the night the President saw satellite pictures of India moving on Pakistan?

> **TOBY**: In the middle of an episode, you were in the Situation Room as commander in chief.
>
> **BARTLET**: I know, I can't believe we're all here.

The two men stare at each other. Toby's wondering how he can joke about that. Bartlet's glare is daring him to object. As a consolation, Bartlet explains the episode was over. Toby asks if Bartlet gets medication. Injections of Betaseron, he answers. From whom? Toby says if none of his doctors know, is his wife medicating him? While temperatures are running a little high, Bartlet instructs tersely, Toby should refer to her as Mrs. Bartlet or the first lady.

Leo comes in from his office with an update on the FAA. Toby's not placated by the fact that Leo was with Bartlet in the Situation Room, along with Fitzwallace and other officers and officials. Toby points out, "None of them was elected." Bartlet shoots back the vice president was and he has the authority . . . "Not last May he didn't," interjects Toby. His mind has settled on the shooting, and the fact that Hoynes didn't take over when Bartlet was under anesthesia. "No," says

Bartlet, "because he didn't sign the letter." "No," Toby says, "if there were a letter, someone would ask why." That night, the President had been attacked and was in surgery. There was a massive manhunt, elements of the National Guard had been federalized, the Republican Guard was moving, and an F-117 was down in the no-fly.

Toby's raising his voice now, overwhelmed by the enormity of what has been revealed to him.

TOBY: And the vice president's authority was murky at best. The national security advisor and the secretary of state didn't know who they were taking their orders from. I wasn't in the Situation Room that night, but I'll bet all the money in my pockets against all the money in your pockets it was Leo. (beat) Who no one elected. (beat) For ninety minutes that night there was a coup d'état in this country.

BARTLET's silent for a moment. It's scary until he bursts into—

BARTLET: (singing) "—*and the walls came tumblin' down.*" (pause) I feel fine by the way, thanks for asking.

LEO: Sir—

BARTLET: No, Leo, Toby's concern for my health is moving me in ways I don't even know what to do.

TOBY: Mr. President—

BARTLET: Shut up. (beat) You know your indignation would be a lot more interesting to me if it weren't quite so covered in crap.

Bartlet asks Toby if he's pissed because he believes Bartlet lied to him, or because fifteen people knew before he did. The tension remains thick even as the President has to take a call with the FAA.

The air in the Roosevelt Room is getting suffocating, and the staff is getting snarky with one another. Sam and Ainsley take a food break, and Ainsley defends her stance on the ERA.

Bartlet and Leo discuss airport security and the fact that terrorists like heightened security because it demonstrates that they're having an effect on the public. Toby sits outside the Oval Office trying to get his head together, and Leo comes to talk him down from the ledge.

Toby asks Leo if Hoynes knows. He does. Leo admits there's a chance Hoynes thinks Bartlet won't run again. Toby realizes, "The first lady was pissed after the State of the Union because it set up the reelection run and she thought that wasn't going to happen." Leo assures him that Bartlet will run. "Okay," Toby asks, his mind moving a mile a minute, "if Hoynes was fourteen, who was fifteen?" The anesthesiologist at GW.

Toby's sure someone's going to leak. Toby states it took him "six days and twenty-three minutes to figure it out," and he thinks Hoynes wanted him to investigate and discover Bartlet's well-guarded secret. Toby says Hoynes is about the only one acting responsible to the party; it's seven-and-a half-months to the Iowa caucus and no party leaders have been told the President might not be a nominee? Leo asks Toby what could unfold in the President's future.

> **TOBY**: (pause) Well . . . I suppose . . . one of five things. The President can decide not to run. He can run and not win. He can run and win—
>
> **LEO**: And what are the other two?
>
> **TOBY**: Leo—
>
> **LEO**: You think he's gonna need to resign?
>
> **TOBY**: There's gonna be hearing upon hearing upon hearing—
>
> **LEO**: He hasn't broken a law.

Toby reminds him you don't have to break the law to be impeached, but Leo tells him it's never going to get that far.

> **TOBY**: Write down the exact date and time you said that.

Back in the Roosevelt Room, Sam finally asks why Ainsley is so vehemently against the ERA. She replies it's humiliating, why does she need an amendment to tell her she's equal under the law to a man? She doesn't have to have her rights handed down to her by "a bunch of old, white, *men*."

Josh is searching through old speeches in his office and brings a mountain of ring binders toppling onto his head. Donna is determined to set Josh straight regarding their anniversary and the history behind it. When she came back the second time, she had a bandage on her ankle. She didn't slip on ice as she originally told him. She was in a car accident. Donna called her boyfriend from the hospital, and he met some friends on his way and had a beer. In the end, she left *him*. Josh took her back when he had no reason to trust her and he didn't make fun of her. Josh starts in on the fact that he stopped for a beer. Donna relents and admits that Josh is better than her old boyfriend.

> **JOSH**: I'm just saying if you were in an accident I wouldn't stop for a beer.
>
> And JOSH is on his way out when he's stopped by—
>
> **DONNA**: If you were in an accident I wouldn't stop for red lights.

In the Oval Office, the President has to make the final call to the FAA.

John Wells

"17 People" became about only a few characters because we had budgetary constraints. We wanted to make sure we had enough money to do what we wanted to do at the end of the year. But that made it very interesting and something that you hadn't seen on the show before. Often, the budgetary limitations will make you come up with even more creative solutions. I'm actually very partial to the episode because it was really just the actors strutting their stuff.

It's beyond tense. Bartlet reflects that he didn't know enough about the situation to make a knowledgeable decision. He's talking about the airports, but Toby says:

TOBY: I know the feeling.

BARTLET: I have no intention of apologizing to you, Toby.

TOBY: Would you mind if I ask why not?

BARTLET: You're not the one with MS, a wife, three kids, and airports to close. Not every part of me belongs to you. This was personal. I'm not willing to relinquish that right.

Toby utters it's seventeen people, by the way. Seventeen people know. You knew, Toby says to Bartlet, "we weren't counting you." At some point, they're going to have to speak with some lawyers.

Kevin Falls

I don't think we had talked about dealing with the multiple sclerosis, when Leo and Toby formed the ad hoc committee to reelect Bartlet, even then we didn't know we were getting into the MS. Because of budget issues Aaron creating this powerful episode dealing with Bartlet and McGarry telling Toby about the MS, it was great.

"That's what usually brings on the episodes," Bartlet responds. Toby smiles. The tension subsides and Bartlet apologizes. "It may have been unbelievably stupid," he concedes. He is sorry. It's a simple, honest apology. Toby says he's got to go.

Toby walks over to the Roosevelt Room. Everyone cheers when he walks in. Now they're in business. Someone throws Toby one of his Spalding balls. He's completely off-balance. Behind him, the Oval Office door is still open. Bartlet is inside. Leo closes the door, and Toby reels back into reality to hear Josh say they have to imagine the President making the joke. "Tell me if you think this is funny."

LEO McGARRY
JOHN SPENCER

In all of Toby Ziegler's righteous ire after he is told about Bartlet's MS, he's most agitated by the thought that while the President was under anesthesia after being shot, it was Leo, not Vice President Hoynes, who was running the show that night in the Situation Room. You bet he was.

Leo McGarry is the second most powerful man in the country. A person is not elected to such a role, they emerge. It's certainly not obvious that a White House chief of staff would ascend to a seat of power. But this is Leo, the President's best friend and confidant, a man who often seems to know what the President is thinking before the President does. How else can you explain two of Leo's essential contributions, both of which looked contrarian at the time: firing all the campaign team except Toby in Nashua and the idea to let Bartlet be Bartlet?

Patrick H. Caddell

Most Presidents have somebody either inside or outside that can actually talk to them in a way where they can really close the door, take off the uniforms, and say, "You're full of crap. You're dead wrong on this." They have to have somebody. We encapsulate that in Bartlet and Leo's relationship. It's a very important one. The subtleties of that relationship capture so much about the reality of a President in the White House.

So how do you find someone to provide this foil for the President? The second most powerful man in the country, a man who just looks in charge.

Aaron Sorkin

To begin with, in casting Leo I said to the casting directors, "What I really want is somebody like John Spencer. Who out there is like John Spencer?" They said, "Well, John Spencer is like John Spencer." "We're never going to get John Spencer, so who can we get?" The next day John Spencer comes in and reads for us. So, that was ninety yards of the battle right there.

John Spencer

When I first read the script, I determined it was something I was really interested in pursuing and doing. Then I just worked on the material. It was great material. I came in and read. And appar-

ently, I say immodestly, after they saw me, they stopped looking for Leo. They cast me on the spot. By the time I came home from the meeting, there was an offer. That was very nice.

Bradley Whitford

The metaphor that Tommy and Aaron have used about John Spencer is that he's like a great Yankee manager. John's the actor's actor. John's been around. John's been up. John's been down. You know when you're doing a scene with John that he's gonna be ready and he's just a great guy to act with.

Many of the cast members did some background reading to prepare for their parts. And the shady mystery of Leo McGarry's past was enough to provide Spencer a firm foundation for his character.

John Spencer

Working on the role, I read thoroughly a book that Aaron gave me called *Chief of Staff*, the writings of five different chiefs of staff. I've always been a political junkie, fascinated by politics and the working machine. My favorite shows are the pundits. Ultimately—it's true of any research you do—bottom line, you've got to play the scene. You research for five months and then you're in there with those words playing the scene. That's basically what I did. I think Leo is the chief of staff that John Spencer would be if he were a chief of staff.

Lyn Elizabeth Paolo

Early on, John and I talked about the fact that Leo's quite wealthy and going through a midlife crisis of some kind. His wife is going to leave him. Also, he's quite well known in Washington and an extremely powerful man. And John is not a big, tall man. He's fairly diminutive compared to some

JOHN SPENCER

The New York Times gave us a bad review on our pilot. They forgot they did, they just turned around at the end of the season. Now the *Times* is a great proponent of ours. There was a transition somewhere that I missed. I don't resent it. You know, you paid your money, you get your ride. We did not come out of the gate in an *ER* fashion, which is the greatest thing that has ever been on television. I remember in our first season, somewhere around the sixth episode, Brad coming out of the trailer—at one point we bumped into each other—and he says, "I guess we're a hit, huh?" And it was like, "Yeah, I think so, I guess." But for us, it's basically one foot in front of the other, these twelve- to sixteen-hour days, and the rest is kind of the accoutrements that attach themselves to the show that we really have no control over.

of our cast. So we decided that for him, he needed to be a really bold, dapper dresser, with the pocket square and a bold tie and the suspenders. Just really put together. To show his world and the fact that he's so terrifically powerful.

Like the rest of the cast, Leo McGarry is at the mercy of Aaron Sorkin's imagination. His ordeal with the public airing of his addictions must vie with this failure of his marriage as Leo's lowest point. Why does the poor man have to lose his wife?

Aaron Sorkin

As far as having Leo's wife divorce him, to be honest, again, the inspiration will start someplace and the result is something entirely different. The inspiration was simply that John Spencer is a leading man—really just an old-school leading man. I wanted to open up the romantic possibilities for him in the show, so I wanted to lose his wife. In doing so, I was able to give him a very emotional story and was able to dramatize just how committed these people are to what they're doing. One of the hardest lines I've ever had to write was when she says to him, "It's not more important than your marriage." And he says, "It *is* more important than my marriage. Right now, it's more important than my marriage."

BAD MOON RISING

Oliver Babish (Oliver Platt) is getting ready to go to an international law summit in Borneo. Staffers are whirling around, trying to get him out the door. The newest White House counsel is brandishing his big hammer, a gavel he says was given to his father's father by Louis Brandeis. Babish babbles aloud about needing a new Dictaphone; his is stuck on record, which, as Babish says, is "just what they want in the White House counsel's office." He's just about to leave when an aide says Leo wants to see him. He's coming over with the President.

By the way he's dragging his feet, it's evident Bartlet doesn't want to have this meeting. On the way, he admits to Leo he's scared of Babish. He's known his fifth White House counsel for years and Babish worked on the campaign, but he is still

intimidated by his intellect and knowledge of the world. Leo advises Bartlet to spit the truth out, but Bartlet hems and haws in the face of his lawyer.

> BARTLET: (pause) Well, Oliver, it really boils down to this. I'm gonna tell you a story, and then I need you to tell me whether or not I've engaged sixteen people in a massive criminal conspiracy to defraud the public in order to win a presidential election.

It takes a minute for this to sink in. Then Babish takes his gavel and smashes the ever-recording microcassette player into five hundred pieces. He exhales, regroups, and says, "Okay."

It's Monday morning and the West Wing is brimming with activity. The Mexican economy just collapsed. Toby is fuming at a quote in the paper on school vouchers. C.J.'s taking questions on it, then she announces that the *Kensington Indio*, a single-hull VLCC* carrying four million gallons of crude oil, ran ashore south of Rehoboth Beach, Delaware, three hours ago. It's leaked 200,000 gallons already and the Coast Guard is trying to contain the spill.

Sputtering, Toby tells C.J. to find out who the "senior White House official" was who said the

---

*A VLCC is a very large crude carrier, or supertanker. The worst such accident in U.S. history occurred on March 24, 1989, when the *Exxon Valdez* hit Bligh Reef in Prince William Sound, Alaska, spilling more than eleven million gallons of crude oil.

President might be ready to compromise on school vouchers. Republican leaders will get ahold of this, and Seth Gillette and a lot of key Democrats are gonna go crazy. He tells C.J. to get the guy's ass in his office by the end of the day.

Babish is trying to get the full picture from the President. He's dealt with some chaos and catastrophes, but this dwarfs everything. Babish starts in on Bartlet's symptoms but then he says he wants to make something clear: They share no attorney-client privilege. Bartlet looks to Leo for deciphering. "Because he's a government lawyer," says Leo. Babish warns the President to

be careful what he says. Bartlet insists he doesn't want to be careful. Babish instantly advises Bartlet to hire private counsel. Bartlet corrects himself: He meant to say he doesn't *need* to be careful.

Babish asks if Bartlet's ever been deposed in a lawsuit. Bartlet shrugs, only a couple of minor things. Did anyone ask about his health in the depositions, because if they did and he lied, that's the ball game. "He never lied," Leo interjects. Babish wants to hear the President say it, and Bartlet acquiesces quietly, "I never lied." He never had to testify under oath about his health? Bartlet says no. Babish speculates on who shares the President's secret: Abbey and the kids, that's four, the six original doctors, his brother, Fitzwallace, the vice president, Leo, who else? "The anesthesiologist at GW," Leo says, "and Toby." Babish asks how Toby's taking it and Leo answers, "Not well."

BABISH: I wouldn't think so. Mr. President, I have some more questions. Is there time now?

BARTLET: Well, the Mexican economy crashed, an oil tanker busted about a hundred and twenty miles from here, and thirteen percent of Americans are living in poverty, so, yeah, I can hang out with you and answer insulting questions for a while.

BABISH: (beat) Good.

Josh is trying to arrange for loans for Mexico while Toby is blasting around the halls slamming doors and shouting at people. He's not making C.J.'s job of finding the leak any easier. Charlie is figuring out which college courses to take for summer session: Theology 201, English 201. Sam looks over his shoulder incredulously, while Charlie explains he has a lot of credits from high school.

SAM: Charlie, just how smart are you?

CHARLIE: I've got some game.

Babish is probing to find out if Bartlet ever signed any form that asked about his health without disclosing his MS. Bartlet says no. The President has to step out to make a phone call. Leo asks Babish what he thinks but Babish tells Leo he's nowhere close to being able to answer that question.

Sam asks Ainsley about the oil spill. She thinks the attorneys general for Maryland and Delaware are going to sue for damages, a hundred million for cleanup, three to four hundred million punitive. "Kensington's going to pay it through the nose," she says. No they're not, declares Sam. He knows because he bought them the boat when he was at Gage Whitney. He wonders if he can be deposed for the plaintiffs because he made the deal but tried in earnest to persuade them to buy a better boat. Sam tells Ainsley this ship wasn't so good, especially in terms of its steering and navigation.

Ainsley stops him. She reminds Sam he didn't abdicate attorney-client privilege when he left the firm. If he gave a deposition he'd be disbarred and no judge would allow the testimony. Ainsley mentions where his liability shield is concerned, maybe he's not as good as he thinks. Sam assures her that he is.

Charlie's filling out endless forms for class. Mrs. Landingham asks if he's taking glee club; Margaret wonders about fencing. Charlie answers no to both. He looks at his pile of forms: financial aid, housing, emergency contacts, transfer of credits, and a fourteen-page form . . . he's looking at the form he was about to complain about when he is struck by something. With urgency, he tells Margaret he needs to speak to Leo right now. She should tell him, "it's an old friend from home." Margaret asks if he's sure. He is.

Leo and Babish are having a prickly conversation. Babish says he's pissed, and Leo responds he was too when he found out, then he remembered he's a drunk and Bartlet didn't give a damn. Babish doesn't know if he's sticking around at this point. But Leo tells Babish he's staying; Leo's running the show and he picked Babish.

LEO: In the two-and-a-half hours we've been sitting here, have you discovered one thing he's done wrong?

BABISH: No.

LEO: So what's your problem?

BABISH: *That's my problem,* **Leo,** *are you outta your mind?!* (beat) He did everything right! (beat) He did everything you do if your intent is to perpetrate a fraud.

Leo returns to his office to talk to Charlie, whose agitation and fright is visible. Very quietly, Charlie says, "Zoey would have had to fill out a medical form for college." There's a long silence as Leo ponders Charlie's mysterious comment. Charlie continues, explaining that the form would have asked for a complete family medical history. Now the awful penny is dropping for Leo, whose first question is, how did Charlie find out? Then Charlie says if the applicant's under eighteen, they need a parent's signature. Now Leo has a bigger problem. Leo tells Charlie he did the right thing. He asks Margaret to collect all of Zoey's admissions paperwork.

Donna confesses to C.J. she leaked the voucher story. And she also kidnapped the Lindbergh baby, whacked Jimmy Hoffa, and framed Roger Rabbit. C.J.'s gotten nowhere with her investigation. Everyone she talked to was offended to be asked. Josh patiently walks the ever-skeptical Donna through the Lend-Lease Act during World War II. He rationalizes, Mexico needs help and they can help them.

Sam is informing Toby about the vast scale of the environmental damage from the *Indio* but Toby isn't listening. C.J. interrupts Sam's tirade and asks if he can give them a second. She shrugs her shoulders at Toby; she gives up. "Leaks happen, things get out." To her surprise, he doesn't seem angry. "This was small potatoes," he replies. He wanted to know if when the big potatoes come, will they be up for it. C.J. asks what could be bigger than what they've been through? Are there bigger potatoes someplace? After a pause, Toby says no.

There's a long silence as C.J.'s expression changes . . .

C.J.: (pause) Toby.

TOBY: Yeah?

C.J.: (pause) Why are you lying to me?

TOBY: I'm not. (pause) Thanks for doing that stuff today. It was—(beat) thanks.

Charlie is waiting for the President on a bench on the portico. He stands up as the President approaches, but Bartlet tells him to sit down and not be scared. Bartlet knows Zoey must have told him about the MS. Charlie says she wanted him to look for certain physical signs so he could tell the first lady. Bartlet tells him it'll be public soon enough.

BARTLET: We won't discuss it except to say this: You're gonna be subpoenaed. I'm confident in your loyalty to me. I'm confident in your love for me. If you lie to protect me, if you lie just once, if you lie just a little, if you lie 'cause you can't stand what's happening to me and the people making it happen, if you ever, EVER lie, you're *finished* with me, you understand?

CHARLIE: Yes sir.

BARTLET: Say you understand.

CHARLIE: I understand, sir.

Back in the Oval Office, Bartlet tells Babish that Zoey had to fill out a family history form for Georgetown and she left off the MS, but Abbey physically signed the form. There's a bad moon rising, and the press and public are going to take him out for a walk. The President tells Babish this wasn't what he signed up for, and if he's going to leave, do it now so it doesn't look like he bailed on the President. Babish says he'll stay if the President does exactly what he tells him. Bartlet answers, "It depends." But Babish is afraid it can't depend. Bartlet needs to step forward and tell his staff, and together, they'll figure out how to make it public. Bartlet agrees.

BABISH: Then order the attorney general to appoint a special prosecutor.

BARTLET: Oh God.

BABISH: Not just any special prosecutor. The most blood-spitting, Bartlet-hating conservative Republican in the bar. He's gonna have an unlimited budget and a staff like an army. The new slogan around here is gonna be "Bring it on." He's gonna have access to every piece of paper you've ever touched, you invoke executive privilege one time and I'm gone. An assistant D.A. in Ducksworth wants to take your deposition, you're on the next plane. A freshman congressman wants your testimony, you'll sit in his kitchen. They want to drag you to the Hague and charge you with war crimes, what do we say?

BARTLET: Bring it on.

BABISH: (pause) I'll be in my office for a while if you need me.

JOSH LYMAN
BRADLEY WHITFORD

If there is an attack dog among the senior staff on *The West Wing*, it has to be Josh Lyman. You wouldn't know it to look at him, but he's the heavyweight. The defectors in "Five Votes Down" find that out. As Josh tells Congressman Katzenmoyer, the President doesn't hold grudges, that's what he pays Josh to do.

As befits someone who fills the role of deputy chief of staff, Josh has a variety of channels and contacts. In "The Short List," when Mandy tells Josh to "talk to whoever it is you talk to," we imagine Josh has a network much like a spymaster's. Josh certainly knows about taking sides. After all, he was on Hoynes's campaign team before he went to see Bartlet speak in Nashua. It's well known that converts are the most fanatical of all.

Bradley Whitford

Josh tends to be pragmatic, a little more pragmatic politically, maybe, than Toby. I feel that Josh is always struggling with this: How dirty do my feet have to get without suffocating in the mud in order to get an inch of what I really want done? Occasionally, I go to the Hill and beat up on a representative. I do that more than someone who really has my job. Part of it is just the logistics of doing a TV show. We can't afford to have a regular that is a legislative liaison, so there's a little fudging.

As with all the senior staff, Josh's job is a little bit of everything, though he won't be running another press briefing any time soon. As Josh, Bradley Whitford has to show the range of a great shortstop. For all the humor—the pratfall in the new shoes in Congress; the pending romance, or whatever it is with Donna and with Joey, it is Josh Lyman who is almost killed at Rosslyn. There is more written into Josh's back story than that of anyone else.

Aaron Sorkin

In Josh's case the tragedies happen out of necessity. "The Crackpots and These Women" was based very loosely on a moment I had with George Stephanopoulos. While I was writing *The American President*, we were having a drink at the Four Seasons Hotel in Washington and he took out his

wallet and he showed me this little laminated card that looked like a bus pass. It was his instructions for where he's supposed to go in the event of a nuclear attack. They either get him up in the air with the President or they get him down underground with the President, but they wanted him with the President.

And he was telling me the story of a Supreme Court justice who was given a similar card. He asked, "And where does my wife go?" And the guy just shook his head no. The Supreme Court justice gave the card back. I thought, boy, I want to write that. So what I was doing was writing a story about Josh, who's been given this card. It's an unsettling card to be given at all, but then he slowly discovers that he's the only one of his friends that's been given this card.

Sorkin knew that Whitford could handle whatever nightmares he concocted for Josh.

Aaron Sorkin

Brad and I have known each other for a little more than a decade now. Even before we met, I knew of him because he went to Juilliard with two women that I know. This was right around the time that I had gotten out of school and I was starting to write. They were saying, "Aaron, there's this actor that you have to meet. He's a great guy and you're going to love him. He can just take what you write and knock it out of the park." I finally did get to meet Brad when we cast him, on Broadway, in *A Few Good Men*, in the role that Kevin Bacon played in the movie. Then he moved up into the Tom Cruise role, in fact, taking over for Timothy Busfield. Brad, also, was the first actor I gave *Sports Night* to. He did *Secret Lives of Women* instead. It all worked out very luckily, because had he done *Sports Night*, he wouldn't have been able to do *The West Wing*.

Bradley Whitford

The experience of the show so exceeds my wildest expectations. Being an actor, to do something (a) that isn't humiliating; and (b) that is so well written and with such a really great group of actors and then for it to do well commercially, is just breathtaking to me. And this spectacular arena is untapped. There's never been a really smart drama, a *Hill Street Blues*, about Washington. The conventional wisdom was that everybody hates politicians. To which, my response was, "More than they hate lawyers?"

Aaron Sorkin has built a lot of his drama around Josh. One thing leads to another. Having decided Josh was going to get the NSA card, a lot of other things fell into place.

Aaron Sorkin

In order to really take him through the kind of journey I wanted to take him through, I gave him another thing in his past. His sister was baby-sitting for him. There was a fire in the house. He ran out of the house. . . .

We heard about his father last year in "Six Meetings Before Lunch." That episode was pretty late in the season, and it's possible that by then I already knew that in the flashback of the season opener his father was going to die. I can't remember whether I was laying it in then or whether I did it then, but I said, "Oh, we've got to show the night of the Illinois primary."

Then for the season opener, I knew that the first flashback scene —in order to set up our whole story—we were going to find Josh working for then-Senator Hoynes, who is far and away the frontrunner in this thing. Because Josh was going to be the first flashback, I knew that Josh was going to have to take one in the chest.

Don't think it's going to get any easier for Josh Lyman. Aaron Sorkin says, "I'm going to shoot him out of a cannon in the third season opener."

THE FALL'S
GONNA KILL YOU

C.J. arrives in Oliver Babish's office at 5:30 in the morning and Babish immediately pounces on her: Did any of the press see her stealth journey to see him? "Not at five-thirty in the morning," she retorts. Babish asks C.J. when she found out about the President's MS. Leo told her last night, she replies. Babish questions if she's ever lied about the President's health. Already, tension is mounting and C.J. wants to know if she should have her lawyer present. Babish is her lawyer, he says. C.J. works from a different angle, asking Babish when the President told him. "Six days ago," he answers. What about Josh? "Two days after that." And Toby? He's known for over a week and Bartlet told Leo a year ago. C.J.'s

known for six hours, so she'd like some breathing room. She wants to know why she should trust Babish. Babish doesn't care if she doesn't.

C.J.: I think this is going really well so far, Oliver, it's almost hard to believe that four different women have sued you for divorce.

Babish, suddenly seeming overworked and exhausted, lays out the bottom line for C.J.: She's going to have to answer questions to him or to a grand jury. It's possible the President has committed multiple counts of a federal crime to which she was an accomplice.

BABISH: So why don't you knock off the cutie-pie crap and answer the damn question.
C.J.: What was the question?
BABISH: Have you ever lied about the President's health; what is your answer?
C.J.: Many, many times.

Nearly doubled over with laughter, Ed and Larry are clutching a fax from NASA. They tell Donna a huge Chinese satellite is coming down to earth and no one knows where or when. They try to control their laughter as they move through the West Wing corridors, leaving a frightened Donna in their wake.

In Leo's office, Leo, Toby, and Josh are discussing how to proceed. Toby wants a poll. They need to know which is worse, the perception Bartlet is not up to the job or the fact that he lied. Josh informs the group, Joey Lucas is on her way. He told her they're polling about subsurface agricultural products: Americans are eating more beets. Leo wants to tell Sam but Toby disagrees; Sam's head is in the speech he's writing, it should stay there. Leo insists the President wants Sam to know by the end of the day. Outside, Toby asks Josh if he trusts Joey and Josh says he does. Toby, on the other hand, doesn't trust anybody right now.

Martin Connelly has been waiting for Josh outside his office. Connelly looks like a man who's been pushing a rock up a hill for a while, and he pleadingly tells Josh the tobacco case is running out of money. Josh asks where it's going. Connelly rattles off for counsel, staff, depositions, witnesses, research. He says Justice has thirty-one lawyers. He says just one of the five tobacco companies has three hundred and forty-two. They've been outspent three hundred and eighty million dollars to thirty-six. "The tobacco companies perpetrated a fraud against the public," Connelly says emphatically. Josh takes pause at these words, looks at him for a moment, and says he'll talk to Leo.

Babish and C.J. are watching a recording of C.J. talking to the press about the President's health which she admits she's done seven times or so over the course of her job. When she talks to the President before the press conferences, does she ask, "Is there anything I should know?" or "Is there anything I need to know?" Babish insists she remember if she used these words, maintaining that the latter implies she wants to maintain deniability. With palpable frustration, C.J. answers she doesn't speak to the President in code. A staffer interrupts and hands C.J. a message about the Chinese satellite. She laughs dryly and shows the message to Babish—the sky is falling down.

Oblivious to the drama echoing through the rest of the White House, Sam is working on a speech about possible tax cuts with the staff in the Roosevelt Room. He gets news that the budget surplus isn't going to be as big as originally expected, and this is great news. With this slight readjustment of the focus of the speech, there's a line the Progressive Caucus and Americans for Tax Justice want Sam to put back in the text.

SAM: (reading) We want a real tax cut for working families to help them pay for higher education and housing, while our opponents want to help the rich pay for bigger swimming pools and faster private jets.

Sam refuses. He took it out because it's bad writing.

Later, Toby is reading a review of a speech, and tells Sam they're called the Batman and Robin of speechwriting.

TOBY: We're Batman and Robin.

SAM: Which one's which?

TOBY: Look at me, Sam, am I Robin?

SAM: I'm not Robin.

TOBY: Yes you are.

SAM: Okay, well, let's move off this.

TOBY: You bet, little friend.

Toby's very happy about the lower surplus when Sam tells him. It means they can lower the bottom rate and stand firm on not cutting the top tax bracket because they might not be able to afford it. Toby thinks Sam can put that line back in, but Sam holds his ground and Toby backs off.

Donna can't get anyone to share her concern about the satellite. Charlie tells Donna he's rooting for it to fall on Zurich. Then he returns his attention to more temporal matters and welcomes back Mrs. Bartlet from a trip.

When Abbey sees her husband in the Oval Office, she starts right in on him, asking why he didn't mention Zoey's medical forms on the phone? Leo brought the topic up but stopped when he realized her husband hadn't told her. Bartlet answers she signed Zoey's form, it's going to be okay. There's a moment of quiet. Bartlet tries easing the tension by changing the subject: Zoey's going to ace her finals, he says. Abbey knows. Bartlet goes on to say he hates Ellie's boyfriend, Abbey replies again she told her. Finally, Bartlet tells Abbey he needs her to speak to the White House counsel. Abbey knows that, too.

Josh informs Leo he needs thirty million more for the tobacco suit. They have contingencies but Josh wants to give them enough to win the case. Leo instructs him to look into it. And with that, Josh heads out to the airport to pick up Joey Lucas.

Meanwhile, Sam tells a bunch of Congressional aides the surplus is two hundred billion less than they thought. They love it. They want to smack down the Republicans by reinserting the planes and pools line. Sam wants to dial down the rhetoric. When he was at Gage Whitney, Sam made $400,000 a year and paid twenty-seven times the average income tax and was happy doing it. But in the end, he doesn't get twenty-seven votes. Sam states the top 1 percent of wage earners pay for 22 percent of the country, they shouldn't call them names while they're doing it.

At the airport, as she emerges from the gate, Josh meets Joey. She's with Dale, a new inter-

preter. Josh asks Dale to step aside a second and asks Joey to read his lips because he can't risk leaking the information to additional sources. Josh explains to Joey she's not actually here to study beets; in fact, she's getting back on a plane in an hour and ten minutes. He whispers to Joey that eight years ago the President was diagnosed with an illness that was never disclosed. Joey asks if it's serious and Josh says yes. When she asks what it is, Josh signs "M," and "S."

Now Abbey is having a nerve-wracking talk with the White House counsel. Babish asks her about Zoey's health form, and she says she signed it without really reading it, and she doesn't remember if the President was in the room. Babish runs through all of Abbey's numerous qualifications: M.D. from Harvard; board certification in internal medicine and thoracic surgery; adjunct professorship of thoracic surgery at Harvard Medical School; positions at Boston Mercy and Columbia Presbyterian. A lawyer's going to ask why, with all that experience, she can't recognize a family medical history form? Abbey repeats that she didn't read it, she didn't think it was important. He hits a nerve: What else has she signed that she didn't think important?

Abbey explains to Babish that MS is not hereditary, so it's irrelevant to Zoey's medical status. Babish points out she's changing her story. Frustrated, Abbey says she just signed it, it's not a big thing. Babish is unrelenting as he tells Abbey she's going to be asked these questions and more. The President's going to be asked if he was in the room when she signed it and he's going to give every-

body's favorite answer from a President who's just announced he has MS, "I don't remember."

Babish asks when they're going public. In a week, probably, replies Abbey, live on TV. Babish parrots the President: He regrets he concealed his condition, he regrets the appearance that he tried to deceive the public. With tremendous gravity he tells Mrs. Bartlet he's not sure she has an appropriate appreciation of what happens next.

Huddled at an airport bar, Josh is telling Joey they need a poll, but not even the callers can understand what it's really about. Joey writes her thoughts on a napkin. She can make it the governor of an industrial state like Michigan. Josh informs Joey that for her participation, she's probably going to have to go before a grand jury, and she seems unfazed. Joey asks how the President is doing and Josh says he's fine. She walks back toward the airline gate—she has quite a job ahead of her.

Donna's still prattling on about the satellite. She sees Mrs. Bartlet, who asks how she's holding up.

DONNA: I'm fine, but there's a giant object hurtling its way toward us at a devastating velocity.

ABBEY: Tell me about it.

The first lady goes to visit C.J. Abbey asks how C.J.'s day was and she replies she got "pretty well bitch-slapped by the White House counsel." Abbey nods. She wanted to be there when C.J. was told. C.J. recollects on the campaign, in Manhattan, Kansas, she came to the Bartlets' suite, and she was almost sure she saw Abbey give the President a shot. Abbey tells C.J. about Betaseron. C.J. grasps for this new reality; she says she just asks the President, "Is there anything else I need to know?" when he has his physical. Abbey nods again.

Josh confides in Leo that Connelly said "they perpetrated a fraud against the public" and he had such a look on his face when he said it. Leo makes Josh draw the line: the White House staff is not big tobacco. Leo's out the door, the President's expecting him.

Bartlet asks Leo why he mentioned the health form to Abbey. He's upset about it and needs to verbalize his disappointment. The President asks if the two of them can be men, they have a bond. With their bond reestablished, attention turns to the looming crisis. Leo

tells the President about Joey's poll. Bartlet thinks it's a bad idea, but knows he doesn't have much choice. He tells Leo to get Sam, it's time to come clean.

Sam seeks out Toby to further debate about the tax cut speech. He starts to explain, but Toby asks if Sam believes he's right, and Sam replies yes. Toby says that's all he needs to tell him, he trusts him. Leo enters and asks Sam to come in to see the President. Toby looks at Leo gravely, and Leo nods. They're telling him now. Toby casually mentions to Sam he'll be in his office when he's done.

C.J.'s walking home, taking advantage of the quiet night after a chaotic day. Josh catches up to her and they walk together. He says the President has Leo worried it'll look like they went public because they did a poll. C.J. smiles. She can't believe the President and Leo are actually worried about that.

C.J.: You guys are like Butch and Sundance. Peering over the edge of a cliff to the boulder-filled rapids three hundred feet below, thinking you better not jump 'cause there's a chance you might drown. (beat) The President has this disease, and has been lying about it, and you guys are worried that the polling might make us look bad?

And now she loses it, half laughing, half shouting—

C.J.: It's the *fall* that's gonna kill ya!!

Josh lets C.J. get it together for a second. Then he mutters "us." Josh says she said, "the fall's going to kill 'you' and you meant 'us.'" C.J. sighs and offers no explanation; she's going home to sleep. Josh says Donna got hold of that fax from NASA. C.J. answers they get one of those a week. Yeah, Josh says, but Donna doesn't know that, and he got a day's worth of entertainment. An object falls out the sky every ten days, seventeen thousand in all since things started being put up there and no one's ever been hit. "Perhaps we're due," he says. C.J. tells Josh he picked her right up there. Josh turns and heads back while C.J. walks on.

Stockard Channing
What emerged in that scene was a deep connection, which is sort of subterranean. Maybe it's because they're both intelligent women. The way we talk to each other has always had a sort of candor, which made the scene very moving for us. At one point we were both crying. Abigail had to keep this a secret from C.J. while being aware of what this disclosure might potentially mean in C.J.'s career. She of all people would be tremendously aware of putting C.J. in that position. We couldn't beat that one down. That was there.

18TH AND POTOMAC

In the White House at 1:20 in the morning, Leo and the President are headed for a meeting in the basement. Bartlet's wondering about the vegetable pretext Josh used to cover Joey's visit for her secret poll on public reaction to the President's MS. He's also worried about looking suspicious by meeting in the basement. On their way to the meeting, Sam tells Toby he thinks the poll numbers will be meaningless. At the door, Toby gives the password, "Sagittarius." Leo and Bartlet arrive. Leo makes sure Joey made no copies of the poll data. Before she can start, Bartlet asks about Kenny's trustworthiness. Joey replies to trust her is to trust him, and Josh backs her up. Then Joey drops the bomb.

JOEY: One thousand one hundred and seventy registered voters in Michigan were

polled, giving their governor a hypothetical, concealed, degenerative illness. These are the results. "Do you agree that it's okay for the governor to lie about his health? Seventeen percent agree, eighty-three percent disagree.

Joey lays out the rest of the results. Seventy-one percent would be less likely to vote for the governor knowing this, the largest block being likely women voters over fifty-five, 78 percent of whom wouldn't vote for a candidate with MS. The questions come flowing forth: first of all, what are the terrible implications? The worst may be that 74 percent of people believe MS to be fatal. Joey adds 62 percent of Democrats aren't going to vote for them, 65 percent of liberals aren't because he lied. Bartlet asks if there is any good news and Joey tells him no.

The bad news doesn't end there: there's a crisis developing in Haiti. The President's told that the renegade Colonel Bazan's soldiers look poised for a hostile takeover and the new President-elect Dessaline is missing. Leo wants to evacuate nonessential personnel from the American embassy, but Dandridge from State is worried that would show they have no confidence in Dessaline's democratic government. Bartlet points out, "At the moment, there is no Dessaline government and there's no Dessaline." He orders the evacuation.

Back in the basement, C.J., Toby, Josh, and Sam are discussing how to tell the nation about Bartlet's illness. They take C.J.'s idea: a live thirty-minute special on a news magazine the day after tomorrow. The President and the first lady will conduct it from the Mural Room. C.J. suggests they have a press conference right after to control the story as long as possible. They'll have medical experts present to combat that front, but the reporters will be more interested in asking if the President is planning to seek reelection. So they'll need an answer on that, too.

Mrs. Landingham is going to buy a new car and Charlie's confidently telling her what she needs: stereo, tow package, tinted windows. Mrs. Landingham wonders why men think women can't buy a car without them. Josh chimes in, did she get an extended warranty?

Leo can't believe Josh's report on the tobacco case. He reels off the figures: Justice has thirty-one lawyers and staff; tobacco, 1,893 lawyers and 2,783 paralegals. Josh explains that the industry's scheduled thousands more depositions and the government can't afford to send anyone. The problem is a subcommittee controls the money, so Leo tells Josh to talk to Ritter, the ranking minority member. Leo wants to know what they've decided downstairs and Josh tells him they'll need an answer on reelection. Leo answers they'll have it by the end of the day.

Quickly changing mindsets, Leo follows the embassy evacuation in the Situation Room. Dandridge gets a call from Peter Bratt on the ground in Haiti. He's got Dessaline in the trunk of his car. In six minutes, he'll be knocking on the door of the embassy asking for asylum. Quickly Bartlet's brought up to speed. The advisers say he shouldn't let Dessaline in because this is an internal matter and they can't choose sides. Leo says they can, Dessaline won the election and there'll never be a real election if the military thinks it can just kill the winner. The car's at the gate and Bartlet orders, "Let him in."

In the basement, an argument brews about whether to put Vice President Hoynes on TV, too. The stakes are impossibly high. Sam wants Hoynes to appear with Bartlet because it shows he anticipated the problem, and Hoynes knew about it, signed off on it, and joined the ticket. Sam strategizes if the President's not going to run, he points to Hoynes and says this is the guy. Toby asks what if Hoynes is asked if Bartlet can function as President till then? Sam responds, "He'll say yes." But Toby counters, "What if he says he's not a medical expert?" throwing back at Sam the reservation he just voiced moments ago.

Fighting on the tobacco front, Ritter tells Josh his committee is against giving any more money for the case. Two Democrats, Warren and Rossiter, are against it on ideological grounds.

Toby brings Donna into his office and says he's going to tell her something shocking, but they don't have time for her to be shocked. They're going to need her to be totally solid for the critical next few days. He tells Donna the news about the President. She's the first assistant to know. Without missing a beat Donna asks if the President is in a lot of pain or discomfort. Toby answers no and Donna goes back to work.

Mrs. Landingham has returned from the car dealer, and Charlie wants to know how much she paid below sticker for her car. Mrs. Landingham replies that she paid the full sticker price. As a government employee she's not allowed to accept gifts over twenty dollars. If the dealership offers it, a nineteen-dollar discount is good enough for her.

In the Situation Room, National Security Advisor Nancy McNally is told there's five hundred well-armed Haitian soldiers outside the embassy versus thirty-seven marines inside. C.J. briefs the press on the emergency: The U.S. is sending ships and aircraft, and the UN Security Council and the Organization of American States are going to meet to discuss further military action. C.J. is asked if the U.S is prepared to invade Haiti but she won't answer that.

Implementing the MS disclosure plan, C.J. meets with television network executive Paul Hacket. He's been in the White House hundreds of times, yet this is the first time he came in through the basement. C.J. is brief but firm. She needs thirty minutes of airtime day after tomorrow, no questions asked.

HACKET: Between friends.

C.J.: Yeah.

HACKET: Is the water over your head?

C.J.: No, the water's exactly at my head.

Josh has arranged a meeting with Warren and Rossiter. With regard to tobacco, they have a problem using the RICO Act that was written to nail mobsters against a legitimate industry. Rossiter states surgeons general have warned the public against smoking since 1964 and cigarettes have carried a warning label since 1966. Josh asks if he is insinuating that people who get addicted to nicotine "are too stupid to live?" "No," says Rossiter, "they're too stupid to be protected by the courts." Warren's position is they're funding a hopeless suit to score points against an industry that funds Republicans. Josh does not relent; what matters to him is, "It's almost three o'clock. By seven, three thousand new people will have taken up smoking and twenty-eight hundred of them will be under eighteen."

In the basement, Sam briefs the first lady on the plan for the live broadcast. Sam wants to hear her story, run it by Oliver Babish, and spend the next couple of days carefully crafting an informative,

brief, and humble message. Abbey tosses out medical terminology to fluster him, referring to partial unilateral nerve paresis, and the like. Sam calls Abbey "Mrs. Bartlet" but she sharply corrects him; it's "Dr. Bartlet." She asks why she's not doing this with the President, is it so their stories can be compared? Yes, it is.

Leo informs the President they shot three Haitian soldiers on the runway and the plane made an emergency takeoff. Bartlet fumes: he evacuated nonessentials so that this very situation could be avoided. He wants to know why the plane was still on the runway, and Leo explains it took more time than expected to get everyone together. So what is it Bazan wants? He wants Dessaline.

Letting off a little steam, the President changes the subject and admits Leo's right, he should be talking to his staff about reelection. Bartlet and Leo plan to meet them in the residence at nine.

Now the President is upbraiding Mrs. Landingham for paying sticker price. Her argument is she works next door to

Stockard Channing

She's a very well-respected physician. On the road she wrote prescriptions for herself and gave the medication to her husband. She's perfectly aware she has put her entire career and reputation in jeopardy. I think she's smart enough to know that this lack of disclosure could last only so long. It's still a big can of worms and it affects her personally in her relationship with him, and professionally. I said to Aaron, "How are you gonna get us out of this one?" She's definitely in hot water, but I have been living with this information almost as long as Abigail has and it's been a concern for me. But if anyone can solve it, it's Aaron.

the Oval Office and "Caesar's wife must be above reproach." She adds the car's a beauty, she's just going to pick it up. Bartlet asks her to come back when she has the keys in her hand. He wants to talk to her about something.

Sam is still with the first lady when Babish interrupts them. Can he have a minute with them? Babish wants Abbey to get a lawyer right away, she shouldn't answer any questions on TV without one. She tells Babish that Sam said they wouldn't be asked questions regarding legality but Babish doesn't know how they can avoid it. He dives into the inquiry, asking if she put her husband on Betaseron. "Yes, in consultation with the specialist." Abbey wrote the prescriptions to herself, filled them in Dunwich, and shipped the drugs various places, like Phoenix and St. Louis. In that case she violated medical ethics rules in three states, and she didn't keep records, either, which is against the AMA Code of Ethics. Abbey says she'd like to be next to her husband when he does this. Babish repeats that she needs her own lawyer.

Donna informs Josh about the meeting in the residence at nine. He starts to fashion an excuse about the Blue Ribbon Commission, but Donna interjects, "Sagittarius." She knows their guarded secret. Is she all right? Josh asks, and she says yes. She put some pillows and blankets in a room downstairs, anticipating a long, stressful night for the staff.

Toby tells Leo it's insane they haven't talked about reelection. They will. Tonight. Josh pulls Toby aside:

JOSH: (quietly) You told Donna.

TOBY: Yeah.

JOSH: Why didn't you let me?

TOBY: You hadn't yet.

JOSH: How'd she take it?

TOBY: If everybody out there takes it the way she did we may be okay. If a few more people in here took it the way she did, that'd be all right, too.

JOSH: Was that for me?

TOBY: That was for me.

Leo wants an update on tobacco, and Josh tells him about Warren and Rossiter. Leo suggests they light a fire under their asses, but Josh says Rossiter's on the Judiciary Committee, and they don't need enemies there.

LEO: We're not gonna stop, soften, detour, postpone, circumvent, obfuscate, or trade a single one of our goals to allow for whatever extracurricular nonsense is coming our way in the next few days, weeks, and months.

TOBY: When did we decide this?

LEO: Just now.

Leo tells the staff the plan to meet at nine. Josh rehearses for Leo his statement about tobacco, saying they won't let the well-fed Appropriations Committee choke off the lawsuit, and it's good. When Leo enters the Oval Office, he sees Charlie standing by his desk, the telephone receiver in his hand, his face pained.

LEO: Charlie?

CHARLIE: Leo, there was an accident. At Eighteenth and Potomac. Mrs. Landingham was driving her car back here.

LEO: What happened?

CHARLIE: There was a drunk driver. And they ran the light at Eighteenth and Potomac. They ran it at a high speed.

LEO: Charlie, is she all right?

CHARLIE: No, she's dead.

Stunned, Leo takes a moment to let the news to sink in. He asks Charlie if the President's alone and walks slowly along the White House portico to the Oval Office to tell his old friend the news.

TWO CATHEDRALS

The staff has been disclosing to Democratic lawmakers Bartlet's bombshell news. Leo's become a sounding board for congressmen, a steady stream of whom have come to voice their reactions. Wakefield and Wade articulate their colleagues' fears. Wade says it's the House Democrats who are going to take it in the throat and the whole House is up for reelection. Democrats are going to tell the President not to come to their district. Wade doesn't want to be the first one to say it but . . .

WADE: I think the President has to strongly consider not running for reelection.

LEO stares at WADE, deadpan but disbelieving.

LEO: (pause) You think you're the first one to say it?

WADE: Leo—

LEO: You are, at minimum, the thirty-fifth in the last two hours.

WADE: Well, we're the ones that are talking to you now. And we're the ones that are asking. Is the President going to run for reelection?

LEO: (pause) Harry, Bill, there's going to be a press conference tonight. I'd watch.

In the Mural Room, Toby is carefully inspecting the broadcast location. As Toby ponders lighting and chair placement, Sam wonders if Bartlet is up to it. But they're already locked in with the networks; they will prep the President after Mrs. Landingham's funeral service. Ginger informs Toby he has a meeting with Greg Summerhays at four. Toby insists he took him off the schedule but Leo's office put him back on. They want him to keep the appointment.

Josh hands C.J. his press release about the tobacco lawsuit. It's very strong, talking about hundreds of thousands of negligent homicides. To C.J., it's like the fire they'd throw in the early primaries. But Josh has to stick it in a drawer, just until the air is a bit clearer. She's about to tell the press a landing ship helicopter assault team is off Port-au-Prince and she's bringing in A.P., Reuters, and *Agence France* for something bigger. Nobody's going to write about tobacco.

Democratic strategists are sitting with Sam, talking about the party's options. One says they're not ruling out Bartlet as a candidate; another says that it would be easier if Hoynes were the incumbent. Fed up, Sam says, okay, he's heard enough, and ends the meeting. He reminds them, "President Bartlet isn't a candidate, he's the President."

In the Situation Room, Nancy McNally tells Leo there are 1,200 troops and four howitzers guarding the perimeter of the embassy, where there's twenty-four hours of emergency power left. Nancy wants to send Fitzwallace down there. With his mind in so many places, Bartlet hears a voice.

*   *   *

The air is calm on the campus of the 1960s New England boarding school, broken only by the chatter of the boys who have just been let out of chapel. Seventeen-year-old Jed (Jason Widener) is called over by his father, Dr. Bartlet (Lawrence O'Donnell Jr.), who reminds Jed to tell his friends not to smoke in chapel. Dr. Bartlet's standing with a young woman dressed for church, hat and all. Dr. Bartlet introduces Dolores Landingham (Kirsten Nelson), as the new secretary in his office.

*   *   *

Back in the Situation Room, Bartlet toys with an unlit cigarette. He agrees to send Fitzwallace down to dissuade a Haitian general from further military action. McNally says Fitzwallace and the general might be able to fracture Bazan's army, which would turn an invasion into a peacekeeping mission. The meeting breaks up.

Bartlet asks Charlie about the tropical storm that's moving up from Florida. Isn't it strange to get one in May? Charlie will find out. The motorcade is leaving for National Cathedral in an hour. As the President walks into the Oval Office, Charlie asks him if there's anything he needs. Yes, Bartlet says in a subdued voice, he needs pallbearers.

C.J. is briefing the press about the American force buildup in Haiti. They haven't exhausted diplomatic options, but Bazan should understand the consequences if he enters the embassy or arrests the democratically elected president Dessaline. When the briefing ends, C.J. requests that A.P., Reuters, and *Agence France* come to her office to discuss seating on Air Force One.

Sam interrupts C.J. to tell her they can't have the press conference in the East Room, which has been closed off due to asbestos. C.J. takes the news in stride, and then tells the agency reporters gathered in her office that they were not invited to talk about Air Force One and closes the door. The leak has started.

In the Oval Office, Leo's discussing the economic implications of Bartlet's MS announcement with two advisors. Bartlet's not really paying attention, he's more concerned why a door to the portico is swinging open. Charlie explains with the right sequence of doors open, there's a wind tunnel effect in the White House. Margaret comes in to announce the motorcade is ready. As for

the markets, Bartlet, trying to stay upbeat, says Leo's pretty rich; perhaps "he can buy some tech stocks and jack up the price." Bartlet overhears Margaret tell Leo it's a non-denominational service.

*   *   *

As he's sorting through files in his father's office, young Jed is discussing chapel with Delores. He's arguing that the services are not nondenominational, because Catholics don't say, "for thine is the kingdom, the power and the glory." She asks Jed why he works in the office after classes. He gets free tuition and he wants to give something back. Then she asks why he calls his father "sir." Jed replies, "Delores, is it going to be a whole afternoon of questions?" Acutely attuned to every aspect of propriety, she says, "Mrs. Landingham, please." With their relationship put back on proper footing, Jed explains his father's the headmaster, he doesn't want to make the other guys uncomfortable, so he calls him "sir."

*   *   *

The storm is building outside, but in the warmth of the limo on the way to the funeral, Abbey tells her husband they released the drunk driver from the hospital. She fractured her wrist and needed a couple of stitches, and it looks like she's going to be charged with vehicular manslaughter. Bartlet is quiet, miles away. Abbey tells him the consensus seems to be that if he steps back and supports Hoynes, there's a decent chance Hoynes will win. "The world'll rest easier," he says. The limo arrives at the National Cathedral. The service begins, "I am the resurrection and the life . . ."

* * *

Young Jed is washing the bottom of a sculling boat outside Deerforth School. Delores comes along and points out a spot he missed. He just hasn't gotten to it yet. She's always telling him he's done something wrong before he's had a chance of doing it. Delores launches into a new project for him: Did he know women are paid less than the men at the school? He didn't.

* * *

The priest's voice echoes through the cathedral. Charlie is giving the first reading from the Book of Wisdom, Chapter 3.

* * *

Delores is pestering Jed about her project. Jed says in his family they don't talk about money, and she counters that's because they have money. Jed challenges Mrs. Landingham, if she wants to convince him, she needs to show him numbers, solid proof.

* * *

Charlie's at the podium. "But the souls of the virtuous are in the hands of God . . ."

* * *

Jed is trying to start a 1960 Ford Falcon. Mrs. Landingham knocks on the window to get his attention: gleefully, she tells him she has the numbers. "Florence Chadwick in English has been there thirteen years and makes $5,900 a year; Mr. Hopkins four years less, and he makes $7,100 . . ."

* * *

As the Mozart *Requiem* begins, Toby, Josh, Sam, and Charlie join two other pallbearers, pick up the casket, and move slowly down the aisle.

* * *

As Jed tinkers with his car, Mrs. Landingham presses on, insisting that he knows she's right and she wants him to bring it up with his father. Women are afraid to mention the discrepancy for fear of losing their jobs. "What is it *you're* afraid of?" she asks.

JED: Why do you talk to me like this?
DELORES: 'Cause you never had a big sister and you need one. (pause) Look at you. You're a boy king. (beat) You're a foot smarter than the smartest kids in the class. You're blessed

with inspiration, you must know this by now, you must've sensed it. (pause) Look, if you think we're wrong, if you think Mr. Hopkins should honestly get paid more than Mrs. Chadwick, then I respect that. But if you think we're right and you won't speak up 'cause you can't be bothered, then God, Jed, I don't even want to know you.

Jed asks if Miss Mueller really gets half as much to teach music as Mr. Ryan gets to coach crew. Sensing she's gotten through to Jed, Delores says he's gonna do it. Jed replies he didn't say that, but she's certain he's come around.

DELORES: Just then. You stuck your hand in your pocket, looked away, and smiled. That means you made up your mind.

JED: It doesn't mean anything.

DELORES: Oh, yes it does.

*   *   *

In the cathedral, Leo consoles the President, his old friend. It was a beautiful service, Leo says. "She was a real dame, a real broad." Now they have to go back to the White House, they've got some decisions to make. The President asks Leo to have the agents seal the cathedral for a minute. He waits to be alone, and then he lifts his face to heaven.

> **BARTLET:** You're a son of a bitch, you know that? She bought her first new car, and you hit her with a drunk driver, what, *was that supposed to be funny*? "You can't conceive, nor can I, the appalling strangeness of the mercy of God," says Graham Greene. I don't know whose ass he was kissing there 'cause I think you're just vindictive. What was Josh Lyman, a warning shot? *That was my son!* (beat) What did I ever do to yours but praise His glory and praise His name?

Bartlet continues his diatribe—there's a tropical storm gaining speed and power, the worst since He took out the tender ship in the North Atlantic last year, killing sixty-eight crew. Yes, he lied, it was a sin. "Have I displeased you, you feckless thug?" He's created 3.8 million new jobs, increased foreign trade, bailed out Mexico, put Mendoza on the bench. They're not at war and he raised three children, and all that doesn't get him out of the dog house? Then, in Latin:

BARTLET: Am I really to believe that these are the acts of a loving God? A just God? A wise God? To hell with your punishments. I was your servant here on Earth. And I spread your word and did your work. To hell with your punishments. To hell with you.

Bartlet lights a cigarette, takes a drag, and blows out the smoke. He throws the cigarette on the floor and stamps it out. Bartlet looks up and says, "You get Hoynes."

Back at the White House, the staff can only wait as Leo is locked away with Bartlet. C.J. says they'll call them Answer A and Answer B. A is "I absolutely will seek another term." B is "Are you out of your mind?" With the ultimate decision still up in the air, Sam still wants to call off the TV appearance. No chance, the story's leaked; it's out there, they're doing it.

In the midst of all this, Toby has to take the meeting with Greg Summerhays, who's a big media player. He pulls out the stops and offers Toby a job as news director on a new twenty-four-hour cable news channel he's starting. Disgusted, Toby thanks him for coming in and walks out of his office.

Overwhelmed and confused, Donna asks Josh if this is how it works, the President and Leo sit in a room and make a decision? Toby storms back toward Josh's office. He's furious. Leo got him a lifeboat, he's going to rip his arms off . . . The look on Josh's face is enough to stop Toby in his tracks: Josh has spoken with Leo. It's Answer B.

The President and first lady have finished the hardest interview of their lives. Leo wants C.J. to do a review with the President before the press conference. He admits he got Toby a lifeboat but he didn't expect Toby to use it. He wanted the President to see that his staff was standing by him. Appeased, Toby realizes Leo thinks Bartlet's gonna change his mind, he's gonna run. Leo doesn't answer.

Meanwhile, Bartlet's hearing Donna's assessment of the public disclosure; she says they all thought it went "very well." The President replies that was the easy part. She tells him tropical storm season is June first to November thirtieth. He asks, How many tropical storms have hit Washington mid-May in the last hundred years? It hasn't happened at all. As C.J. comes in, Donna departs.

C.J. tells the President she wants to review a few things. He should take the first question from the *Times* chief medical correspondent, who is guaranteed to question the medical aspects before politics. He'll be in the front row, first seat to the right.

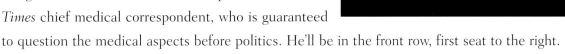

*   *   *

Young Jed has gone to his father's office. He wanted to talk about salary inequality, but his father's furious about an article Jed wrote in the school newspaper. He is criticizing a professor for banning books from the library: Henry Miller, D. H. Lawrence, *Howl*, *Giovanni's Room*. Jed says the professor banned *Fahrenheit 451*, which is about banning books. Dr. Bartlet's patience is short—he

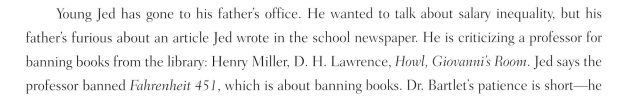

Alternate scene:

Before C.J. comes in, DONNA tells BARTLET a story about three candidates for world leader. The one with crooked associates and two mistresses who chain smokes and drinks eight to ten martinis a day; the one who was kicked out of office twice, used opium in college, and drank a quart of whiskey a night; and the vegetarian, teetotaling, nonsmoking war hero who never had an extramarital affair. BARTLET knows they're FDR, Churchill, and Hitler.

BARTLET: You're a good kid, Donna. Don't get married to a guy until he comes along. Makes me crazy when a woman gets married to a pair of pants.

DONNA: Problem is Abbey Barrington got to you first. That didn't leave much for the rest of us.

asks Jed if that wordplay was supposed to be funny? *Crack*—he smacks Jed across the face.

Dr. Bartlet asks if there's anything else. Yes, there is. Jed pipes up, "It's not a nondenominational service." His father shoots back that Jed's the only one who seems to mind. Jed answers he's the only Catholic. Intent on keeping the upper hand in this exchange, Dr. Bartlet growls he's Catholic because his mother is, and Jed's at the school because he's headmaster, and how's that for clever with words? And leaving Jed no chance for another word, he asks him to close the door behind him.

* * *

Bartlet has returned to the Oval Office. The door to the portico swings open loudly into the storm. Without thinking, he shouts, "Mrs. Landingham!" And she comes in.

MRS. LANDINGHAM: I really wish you wouldn't shout, Mr. President.

BARTLET: (pause) The door keeps blowing open.

Mrs. Landingham reprimands Bartlet, explaining he should use the intercom but he doesn't know how. Bartlet says he just hasn't learned yet. Bartlet confesses he has MS and he didn't tell anybody. He's having a little bit of a day, she says. Mrs. Landingham tells Bartlet that God doesn't make cars crash, stop using her as an excuse. She says he'll get the party back. Bartlet has a secret for her; he's never been the most popular guy in the party. She's got a secret for him: His father was a prick. He's in a tough spot? Yes. Does she feel sorry for him? She does not. There are peo-

ple worse off. He brings her argument around full circle. "Give me numbers," he says. She doesn't know them, he should give them to her.

Bartlet starts to recite the statistics. A child has a one in five chance of being born into poverty. Now she's asking: How many Americans don't have health insurance? Forty-four million. What's the number one cause for death among black men under thirty-five? Homicide. How many Americans are behind bars? Three million. How many Americans are drug addicts? Five million. Mrs. Landingham says one in five children, that's . . .

BARTLET: Thirteen million American children. Three and a half million kids go to schools that are literally falling apart, we need a hundred twenty-seven billion in school construction, we need it today.

MRS. LANDINGHAM: To say nothing of fifty-three people trapped in an embassy.

BARTLET: Yes.

MRS. LANDINGHAM: You know, if you don't want to run again, I respect that. But if you don't run because you think it's gonna be too hard . . . or you think you're gonna lose . . . (pause) . . . well, God, Jed, I don't even want to know you.

Bartlet looks down and back up, and she's gone, as he knew she would be. The President walks outside into the teeth of the storm. Charlie finds him; it's time for the press conference. Bartlet and his staff head over to the Commerce Department, where C.J. is holding down the fort with the press. She announces, "Tomorrow a special prosecutor is going to be appointed. A three-judge panel chooses from a list of three prosecutors, all of whom were appointed by Republican

presidents." C.J. imagines subpoenas will be issued to most of the White House staff, herself included. As the President watches from the window of his limo, thunder and lightning come with the driving rain and the wind.

C.J. introduces the President of the United States. Bartlet is at the podium. C.J. indicates the man she set up for the first question. Bartlet looks at him, then looks up, and, to C.J.'s surprise, picks out someone else.

BARTLET: Yes, Sandy.

REPORTER (SANDY): Mr. President, can you tell us right now if you'll be seeking a second term?

And BARTLET doesn't answer . . . the staff is getting curious . . .

BARTLET: (pause) I'm sorry, Sandy, there was a little bit of noise there, can you repeat the question?

The staff is collectively thinking, Please, God, come to Papa . . .

SANDY: Yes, sir, can you tell us right now if you'll be seeking a second term?

Again BARTLET is silent . . . LEO smiles and leans in to TOBY . . .

LEO: Watch this.

And BARTLET thinks . . . looks away . . . sticks his left hand in his pocket . . . and just as he smiles we . . .

FADE TO BLACK

END OF SHOW

INTERVIEWER: One last question. I realize that there are contracts and pickups and other things to worry about, but yes or no, do you know who's going to win the 2002 election?

AARON SORKIN: Yes.